# 1996 • 1997

# Annual

## California
## Government
## & Politics

ISBN: 0-930302-39-7
ISSN: 0084-8271

# INTRODUCTION

## The California Phenomenon

The California system of government is the same in bold outline as the government of the United States, with three theoretically equal branches of government operating under the supreme law of the land, the Constitution. Nevertheless, there are some significant differences:

• The California Constitution is far more detailed than the United States Constitution and, thus, the Governor and the Legislature have far less power and freedom than the President and Congress. Matters that are left to the statute-writers in Washington are covered in detail in the California Constitution, taking these issues out of the hands of the Governor and Legislature. The judiciary, on the other hand, may be even more powerful because this branch is in charge of interpreting the constitution.

• Normally, the speaker of the Assembly has far more power in Sacramento than any single member of Congress in Washington because this official controls virtually all committee appointments. Few bills pass over the speaker's objection. However the power of particular speakers ebbs and flows depending on factors such as their personalities, the size of their party's majority and the loyalty of their parties caucus. Moreover, under Prop. 140's term limits, speakers succeeding Willie Brown will not be as powerful because they will have a much shorter term in that office.

• The people at large have much more control over California government than over national government because they have the powers of initiative, referendum and recall, giving them the ultimate voice in all matters that are not in conflict with the United States Constitution. Most major fiscal decisions, such as the enactment of general-obligation bond issues and the raising of local taxes, also cannot be made without voter approval.

Other factors make California unique as well. It has been the land of superb climate, breathtaking natural scenery, rapid growth, and the glamor of movie stars and the radio and television industries. Its government and politics reflect the excitement of a land of opportunity and colorful characters, and the news media look to California for the bizarre and offbeat. These unique characteristics may be fading, however. No longer is California the promised land; smog has dulled the horizon; unemployment runs higher than elsewhere; and the movie industry is far from what it used to be. California is experiencing the ills of a mature society: slowed financial growth, reduced national defense spending with the end of the Cold War, declining infrastructure, burgeoning population, especially among new immigrants from foreign lands, and the need for urban renewal. The Los Angeles race riot of 1992 (the worst ever in the nation), sparked by the beating of African-American Rodney King by four white police officers and their acquittal by a Simi Valley jury, is indicative of California's urban malaise. California, in short, is no longer the land of milk and honey.

## Constitution

Every few years the California Legislature prints a paperback book with up-to-date versions of the United States and California Constitutions. The document that is the basic law of the entire nation takes up 27 pages; but the California Constitution takes up three times as much space (and twice as much just for the index).

The state constitution contains 21 articles describing, in great detail the bill of rights, the powers of various branches of government and basic state law in such fields as education, local government, corporations, taxation, water, harbor frontages, state debt, homesteading, motor vehicles, civil service, open space, public housing, and even the minimum drinking age.

The California Constitution wasn't always such a long-winded document. The first constitution, adopted in 1849 (one year before California was admitted into the Union), was a basic statement of the rights of the people and the responsibility of the three branches of government. Peter H. Burnett was elected California's first governor in November 1849, and the first Legislature convened shortly thereafter to levy taxes, establish cities and counties, put the courts into operation, and borrow enough money to grease the wheels of state government. Over the next 30 years, only three major changes were made to this constitution. This stands in sharp contrast to the current practice of adopting amendments every election year.

Massive unrest produced a greatly expanded new constitution in 1879. There was tremendous distrust of the state government, especially the Legislature, and demands were made for greater public control over taxation. The state's population had increased 17-fold in its first three decades. A drought and unfavorable economic conditions had produced mass unemployment. The railroad bloc practically ran the state and was an obvious target. Farmers were in revolt against the railroads and other businessmen. Unemployed whites joined the Workingman's Party to seek a ban against imported Chinese labor. Constitutional reform was seen as a solution, and a convention was called in 1878. The result was an extremely detailed document, which was adopted the next year by a comfortable but not overwhelming margin. The document remains the basic law of California, although it has been amended hundreds of times.

But despite the goals of those who demanded the convention, the second constitution did not provide major reform. That was to come later with Hiram Johnson and the Progressives, who instituted the initiative, referendum and recall.

**Amending the Constitution**

There are three ways amendments to the California Constitution may be placed on the ballot for approval by a majority of the voters: by initiative petition now requiring nearly 700,000 signatures of registered voters, by legislative proposal, and by constitutional convention.

• *The initiative.* Almost every election California voters decide the fate of one or more measures placed on the ballot through the initiative process. The initiative was designed as a method of exerting public control over the Legislature, so that bills ignored by the lawmakers could be put into effect. In recent years, elected officials themselves have sponsored initiatives when they are unable to get their way in the Legislature. Beginning in the late 1970's the initiative has been used more and more frequently by special interest groups, the very element the initiative was created to counter. The initiative can also be used to enact statutes.

• *Legislative proposal.* Every year, legislators introduce dozens of proposed constitutional amendments. A small percentage receive the necessary two-thirds vote of each house to qualify for the ballot. A 1983 law requires that ballot measures be numbered consecutively from election to election, starting with November 1982, to avoid confusion. Thus, for example, the November 1994 ballot measures were numbered 181 to 191.

• *Convention.* The constitution provides that the Legislature may call a constitutional convention by a two-thirds vote of both houses. However, it has not done so since 1878. Instead the Legislature has chosen to form a revision commission because it can control the commission and its recommendations. Such a commission existed from 1963 to1970. The commission had some successes during those years and managed to reduce the size of the constitution considerably. A new constitutional commission was established in 1994 to evaluate and recommend structural reforms in California government. 🏛

# The Abiding Dream

## By Lou Cannon

Reprinted from *California Journal*, January 1995

alifornia has long been celebrated as a land of limitless possibilities, but the current wisdom is that the state's best days are history and that the shining, California dream is dead.

Three years ago *Time* magazine devoted an entire issue to a blunt obituary called "California: The Endangered Dream." Since then, the state has survived drought, riots, fires and earthquakes while suffering from business exodus, white flight, and hyperbolic fears of being overwhelmed by illegal immigrants. Public opinion surveys by venerable California pollster Mervin Field have found record levels of pessimism.

"Everywhere you go, you see people giving up on California," said Kevin Starr, one of the few historians who does not share this pessimism.

Certainly, the implicit premise of the 1994 gubernatorial race was that the good life is gone in California. Republican Governor Pete Wilson blamed immigrants, crime and a federal government that mandates programs without paying for them. Democratic challenger Kathleen Brown blamed Wilson and declining opportunities. Wilson won handily, partly because he has been a capable governor under difficult circumstances and partly because his campaign was as skillful as his opponent's was inept. But even Wilson acknowledges that California faces continuing hard times.

> "With our diverse population and the kind of new businesses that are being generated, we could become the first universal nation."
> —James K. Didion

What has happened to California's fabled optimism? Is the California dream susceptible of restoration or is it destined to be only a memory of a happier time when solutions to the state's problems seemed within the grasp of its citizens and their political system? These questions are the subject of this essay, which examines issues of population, immigration, economic change and political attitudes as they relate to the California dream.

The dream was born in 1848, when California exploded into national consciousness with the discovery of gold, the enduring international symbol of wealth and independence.

A poor man's gold rush ensued, bringing risk-takers to California from every corner of the globe. As Carey McWilliams observed, the discovery of gold coincided with a revolution in transportation and communication that made mass migration possible, "catapulted California into the national limelight ... increased its population 2500 percent in four years" and gave it statehood within two years.

The state has been on the cutting edge of change ever since. Elsewhere in America, economic and political development gradually accelerated as energy accumulated. "But in California," wrote McWilliams, "the lights went on all at once, in a blaze, and they have never been dimmed."

From California's adventurous beginnings the state became a magnet for immigrants of energy and talent from every race and ethnic group. Other "gold rushes" followed, attracting new waves of risk-takers: the "green gold" of agriculture, the "black gold" of oil, the dream machine of the movies, and the war machine of defense and aerospace.

Individualism was the social corollary of economic opportunity. Entrepreneurs were valued and honored. Politicians were nourished on the cult of "the man, not the party." William Faulkner had defined the American dream as "a sanctuary on earth for individual man," and the California dream was the American dream writ large and made accessible to everyone. "Mister, this is dreamland," declared a *Life* article in 1943 that described how Southern California was "irresistibly attractive to hordes of people."

The entire population of the state was then seven million people, and even the most visionary Californians could not foresee the full dimensions of the boom to come. When social historian McWilliams in 1949 wrote "California: the Great Exception," from which the comments attributed to him in this article are taken, he anticipated an "eventual" population of 20 million.

The eventuality arrived by 1970 without dimming California optimism. When newly re-elected Governor Ronald Reagan delivered his State of the State message in 1970, an address reprinted in the first issue of *California Journal*, he talked almost routinely about preserving "the magic of California."

But a quarter century later, the magic seems to have disappeared, without anyone knowing quite where it went or when it vanished. Some believe that the magic is a casualty of overcrowding. California extends 800 miles from corner to corner, and its size enabled it to absorb early waves of immigration with relative ease. But the population pessimists contend that the state will soon exceed its carrying capacity, or, at a minimum, that the easy-going California lifestyle will be damaged beyond recognition.

Finding living space for new residents has been a California preoccupation since the early days of the century. The historic response of urban planners to population pressure was to spread out, providing cheap homes for newcomers at the cost of farmland and desert. Los Angeles became "40 suburbs in search of a city" and was emulated in the suburban sprawl of the Inland Empire and the Santa Clara Valley.

The suburbanizing process encouraged an automobile culture that was simultaneously egalitarian and destructive. The sprawling city-suburbs provided inexpensive and often comfortable housing for millions of working-class and middle-class Californians whose home equities became passports to prosperity. But the atomized communities in which they lived were too often unsatisfactory pseudo-cities inhabited by weary commuters who left before dawn to reach their work places and arrived home after dark on congested freeways that clogged the skies with smog.

In today's California, that commute is actually changing for the better. Business decentralization and telecommunication have brought work places nearer, reduced driving distances, and encouraged a new sense of community. Meanwhile, after succeeding in the San Francisco Bay Area, rapid transit finally has caught on in Southern California, where bus and light rail use is expanding faster than automobile traffic. *Time's* report on the endangered dream declared that "mad, fit joggers must run at night if they hope to breathe freely," but Southern California smog levels are lower than in the '70s, when the dream was flourishing, and they are likely to decline even more with the recent introduction of reformulated gasoline.

Weighing more heavily on the dream than population pressure has been the bitter dispute over population composition, much of it framed as a debate about illegal immigration. An analysis of driver's license records in 1992 showed a record exodus of 580,000 persons from California and prompted *The Sacramento Bee* to suggest renaming the state song, "California, There They Go."

The exodus has been primarily of white, middle-class and older Californians. High birth rates, particularly among young immigrants, have pushed California's population above 32 million and increased tax burdens to pay for the schools and social services.

It is not a new problem. *Newsweek* magazine, in a 1948 article called "Crowded California," said that "climate-minded, population-conscious, real-estate mad California has burst its breeches" and "is suffering from the worst case of economic growing pains in American history..."

These growing pains did not trouble three-term Republican Governor Earl Warren, who was quoted by the magazine as saying that California was getting "the greatest population bargain in history." When it was pointed out that most newcomers were young families with debts, Warren said, "I would rather have the production of the best years of the young people now migrating to our state than the dollars the retired people earned elsewhere."

Now, however, young foreign-born immigrants are becoming part of the economy without becoming part of the electorate. Latinos are 26 percent of California's population and 14 percent of registered voters but, according to *Los Angeles Times* exit polls, were only 8 percent of those who cast ballots in last November's election. This minimal participation assured passage of Proposition 187 and abetted scapegoating of illegal immigrants before and after the campaign.

Studies by the Urban Institute, RAND and Los Angeles County impeach the widely held notion that illegal immigrants cost more than they contribute. But the economic contributions (largely Social Security taxes that are collected and never repaid as benefits) are distributed nationally while costs of social services are disproportionately shouldered by border states and counties.

A historic dark side of the California dream has been the scapegoating of minorities during economic crises. When Chinese imported to work on the transcontinental railroad competed for jobs during a recession in the 1870s, labor agitators raised the cry, "The Chinese must go." Chinese were denounced at rallies and lynched by mobs. In successive decades this agitation was extended to imported Japanese, Filipino and Korean workers and to Mexicans brought in as farm workers. The latter were imported during the labor shortages of the two world wars but rounded up and dumped at the Mexican border during the Depression.

The reputations of two great California leaders — Progressive Hiram Johnson and Warren — were blemished by racial demagoguery. As governor in 1913, Johnson signed the Anti-Alien Land Act, which prohibited Japanese ownership or tenancy of agricultural land. As state attorney general in 1942, Warren participated in efforts to intern Japanese-Americans during World War II, an action retrospectively recognized as disgraceful and unjustified.

Governor Pete Wilson's popular campaign against illegal, mostly Latino, immigrants is reminiscent of these sad episodes, which also were immensely popular at the time. And like anti-Chinese agitation, the Anti-Alien Land Act and the Depression exportation of Mexicans, the present demonizing of illegal immigrants is a byproduct of economic frustration.

The collapse of the Cold War triggered aerospace layoffs, punctured the overblown California real estate boom, sent the state into its worst economic slump since the Depression and arguably did more to diminish the California dream than any other single event. Aerospace workers were the elite troops of a work force made necessary by hot and cold wars. From the military buildup before World War II until the demise of the Soviet Union a half century later, the defense industry was an economic cornucopia for California, providing so many jobs that a myth arose that the state was recession-proof. "The California economy was on steroids," said Starr.

Then the aerospace collapse rippled through the California economy, accounting for one-fourth of the 800,000 jobs lost in the state during a three-year period that began soon after Wilson took office. But the structural economic changes caused by the aerospace collapse were even more significant than the job losses.

The structural change can be illustrated by a comparison of aerospace to the apparel industry, the state's fastest-growing manufacturing sector during the economic downturn. In 1993 the median aerospace wage rate was $45,000 a year compared to $34,000 for all California manufacturing jobs. But the median wage in apparel, with a heavily Latino and Asian work force, was only $17,000 a year. While more than two and one-half garment jobs were needed to equal the purchasing power of a single lost aerospace job, aerospace declined at about the same rate that apparel manufacturing was growing.

Reporting on the California economy for *The Washington Post* in 1993, I interviewed Southern California aerospace workers while my colleague Jessica Crosby talked to Spanish-speaking garment workers in the Los Angeles apparel district. Many of the aerospace workers were disillusioned by crime, congestion and lack of economic opportunity. They talked of retiring, retraining for other work or leaving California. The garment workers,

*Detail Computer illustration by Perry Babasin*

while working for low wages under poor conditions, were imbued with the ambitions of immigrants: education for their children, a home or a car, a chance to make something of themselves.

"I want everything," said Hugh Gonzalez, 22, who had come to Los Angeles from Guadalarjara. He cut out vest patterns on a hand-held machine by day, attended night school to improve his rudimentary English and said he wanted to become a veterinarian.

Reading such interviews, I realized that the garment workers were as captivated by the California dream as any 19th Century gold-seekers. Soon afterward I discussed this with Assemblyman John Vasconcellos (D-San Jose), who said: "A new society is emerging in California, but its shape isn't clear. We're in a chasm between two shores. We can't go back to the shore we've left, and the other is too far away for us to see it clearly."

While 1994 was the year of Proposition 187, it was also the year when the Greater San Diego Chamber of Commerce (and the *San Diego Union*) opposed the measure in part because of its potential damage to U.S.-Mexican relations. It was the year when the North American Free Trade Agreement proved its worth and when the General Agreement on Tariffs and Trade was approved by Congress. It was a year of vast expansion of trade with nations of the Pacific Rim, California's natural partners as the tide of the commerce continues westward.

The private sector clearly must provide leadership if California is to navigate the shoals of cultural change and reach the other shore, for the public has lost confidence in the government solutions that were widely accepted a quarter century ago.

When *California Journal* for its 20th anniversary issue asked prominent Californians to look ahead at the next two decades, Reagan talked about increased telecommuting, work decentralization and "privitization of many functions of government." Jerry Brown said the Russian concept of *perestroika* would become a metaphor for worldwide restructuring.

Their comments were prescient, perhaps because both Reagan and Brown had advanced variants of these ideas during their governorships. Under Reagan, the growth of the state work force slowed for the first time since World War II. Brown advocated an "era of limits" that voters enforced in 1978 with Proposition 13, the initiative that ignited the nationwide anti-tax revolt and still restricts public expenditures in California.

Diminished government and the anti-politics revolution is a worldwide phenomenon. The seminal event was the collapse of the Soviet Union, which reduced the perceived need for a powerful, intrusive and military-oriented U.S. government and arguably had as much impact on national public attitudes as the aerospace collapse had on the California economy.

According to Department of Finance projections, California's population will surpass 40 million by 2006, reach 50 million by 2022 and 60 million by 2036. Latinos will become the largest ethnic group in the state by 2020. By 2002, the state will have no racial or ethnic majority.

"Look at it another way," said Vasconcellos. "By the year 2010, three-fourths of the people on retirement will be Anglo whites and two-thirds of the work force supporting our retirement will be people of color."

Can California deal with such changes? Versions of this question have been put to Californians ever since the gold mines gave out, and the answers have always been affirmative.

The best answers today come not from think tanks but from the sweat of people such as Alicia Aguilar, an immigrant from Toluca, Mexico, who works 11 hours a day making blouses at piece-work rates in a Los Angeles garment factory that is literally a sweatshop because of the lack of air conditioning. Aguilar's three children are learning English, however, and they will be part of the new California.

Answers also are coming at the other end of the economic spectrum by the growing high-tech health care industry, which in California today accounts for nearly 150,000 jobs. "The state has a toehold in the industries of the future," said Kirk West, president of the California Chamber of Commerce.

James K. Didion, chief executive officer of CB Commercial Real Estate Group of Los Angeles and a lifelong Californian, believes that the state's natural advantages and the "renewal of energy" provided by legal immigration will lead to a California revival.

"I look back with great nostalgia to the way California used to be," said Didion. "But with our diverse population and the kind of new businesses that are being generated, we could become the first universal nation. California's future could be even brighter than its past."

That is what Reagan believed a quarter century ago. Delivering his State of the State message in 1970, Reagan said: "We seek ways to accommodate those who want to share in the magic of California without allowing that magic to be swept away by a wave of people and pollution."

The accommodation is still being sought despite more pollution and many more people. The magic of California is being rediscovered. The dream abides. 🏛

*Lou Cannon is a veteran political reporter and the author of numerous books, including "President Reagan, the Role of a Lifetime." He currently is writing a book on the aftermath of the Los Angeles riots and the Rodney King trial and is on leave from The Washington Post.*

# Remodeling the Constitution

## Revision Commission is poised to offer a bold revamp of the state constitution.

## by Steve Scott

Reprinted from *California Journal*, April 1996

For most of the last two years, the California Constitution Revision Commission has occupied the policy equivalent of the land of the architects. Convened in 1994 with a mandate to fix what's broken about the state's Rube Goldberg system of governance, the 20-member commission has produced a set of recommendations remarkable in its breadth and sophistication. But as the commission prepares its final reform package this month, its role has changed. No longer mere architects, the commission members must now find a way to get the thing built despite a growing chorus of special-interest doomsayers, each with their own particular nit to pick. They must also make believers of the Legislature, which will decide how much of the commission's work will be placed before voters on the November ballot, or whether any will be placed there at all.

"It would be much easier to do this job in Nevada," conceded Commission Chairman William Hauck.

For most of the revision commission members, the journey they have taken over the last two years must seem every bit as long as Gulliver's travels, if not quite as strange. Hauck —a vice president for StateNet, *California Journal*'s parent company — and executive director Fred Silva spent more than a year guiding the commission through what may have been the longest-running policy seminar in the history of state government. Every internal organ of the state constitution was examined, dissected, reassembled and dissected again. Commission meetings were taken on the road, public hearings were held via satellite, and every interest group with a stake in the system weighed in, often several times.

Out of that process emerged a remarkable level of consensus and a thick set of preliminary recommendations. While many of the suggestions reflected ideas that had been kicking around the Legislature for years, some bear the commission's own unique stamp. Almost from the moment the findings were released, however, fax machines started spitting out notices praising the process and scorning the specifics. The earliest casualty was the commission's most visible suggestion—movement from a two-house to a one-house legislature. Many commission members saw the unicameral legislature as a magnet to draw media attention to their efforts, but most of the serious attention came from recalcitrant legislators, who let it be known unicameral meant certain death for the commission's efforts. Another area in which little headway appears possible is in expanding the state's ability to contract services with the private sector.

Even without a unicameral legislature, the commission's recommendations, which were scheduled to be finalized at the end of March, remain extensive, reaching into every cranny of governmental structure (see page 16). "You've got to give them high marks for gaining a modicum of consensus that has escaped the Legislature," said Assemblyman Phil Isenberg (D-Sacramento), a commission member until he was dumped off by new GOP Speaker Curt Pringle.

While reaching consensus among 20 board members of varying philosophies is, indeed, an accomplishment, the degree of difficulty pales in comparison with the challenge of gaining consensus among 120 lawmakers, one governor and a phalanx of interest groups. Since the year began, the commission's findings have been picked at by critics from both ends of the political spectrum. The Howard Jarvis Taxpayers Association, guardian of that political sacred cow, Proposition 13, sees danger lurking in

the commission's retreat from a two-thirds vote requirement on local school bonds and its plan to give local school districts more taxing authority. "What happens when the police come in and say, 'Hey, what about us?'" noted HJTA President Joel Fox. And what about the school community, guardians of that other sacred cow known as Proposition 98? They're even less impressed than the Jarvis folks.

"There definitely is an anti-Prop. 98 tone to the work," said California Teachers Association lobbyist Owen Waters. "Obviously, we didn't see any real change in tax policy."

In truth, it seems that for every recommendation, there is a force resisting the recommendation. Anti-tax and anti-government activists object to the call for a majority vote on the state budget. The initiative industry bitterly opposes plans to let the Legislature tinker with initiatives before they go to the ballot. The three constitutional officers whose functions would become

# Constitutional Checklist

## key recommendations of the Constitutional Revision Commission

### Legislative Branch
- Lengthen term limits, giving legislators three, four-year terms in each house.
- Shorten legislative sessions
- Forfeit pay when budget is late
- Provide state retirement benefits for legislators

### Executive Branch
- Gov. and Lt. Gov. run together as ticket
- Gov. still in power, even when out of state
- Treasurer, Ins. Comm. Supt. of Pub. Instr. appointed, rather than elected
- Consolidate Bd. of Equalization and Franchise Tax Bd.
- Reduce terms of UC Regents

### State Budget
- Majority vote to pass budget
- Two-year budget, with rebalancing act after first year
- Authorize single trailer bill for budget
- Require phased-in 3% budget reserve
- Limit short-term borrowing authority
- Outcome-based performance criteria
- Five-year capital outlay plan

### K-12 Education
- Declare K-12 education a "fundamental

state interest"
- Allow override of Prop. 13 property tax limits for school spending
- Authorize local sales tax for schools on majority vote
- Give Leg. and governor greater flexiblity to adjust Prop. 98
- Remove authority for state Bd. of Education and local county Bds. of Education from constitution
- Establish authority for local school boards

### Local Govt.
- Authorize Multi-Agency "Community Charters" to consolidate local govt. functions
- Authorize additional revenue stream as an incentive to consolidate
- Require governor and Leg. to draft a state/local realignment plan, detailing specific functions of each level of govt.

### Initiative Process
- Put all constitutional amendments on the November ballot
- Allow Leg. to amend initiatives prior to election, provided amendments are "consistent with the purpose of the initiative."
- Allow Leg. to amend any statutory initiative after six years

**William Hauck**

appointed rather than elected—treasurer, insurance commissioner, and state superintendent of public instruction—all oppose the move. "I have a $27 billion checkbook," said state Treasurer Matthew Fong. "The voters have every right to have that office be directly accountable to them." Perhaps most vociferous in their objections are term-limit advocates, who object to the commission's proposal to allow both Assembly and Senate members to run for up to three four-year terms.

"I think it is unfortunate that the commission would essentially pit itself against the will not simply of a transient majority of the people but what is by every measure a growing majority of the people," said Alan Heslop of the conservative Claremont Institute, who also sits on the commission.

Interestingly, the one area given the best chance of achieving consensus is arguably the commission's toughest nut—local government restructuring. Some 7000 different governmental agencies operate within California, each jealously guarding its autonomy and often duplicating services. To prod these entities into taking advantage of the economies of scale, the commission proposed that local regions establish "community charters," in which counties, cities, school districts and special districts would identify cross-jurisdictional functions and pool resources to pay for them. Successfully enacted charters would be given a carrot for their good behavior—a guaranteed piece of the property tax and the ability to pass general obligation bonds by a majority, rather than a two-

thirds vote. The state, meanwhile, would be required to lay out a specific "job description" for state and local government, so each knows what it's supposed to do, and where the money is supposed to come from. While charter cities remain worried their own taxing authority may be restricted by the charters, commission leaders are cautiously optimistic about working out a compromise.

"What they landed on with local government was that they proposed processes to be conducted locally in the future, rather than imposing something themselves," said Steve Szalay, executive director of the California State Association of Counties.

**Fred Silva**

With all but the final "i-dotting" and "t-crossing" completed, the focus now turns to state lawmakers, who must take the commission's recommendations and fashion them into something that can go before voters this November. The Legislature's track record for embracing big-picture government reform at any time is, at best, mixed, and such reforms are even harder to achieve in election years, of which 1996 is one. "All great changes are irksome to the human mind, because they have uncertain effects," conceded Silva. With special interests hounding them on both sides, the temptation for lawmakers to "cherry-pick" recommendations out of the commission's report will be strong.

"I'd say it's zero," said Senator Bill Leonard (R-Redlands) of prospects that the commission's ideas would survive the Legislature intact. "I think what will happen is that members who agree with individual recommendations will use that to advance their own proposals."

The commission is meeting this urge to purge head on, taking the breadth of opposition as a sign they are on the right track. "My pitch to people will be, 'If everyone's screaming over the recommendations, then it must be good,'" said Hauck. There are also

some tactical advantages to pushing the report as a package. As a package, legislators can justify voting for things they don't like by pointing to things they do, taking the bitter with the sweet. Picked apart, all they get to take is bitter and nothing happens. "If you try to do it piecemeal, it never happens," said Tim Hodson, director of the Center for California Studies at Sacramento State University.

"Everyone's going to want to focus on one point and change it," said Isenberg. "Eventually, members will have to sit back and look at these as connected issues in the sense of creating a high-wire balancing act."

So what happens if nothing happens and the commission sunsets as scheduled sometime later this year? Will the California Constitution Revision Commission see its ideas become catalysts for broader debate about the way the state is governed? Or will its report be dispatched to the dusty, ever-lengthening shelf of studies that sounded good on paper but never made it into practice? Critics of the commission's findings predict it will become another dead letter. "It looks like another report that has a lot of pieces, none of which particularly go together," said Waters. For supporters of the effort, however, there are signs of encouragement. CSAC has launched its own public-private council aimed at restructuring local government. An even more ambitious effort, the California Governance Consensus Project, aims to use dispute-resolution tactics to forge compromise among conflicting governmental entities. Both efforts figure to use the commission's findings as a framework.

These signs give many commission members the conviction that it was worth all the effort. Hauck says the commission has already "set the discussion in motion" that could ultimately lead to the kind of structural change the commission sought. While such optimism may be excused of the commission's chair, it is also shared by many who have watched from the outside.

"You cannot look at the CCRC as just another think tank," said Hodson. "Even if the commission's proposals are not acted on, they've performed a great service by putting many of these things on the table in a manner that it will not be easy for them to be taken off the table." 🏛

# EXECUTIVE BRANCH & STATE FINANCE

California's governor has, as does the President of the United States, power that is counter-balanced by power of the other branches of government and the electorate. The governor reigns supreme in very few areas. One of them is appointments, but many of these are subject to confirmation by the state Senate. California's governor has remarkably few appointments compared to other states because the civil service system has long been established for all but the top policy posts. The governor also has prime responsibility for the fiscal affairs of state, but his budget is subject to alteration by the Legislature. The governor can reduce or eliminate items in the budget passed by the Legislature. This "line-item" veto is a very powerful tool of California Governors. These vetoes, like any others, are subject to override by two-thirds vote of the Senate and Assembly, through this happens only rarely. Former Republican Presidents Ronald Reagan and George Bush supported a line-item veto federal amendment to strengthen the executive's fiscal power. Democratic President Bill Clinton is also an admirer of the line-item veto.

Governors are elected for four-year terms, with a two-term maximum (established by Proposition 140 in November 1990). Historically, only Earl Warren was elected more than twice. The order of succession is the lieutenant governor, Senate president pro tempore, Assembly speaker, secretary of state, attorney general, treasurer and controller. The governor serves as the ceremonial chief of state, as president of the University of California Board of Regents and the State University and Colleges Board of Trustees, as unofficial leader of his party, and as the head of most administrative agencies through his subordinate appointees. The governor is deeply involved in the legislative process, through presentation of the budget, the office's veto power and the traditional presentation of a package of bills constituting a legislative program (and usually outlined in the annual "state-of-the-state" message). When stymied by the legislature, Governor Pete Wilson has also authored initiatives.

## Veto power

The veto is perhaps the governors most potent weapon, but it is essentially a negative power. Governors usually wield considerable influence with members of their own party (because they often control the party structure, weak as it is, and because lawmakers like to stay on the good side of a governor so they can get projects for their districts and appointments for their friends). Consequently, vetoes are rarely overridden. When Governor Ronald Reagan had a veto overridden during the 1973-74 session, it was the first over-ride since 1946. Jerry Brown was overridden during his first term on a death-penalty measure and overrides became almost commonplace in 1979, especially on fiscal issues. Neither George Deukmejian nor Pete Wilson has had a veto overridden.

Governors have the power to organize the administrative agencies of state government as they see fit, although the Legislature can veto major reorganization plans. Reagan organized his administration into four agencies headed by the secretaries of health and welfare, business and transportation, agriculture and services, and resources. The Department of Finance reported directly to the Governor. The cabinet met regularly and established policy for the administration.

The Jerry Brown administration employed the case-study method for solving problems and establishing policies. Cabinet sessions at the start were frequent, lengthy and argumentative — far less business-like than in the Reagan years. However Brown put agency executives on a loose leash once they learned what he expected from them. Jerry Brown created a fifth agency, the Youth and Adult Correctional Agency.

George Deukmejian, it was assumed, would be willing to bargain and compromise with the legislature on issues since, as a former legislator, he was used to a give and take process. His unyielding stance during his first year in office on issues like taxes and community college fees surprised many. Despite the fact that he was the sole Republican among the state's statewide officeholders and both houses of the Legislature were Democratic-controlled, Deukmejian wielded the powers of his office with considerable effect.

Deukmejian's Republican successor, Governor Pete Wilson, selected a more moderate and pragmatic group of Cabinet secretaries. Wilson has also established three new cabinet-level agencies: Environmental Protection, Child Development and Education, and Trade and Commerce.

Sharing executive power with the governor are a number of boards and commissions. The governor appoints most of their members and they in turn exercise independent

# CALIFORNIA EXECUTIVE BRANCH ORGANIZATION

## GOVERNOR

### EDUCATION POLICY BOARDS

Board of Education
U.C. Board of Regents
State College and University Trustees
Community College Board of Governors
Postsecondary Education Commission
Commission for Teacher Preparation and Licensing

### BUSINESS, TRANSPORTATION AND HOUSING AGENCY

Dept. of Alcoholic Beverage Control
Dept. of State Banking
Dept. of Corporations
Highway Patrol
Dept. of Housing and Community Development
Dept. of Motor Vehicles
Dept. of Real Estate
Dept. of Savings and Loan
Dept. of Transportation
California Housing Finance Agency
Stephen P. Teale Data Center
Office of Traffic Safety

### RESOURCES AGENCY

Dept. of Conservation
Dept. of Fish and Game
Dept. of Forestry & Fire Protection
Dept. of Boating and Waterways
Dept. of Parks and Recreation
Reclamation Board
S.F. Bay Conservation and Development Commission
Dept. of Water Resources
California Conservation Corps
Colorado River Board
Coastal Commission

### HEALTH AND WELFARE AGENCY

Dept. of Alcohol and Drug Programs
Employment Development Dept.
Dept. of Developmental Services
Dept. of Health Services
Dept. of Mental Health
Dept. of Rehabilitation
Dept. of Social Services
Dept. of Aging
Office of Statewide Health Planning & Development
Emergency Medical Services Authority
Health & Welfare Data Center
Dept. of Economic Opportunity

### STATE AND CONSUMER SERVICES AGENCY

Fire Marshall
Franchise Tax Board
Dept. of General Services
Personnel Board
Dept. of Consumer Affairs
Public Employees Retirement System
Teachers' Retirement System
Dept. of Veterans Affairs
Dept. of Fair Employment and Housing
Building Standards Commission
Museum of Science and Industry

### TRADE AND COMMERCE AGENCY

World Trade Commission
California Film Commission
Office of Tourism
Office of Small Business Development

### YOUTH AND ADULT CORRECTIONAL AGENCY

Board of Prison Terms
Dept. of Corrections
Board of Corrections
Prison Industries Authority
Youthful Offender Parole Board
Dept. of Youth Authority

### ENVIRONMENTAL PROTECTION AGENCY

Air Resources Board
Integrated Waste Management Board
Water Resources Control Board
Dept. of Toxic Substance Control
Dept. of Pesticide Regulation
Office of Environmental Health Hazard Assessment

### INDEPENDENT COMMISSIONS

Agricultural Labor Relations Board
Arts Council
Lottery Commission
State Lands Commission
Coastal Commission
Fair Political Practices Commission
"Little Hoover" Commission
Public Employment Relations Board
Transportation Commission

### SECRETARY OF FOOD AND AGRICULTURE

### DEPARTMENT OF FINANCE

### DEPARTMENT OF INDUSTRIAL RELATIONS

### SECRETARY OF CHILD DEVELOPMENT AND EDUCATION

Office of Administrative Law
Office of Planning and Research
Office of Emergency Services
Office of Personnel Administration
Military Department
Office of Criminal Justice Planning
State Public Defender

authority. Among them:

*University of California of Regents.* Aside from the power of the purse, the Regents control the university system.

*State University Trustees.* This board has less power and prestige than the UC Regents but has been seeking increased independence.

*Public Utilities Commission.* The PUC sets rates for public utilities and also exercises allied responsibilities.

*Franchise Tax Board.* This board administers the state income tax and handles other revenue matters.

*State Lands Commission.* This commission exercises control over the state's oil-rich tidelands and other public properties.

*Fair Political Practices Commission.* This powerful agency was created by voters in June 1974 to police the state's Political Reform Act covering lobbyist activities, campaign contributions and conflicts of interest.

*Energy Resources, Conservation and Development Commission.* This commission also went into operation in 1975. It is charged with establishing overall state power policy and with the selection of sites for new power plants.

*Agricultural Labor Relations Board.* This agency supervises management-labor activities for the agricultural industry.

*Lottery Commission.* Created by the 1984 initiative to run what is, in effect, one of the nation's largest businesses.

*Citizens Compensation Commission.* This governmental unit was established by voters with the adoption of Prop. 112 of June 1990. This commission is charged with setting the salary level of all state elected officials except judges.

In a special category is the *State Board of Equalization,* composed of the state controller and four members elected by district. It collects the sales tax and other levies, and supervises county administration of the property tax. From time to time, governors propose elimination of the Board of Equalization and the Franchise Tax Board in favor of creating a Department of Revenue under the governor's control.

**Statewide offices**

In addition to the governor, the state Constitution requires the election of seven other statewide officials. All are limited to two four-year terms by Proposition 140. See box for a list of current incumbents, the individuals they defeated and their predecessors.

Here is a brief rundown of the duties of these other statewide officials:

• **Lieutenant Governor:** presides over the Senate, serves as a member of numerous state boards and commissions, and exercises the powers of chief executive when the governor leaves the state or is incapacitated.

• **Secretary of State:** the state's chief election officer; maintains all the state's official files and historical documents, including articles of incorporation; receives lobbyists' registrations and their monthly reports; receives campaign-contribution and conflict-of-interest disclosure forms.

• **Attorney General:** the state's chief law enforcement officer, legal advisor to state agencies.

• **Treasurer:** provides all banking services for the state, including sale of bonds and investment of securities.

• **Controller:** the principal accounting and disbursement officer for the state; administers inheritance and gift taxes and performs a variety of functions assigned by the Legislature, including publication of statistics on local government.

• **Superintendent of Public Instruction:** heads the state Department of Education, but most of the public schools are administered by local boards; state education policy is established by the state Board of Education, composed of gubernatorial appointees.

• **Insurance Commissioner:** This is a relatively new position created by the passage of Proposition 103 in 1988. The commissioner oversees the operations of the state Department of Insurance and has wide authority to approve or disapprove many types of insurance rates.

# Constitutional Officers

|  | Incumbent (year first elected) | Defeated Nov. 1994 | Predecessor |
|---|---|---|---|
| **Governor** | Pete Wilson (R) 1990 | Kathleen Brown (D) | George Deukmejian (R) |
| **Lieutenant Governor** | Gray Davis (D) 1994 | Cathie Wright (R) | Leo McCarthy (D) |
| **Secretary of State** | Bill Jones (R) 1994 | Tony Miller (D) | March Fong Eu (D) |
| **Attorney General** | Dan Lungren (R) 1990 | Tom Umberg (D) | John Van de Kamp (D) |
| **Treasurer** | Matt Fong (R) 1994 | Phil Angelides (D) | Kathleen Brown (D) |
| **Insurance Commissioner** | Chuck Quackenbush (R) 1994 | Art Torres (D) | John Garamendi (D) |
| **Controller** | Kathleen Connell (D) 1994 | Tom McClintock (R) | Gray Davis (D) |
| **Superintendent of Public Instruction** | Delaine Eastin (nonpartisan)1994 | Maureen DiMarco | Dave Dawson* |

Note: Minor-party candidates omitted.     *Acting upon conviction of a felony of Louis (Bill) Honig

## State Finance

The governor is required by the state Constitution to present a budget each January — an estimate of the state's expenditures and revenues for the fiscal year starting the following July 1st. In a state growing as fast as California, the budget increases dramatically no matter who is governor.

During the eight years Ronald Reagan was governor, the total budget doubled from $5 billion to $10 billion. Jerry Brown's first budget (1975-76) totaled $11.4 billion, and his final budget (1982-83) totaled $25.3 billion. George Deukmejian's first budget (1983-84) totaled $26.8 billion and his last budget (1990-91) was $51.4 billion. Governor Pete Wilson's 1996-97 budget totaled $58.5 billion.

These figures can be misleading because they do not show how much the cost of state government has risen. Many of the increases were for the exclusive purpose of relieving-pressure on the property tax or on local government, especially after the passage of Proposition 13 in 1978. In fact, about two-thirds of each year's budget consists of allocations to schools and other elements of local government, and about half the state budget is for public education.

### Budget process

The budget process in the Legislature involves detailed study of items that are questioned by the Legislature's fiscal specialist, the legislative analyst. For months, subcommittees of the Senate Budget and Fiscal Review Committee and the Assembly Budget Committee pore over the budget and decide which items should be increased, reduced, added or eliminated. Eventually, the budget is packaged by the fiscal committees and sent to the floor of each house. As a practical matter, either the Senate or the Assembly bill becomes the vehicle for enactment of a budget. The first house to act sends its version of the bill to the other, which then puts its own figures into the legislation and sends it back to the house of origin. The changes are routinely rejected, and the budget is placed in the hands of a conference committee composed of members of both chambers. Even though the constitution requires that the budget be sent to the governor by June 15th, it is often much later before both houses are able to adopt a compromise because passage by a two-thirds majority is required.

### Revenue

One major portion of the budget — estimated revenues — is not considered at all by the Legislature, except to verify that funds will be sufficient to meet anticipated expenditures. The difference between revenues and expenditures (with any carry over from the previous year taken into account) produces the projected surplus for the fiscal year.

About 75 percent of the revenue goes into the state general fund. The remaining 25 percent is collected from specific sources and placed in special funds (notably the motor vehicle fund) to be spent for specific purposes. Estimates in the governor's proposed budget for the 1996-97 fiscal year show anticipated revenue from all funds of $58.9 billion ($45.6 billion general fund; $13.3 billion special funds). Specific fund sources and their percent of total revenue are as follows:

Personal income tax, $20.6 billion (35.0%);
Sales tax, $18.1 billion (30.8%);
Bank & corporation taxes, $5.6 billion (9.6%);
Insurance, $1.1 billion (1.9%);
Motor vehicle (inc. gas tax), $7.9 billion (13.4%);
Tobacco, $630 million (1.1%);
Liquor, $262 million (0.4%);
Estate taxes, $578 million (1.0%);
Horse racing fees, $105 million (0.2%);
Other, $3.9 billion (6.6%).

### Expenditures

Total proposed 1996-97 expenditures are $58.5 billion, not counting bond funds. Here are the major items of expenditure as proposed by the governor in January 1995:

Aid to schools K-12, $17.9 billion (30.5%);
Health and welfare, $16.6 billion (28.4%);
Higher education, $6.5 billion (11.0%);
Business, transportation and housing, $4.2 billion (7.2%);
Youth and adult corrections, $4.1 billion (7.0%);
Other, $9.3 billion (15.9%).

While the Legislature can revise the budget in any way it sees fit, the governor has only two choices when he receives the bill act at the end of June: he can veto it in its entirety and thus force the Legislature to pass a new bill, or he can reduce and eliminate specific items (this is known as blue-penciling the budget through line-item veto). This latter is the practice traditionally used.

Until the budget is enacted, the Legislature cannot pass appropriations measures unless the governor provides a letter saying that the expenditure is needed on an emergency basis. Once the budget is passed, however, the Legislature can — and usually does — send the governor numerous bills containing appropriations. The governor can cut the entire appropriation or reduce the amount. (Each of these bills can contain only a single appropriation.) 🏛

# Last in, First out

Pete Wilson entered the 1996 presidential sweepstakes with an impressive string of political victories. But the way he and his minions conducted what ultimately became a failed campaign has temporarily shattered his myth of invincibility.

## By Steve Scott

Reprinted from *California Journal*, November 1995

While the nation will doubtless recall 1995 as the year of the O.J. trial, there's a case to be made for Califor-nians remembering 1995 as "The Year of the Crash and Burn." Consider, for example, the California Angels. After bursting to an 11-game lead in the American League's Western Division in mid-August, the Angels suffered through the slow-motion calamity of watching that lead disappear. They eventually lost the flag to the Seattle Mariners.

While the Angels were teaching baseball how to choke, Governor Pete Wilson was giving a national political clinic on the same subject with his presidential campaign. From the time he informally announced last spring (see *CJ*, May 1995), Wilson's White House campaign bus was beset with a seemingly unending series of disasters. Finally, late last month, the governor mercifully put an end to his effort. "As much as your hearts and mine tell me to fight on," Wilson told supporters in Sacramento, "that would be unfair to all of us."

It's tempting to compare Wilson's demise with that of the Angels — both started with high hopes only to become victims of bad luck and their own inability to execute. There is, however, one important difference. The Angels, at least, had a chance.

Never in Wilson's political career has so much time, effort and money been exerted with so little effect. For the better part of a year, Wilson was riding a White House campaign bus that was up on blocks. A seemingly routine throat operation turned into a months-long water torture, as Wilson was unable to speak publicly or raise money privately. The chronically weak fund raising eventually forced Wilson's top staffers to go off salary, and prompted the governor to abandon his campaign in the first caucus state — Iowa. While he flirted briefly with double-digit poll ratings during the summer, by September a *Time*/CNN survey put him at 5 percent nationally. His poll numbers in New Hampshire, the first primary state, were equally dismal. Perhaps most strikingly, Wilson's vaunted campaign team was rocked by an internal power struggle that ended with the resignation of campaign manager George Gorton — a fixture in the Wilson camp for a quarter of a century.

For those who have watched Wilson bulldoze his way through California politics, the question most often asked in the wake of Wilson's failure is, "What happened?" Why did one of the most disciplined politicians in the state suddenly start taking his plays from Kathleen Brown's campaign playbook? The answer, by and large, lay in the "three M's" — money, management and the man himself.

Financially, Wilson found himself trapped in the ultimate paradox of any national campaign: To raise enough money, a candidate must prove he or she has a chance to win. Unfortunately, the clearest measure of that "viability" is the amount of money a candidate has raised.

For many, the roots of Wilson's "viability" problem stretched back to the beginning of his campaign and what been described as "the original sin": breaking his pledge not to run. Not only had Wilson publicly promised not to run during the 1994 re-election campaign, he made the same vow privately to prospective donors. Breaking that vow alienated not only the conservative Republicans who already disliked him, but also several of his long-time backers, who felt betrayed and used. "After he promised the people of this state he wasn't going to run, people outside the state took him at his word," noted University of California, Irvine, political science professor Mark Petracca.

"It says to people that this guy is so cynical, he thinks people won't care a whiff if he turns 180 degrees on his pledge," said University of Virginia political scientist Larry Sabato. "Even a cynical public found that too cynical by half."

His universe of potential donors was further diminished by the lateness with which he started to actively campaign, as many potential donors had already been lined up by other candidates. "We entered late," admitted Wilson. "We found that too many donors had signed on with other candidates and were commendably loyal to them."

Another lead weight around the governor's campaign was his flagging reputation in California. Wilson consistently trailed Kansas Senator Bob Dole among Republicans, and President Bill Clinton among all voters, and his approval ratings ran about 20 points behind Clinton's. Then there was the revelation in the spring that Wilson had, at one time, employed an illegal housekeeper and failed to pay Social Security taxes for her. While most candidates might have sloughed off such a revelation, for Wilson it was a sore point, given his vocal advocacy of cracking down on illegal immigration.

With all his external problems, however, the real enemies to the governor's fund raising were his vocal cords. In April, Wilson, whose voice has long been plagued by squeaks and cracks, had "minor" surgery to have a node removed from his throat. All he had to do was stop talking for a few weeks, said doctors, and everything would be good as new. Wilson didn't listen, and shortly found himself presented with an ultimatum — stop talking for two months, or forget talking altogether. While Wilson obeyed the second dictum, his refusal to obey the first cost him two months on the phone raising money.

"We thought he was going to be out for three weeks," said Bob Naylor, former state GOP chief and one of Wilson's California fund raisers. "Instead, he was out for close to three months. Commitments were being made [to other candidates] and the momentum was lost."

Wilson's fund-raising trouble was somewhat surprising, given his previous success in both the unrestricted gubernatorial campaigns and contribution-limited races for U.S. Senate. Even more surprising, however, were the miscalculations and tensions that plagued the governor's campaign-management team. Unlike other national campaigns that center on direct regional appeals, the central calculation of Wilson's campaign was always "California times 50." As they successfully had in California, Wilson forces thought they could win by identifying an issue — in this case, affirmative action — and then beating it to death with TV ads. While Wilson's opposition to affirmative action did resonate, many experience in national campaigns say such a strategy was doomed from the beginning.

"Running for national office is very different from running statewide in California," said Democratic consultant Darry Sragow, a veteran of both types of campaign. "It is hubris to think that because you can win a gubernatorial race on illegal immigration and the death penalty, you can win the presidency like that."

If, as Sragow and others suggest, the strategy was flawed, those flaws were magnified by a polarizing power struggle within the campaign. Recognizing the lack of national experience among his veteran team of California hands, Wilson hired Craig Fuller, a long-time national GOP hand who was chief-of-staff to then-Vice President George Bush and helped run Bush's winning 1988 campaign. The importation of Fuller incensed the mercurial Gorton, who disappeared for a week before returning to the race. The two men were never able to work together, and some close to the campaign said it was like stepping into "two armed camps."

The fissures became public when it was learned in September that Wilson's campaign was roughly $1 million in debt. "[Fuller and Gorton] weren't speaking to each other, and each thought the other was watching the money," said one source on condition of anonymity. Ultimately, Wilson chose to elevate Fuller over Gorton, prompting Gorton's bitter resignation from the campaign, but by then, it was too late. Less than two weeks after Gorton and chief fund raiser Anne LeGassick were purged, the campaign itself ended.

While money and management may go a portion of the way toward explaining Wilson's failure, there is another crucial element — the man himself. In 1994 Wilson's campaign forces clucked over Democrat Kathleen Brown's futile efforts to move to the right to appeal to a broader constituency in the race for governor. Among other things, Wilson aides pointed out, Brown had abandoned her base of support among Democrats. Well, fast forward a year and you find Wilson making exactly the same mistake, abandoning his presumed base in California and among moderate voters and competing for support from the GOP's conservative wing.

"It's 'Politics 101,'" said Orange County Republican strategist Eileen Padberg. "Solidify your base, go after the undecideds, and forget about the people who are never going to vote for you. Have they solidified their base? I don't think so."

Wilson's critics say the reason Wilson had problems solidifying his base was that he doesn't have one to solidify. For them, Wilson's presidential campaign merely highlighted the growing perception of Wilson as a man in search of a vision. His broken promise was the first in a series of shifts in philosophy and emphasis that cast Wilson as an opportunistic automaton, whose positions were determined by focus groups, rather than any ideological core. "Who is this guy?" wonders veteran Democratic consultant Bill Carrick. "Is he the moderate guy who ran in 1990, or is he this mean-spirited guy we got [in 1994 and 1995]."

Wilson and his backers bristle at the suggestion that the governor lacks vision. His position changes, they say, are simply the hallmarks of a pragmatic individual who is responding to changing times. "Most voters realize that, when the world changes, sometimes different measures are called for," said longtime Wilson press aide Dan Schnur. Still, even some of those predisposed to support Wilson were disenchanted with the ease with which Wilson repositioned himself on such issues as affirmative action and abortion funding.

"Pete has an awful lot to offer," said Padberg. "But he needs to come down and be a person of purpose. Nobody feels like he's really rooted to anything. You like Pete Wilson, but you don't march over the mountain for him."

How well he can get people to "march over the mountain for him" will policy direction, Wilson must also soothe the lingering anger among California Republicans over his broken pledge. Wilson can be expected to spend considerable time and energy helping to get Republicans elected to the Legislature next year. "Governors have an influence in legislative races where presidents don't," noted Tony Quinn, a Republican consultant and former legislative staffer. "If Wilson can rehabilitate himself, he can help get Republican votes for legislative candidates." Wilson can also be expected to actively support initiatives, such as the anti-affirmative action California Civil Rights Initiative and his own effort to institute a 15 percent income-tax cut.

If 1995 proved one thing, however, it is that Wilson's policy success depends on his personal commitment to it. Privately, many Republicans secretly fear the possibility that Wilson might be angling for a vice-presidential nod. Campaign Chairman Craig Fuller insists one doesn't "run" for vice president, but didn't rule it out. "My own personal advice to our nominee is to look seriously at Pete Wilson, but that's an issue he has not discussed with us," said Fuller. "I think that's wide open." Supporters and detractors of Wilson's cau-

Photos: Rich Pedroncelli

George Gorton

Craig Fuller

ultimately determine where Wilson goes from here. Most anyone listening to his withdrawal speech heard someone still very much bitten by the presidential bug. "There is one hell of a lot of fight left in this old Marine," said Wilson to his supporters. But in ending his fling with national politics, Wilson must now face some unpleasant music from the jilted spouse — California. His standing to try again in 2000 could hinge on how well he rehabilitates himself with his ambivalent constituents.

"If he's not trying to do things to get national visibility, the potential is there to exert leadership," said political scientist Larry Berg, retired former director of the Unruh Institute on Government at the University of Southern California. "He really needs to do it."

In addition to restoring faith in his tion against such a move, however. "I think that's out for all the reasons he was out for president," said Quinn. "All the problems with unhappy Republicans, which have been put to rest, would come right back."

Even if Wilson is not positioning for a spot on the ticket, anyone hoping for a return to the pragmatic Wilson of the 1990 campaign is in for a bit of a wait. But if Wilson is to ever be a credible national contender, he must at least do a better job of projecting himself as a leader with a vision, rather than a politician with a runaway ego. The best way for the governor to make that case is to direct attention toward one goal between now and the end of his term. Results. 🏛

# Two green threads

## The Wilson administration has made an attempt to braid together environmental and economic interests, but the effort has proved difficult. And staff complain that science has sometimes been suppressed in the name of regulatory reform.

### By John Borland

Reprinted from California Journal, January 1996

Two green threads run through the history of environmental protection. One is the green of old growth forest, of the habitats of endangered species, of environmental interests. The other is the green of dollars: economic interests that have political clout and the ability to promise jobs for voters.

When Governor Pete Wilson came into office in 1991, he told the world he would braid the two together. "There are a number of people who think environmental quality and economic health are mutually exclusive," he told reporters. "On the contrary, they are interdependent."

This has proven to be a difficult task. The administration has exerted an iron control over its regulatory departments, making it clear at the lowest levels that departments are to balance thè sometimes-competing interests in their actions. But staffers inside these bodies say they see immense political pressure to protect the interests and good will of "stakeholders" — the businesses and other economic players of the regulated community — often at the expense of the departments' public trust.

"A lot of my time [is spent] justifying what my job is," said one water-related agency employee, who like several others in state service asked not to be identified for this story. "You can't take for granted that a statute is on the books. You have to justify it every time to enforce it."

The pressure sometimes goes farther, some say: In seeking the politically feasible balance between the environment and economics, the science produced by staff sometimes gets watered down or ignored to make compromise easier. "More than once, the best information has been diluted by higher-ups," said one Department of Fish and Game biologist. And staff is loathe to complain, for fear of retribution from above. "We're in an era now where punishment is one of the tools being used," explained another Fish and Game employee.

Wilson came into office with grand environmental schemes. A politician who had often sided with environmentalists in the past, he touted his newly-created California Environmental Protection Agency (Cal/EPA) as "a single point of accountability for all of the state's environmental programs ... [enforcing] vigorously what will be high standards — standards based upon honest, scientific assessment." The agency's objectives included a link between environmental protection and economic progress, also stating that priorities would be based on rigorous science and supported by vigorous enforcement.

The Republican governor's first years in office were marked by recession, exacerbated in California by the gradual pullout of billions of federal and private military-industrial dollars. The downturn drove business and the public to focus on the green of dollars-and-cents issues more than the green of the environment; the administration responded with a drive to prune regulatory red tape.

Wilson was insistent upon the appearance of a unified team in these and other efforts. "Talking Points," or memos listing the governor's goals and accomplishments, were regularly sent out to high-level appointees, sometimes with pointed cover sheets alluding to recipients' "duties as a member of the Wilson administration." Early in 1993 all cabinet officials were told that any official report or document released to the public first had to be cleared with the Cabinet Affairs Unit.

Always a high priority, Wilson's regulatory reform efforts redoubled last year in tandem with his short-lived presidential bid. An early July memo from Cal/EPA Undersecretary Jack Pandol lists several key administration goals for the environmental agency: reducing the excessive burdens of regulations, ensuring that costs of compliance are equal to benefits, and producing regulations "written and organized in a user-friendly manner."

Pandol's memo outlines several potential approaches to these tasks. Departments might simply ask themselves if each regulation was reasonable. They could conduct meetings with business and other affected individuals to solicit ideas on how to relieve excessive burdens. Departments could propose the repeal of all regulations — or just those that hadn't been amended in three years — and hold hearings to "see if substantial justification is forthcoming to save some of them." Or, Pandol said, the administration could simply instruct departments to reduce regulation by 30 percent and let them figure out how to do it.

**W**ilson codified his new campaign in a mid-September executive order directing each department to review every regulation affecting the business sector, identifying those suitable for repeal. This should be done, he added, with the input both of the affected business and environmental communities. The result has been massive review and reorganization projects throughout the departments, which will culminate some time next year.

But in its drive to roll back red tape, the administration has alienated much of its own regulatory staff. Staff scientists grumble that science is being ignored or diluted for the sake of political expediency. And in several environmental departments, staff reports that the pressure to be a "team player," to refrain from questioning the administration's objectives, has reached unprecedented levels. One Fish and Game biologist recounted a recent assignment evaluating the effect of a large timber company's cutting plans on a threatened species.

"We were told — not in so many words — that this timber harvesting plan must go through," the biologist said. "We were told, 'Trees are going to be felled, so do a mitigation plan.'" She

did what she felt she was expected to do, writing up a report that would allow the timber to be cut, but which went against the grain of her scientific instincts. "A lot of what I wrote or what I was told to write isn't what I would have written [based on science alone,]" she said.

Another biologist described a similar incident. He and a supervisor had agreed that research justified beginning the consideration process to list a new endangered species. Opponents of the listing countered with testimony at a public hearing, but the scientists concurred that this evidence was neither new nor persuasive. A bit later, while both were out of state, the department announced that the scientists had changed their minds based on the new information, and that there was no need to begin the review process. "Changing a recommendation is always management's prerogative," the biologist said. "But that was inexcusable."

As a 20-year veteran of the department, the scientist said he has long seen and expected some politically influenced decisions. Government work does, after all, take place in a political environment. But "there has been no governor before Wilson that has interfered with the mandates of the department like Wilson," he said. "This is insidious, both in frequency and in significance."

In mid-February of last year, a pair of Fish and Game Wardens testified in front of Senator Tom Hayden's (D-Santa Monica) Natural Resources and Wildlife Committee, citing political pressures that curtailed some enforcement efforts. "We are in competition with other water interests for the resources, and essentially, fisheries seems to have taken a back seat," said warden Will Bishop. "Agricultural interests ... have a bigger voice, apparently. When I try to, or we as wardens generally try to enforce the provisions of the code that the Legislature has given us ... we're told to work with these people." He gave only past incidents as specifics, but Warden's Association legislative director Dave Gardner later said that small examples still continually arise. "We see little pieces of it all the time," Gardner said. He cited a few areas, such as streambed alteration decisions, where decisions made in Sacramento are often at odds with what field staff recommend. "To a certain degree those pressures are still there."

Jeff Weir is Fish and Game's Deputy Director for Conservation Education. He admitted that politics are necessarily involved in the workings of the department, since it operates in and is funded by a politically driven world. "I would be happy to say we're as politically astute as possible," he said.

Weir says he is aware of the perceptions of upper-level "conspiracy" in some of the department's lower ranks. "It is just their lack of knowledge," he said, casting the critics in the role of the allegorical blind men trying to picture an entire elephant from a single touch. Rank-and-file critics are simply mistaken, he said, in assuming that outside political powerhouses pull the strings on agency decisions. "If management doesn't do what they want, they think [the decision] is politically tainted," he said. "That's a naive point of view."

Reports are routinely edited, sometimes by him, Weir noted, but primarily for stylistic reasons or to take out loaded language or unwanted policy statements. "My role is to destigmatize information, so it becomes a legitimate resource,"

> But in its drive to roll back red tape, the administration has alienated much of its own regulatory staff.

he said. "I am unaware of a single report that has been politically changed or changed for political reasons."

That there is currently pressure on wardens to refrain from enforcement for political reasons is "not true," said Fish and Game chief of wildlife protection De Wayne Johnston. "We enforce all the rules," he stated. "The only reason there is any less emphasis on enforcement is that we have about 50 less wardens than we used to have." Budget cuts have hit all departments hard, he said, and make it increasingly difficult for everyone to do their job.

Weir did note the need to bow to political winds at times, if the department is to keep its funding and be able to operate in a hostile climate. "It's pretty obvious that when the environment and economics clash, people vote for economics," he said. "We represent 32 million people with a lot of different values. ...From a public survivability point of view, we as an agency have to recognize that."

Resources Agency Deputy Secretary Andy McLeod attributed the charges of political pressure to those opposed to the administration's compromise-based policies. "Some people will inexorably oppose [innovation] because it is change," he said. "We're trying to improve things."

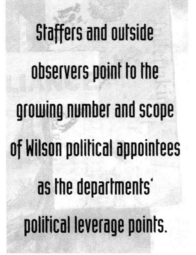

**Staffers and outside observers point to the growing number and scope of Wilson political appointees as the departments' political leverage points.**

The administration's identification with economic interests is found in other agencies. A former Air Reseources Board employee tells of being caught in a political battle between the board and the California Truckers' Association (CTA). The board had mandated an additive to diesel fuel, which raised the fuel's price and the truckers' hackles. Much of the new fuel turned out to damage truck engines, and the truckers blamed the air board, releasing a barrage of publicity and lobbying the administration to end the experiment. The ARB appeared hard-pressed to defend itself. "Every time the facts ran contrary to what the CTA was saying in public, the administration was restricted from protecting itself," the staffer said. "It even got to the point where some of the comments from [Cal/EPA head James] Strock reflected comments of the CTA. ...If you look at some of the wording of some of the CTA press releases and then some wording of Stock's speeches, the wording is the same."

An independent panel of experts was called to evaluate the CTA's claims. It cleared the ARB, putting the blame on a large producer of diesel fuel. But when the employee released the finished report on his own volition, he was called by a high-level ARB official and reprimanded. "There was some displeasure that the CTA was unhappy," he said. "The message I got was that I didn't get the message. The message was, 'Don't piss off the truckers.'" After more than 20 years in government service, he left the board for the private sector soon after this incident.

Another example of questionable commitment to fact was recently brought to light by the *Sacramento News and Review*, an alternative weekly newspaper. In late 1994 state Water Resources Control Board inspector Boris Trgovcich examined an El Dorado irrigation plant, finding significant pollution and evidence of hundreds of code violations over the past few years. He wrote a report on the plant, as his supervisors requested, but as he neared completion, word came from above that the report would not be released to the public because it would embarrass the Regional Water Board. Trgovcich kept writing. When he turned it in, he was told it would not be needed — and when the press and public asked a supervisor if the report was ready, they were told that only a "bunch of notes" had been prepared.

Trgovcich had recently — and successfully— fought a different whistle-blower case after being transferred to a unit where he was told he "would not cause any more problems" for himself. This time, he sent a caustic letter to his division chief. "During the last few years, I have frequently been instructed not to criticize or embarrass the [regional water quality boards] when they fail or refuse to enforce their [responsibilities]...," he wrote. "My duty statement (or that of my supervisors) says nothing about protecting [regional board executive director William] Crook's reputation, covering up our own mistakes, denying the taxpayers access to public records or writing 50-page reports destined for the wastepaper basket." Trgovcich's report was eventually released, in what he calls a somewhat "sanitized" but acceptable form.

Staffers and outside observers point to the growing number and scope of Wilson political appointees as the departments' political leverage points. "As long as the director is appointed by the governor, the governor and the Legislature will put pressure on the department," Fish and Game warden Bishop recently said, reiterating his testimony earlier.

Many state environmental employees believe they are subject to retribution if they speak out critically. "I can say that the fear is palpable. People are afraid to talk," said Chris Voight, a consultant for the California Association of Professional Scientists, the government scientists' union. "There has been retaliation in the past."

Civil servants can't legally be fired without good cause. But there is a widespread staff feeling that other means can and will be used, including transfers, assignment to unwanted or make-work projects, or black marks in their records that might prevent future promotions. Several staffers point to the example of Fish and Game's Jerry Mensch, who was transferred against his will to the Sacramento headquarters after reporting a supervisor for code violations. Mensch is currently suing the department. "That is not a routine transfer," one wary biologist said.

Fish and Game asks staffers to fill out a standard form after talking to the media, naming the reporter and detailing the topic of conversation. Whatever the intended effect of this procedure, it too has a chilling effect on many staff members.

The tension inside these departments indicates that Wilson's marriage of environment and economics is done with a shotgun as often as with a ring. Wilson's attempts to dramatically revise the state Endangered Species Act and the California Environmental Quality Act, and charges by environmentalists that the massive departmental regulatory reviews are being dominated by business interests, don't promise a quick rapport.

But state employees are used to keeping their heads down through such political cycles. They will do it for a few more years. 🏛

# California's "morphing" economy

## By Susan F. Rasky

Reprinted from *California Journal*, March 1995

**E**conomics, like all great religions, is largely a matter of faith and assertion — a constant redefining of observable phenomena to explain the past, to predict the future and to make living in the unpleasant or confusing present a little more tolerable.

This is perhaps better understood elsewhere in the country. Here in California, we have never had to bother much about complicated economic explanations or redefinitions. Until recently, we had a perfectly serviceable myth that covered all contingencies. Our mythical past was an unbroken line of successes from the gold rush, to the oil boom, to the rise of Hollywood, the flourishing of the defense industry, the emergence of Silicon Valley and the spectacular rise in real estate prices. Our future was, well, just like the past, the only uncertainty being what precise form the next boom might take. And our present punctuated how special we were. In a state that can swing so easily from the politics of Jerry Brown to the politics of Ronald Reagan, why be overly concerned about the fulminations of Mother Nature?

Three-plus years of recession that began in 1990 changed all that, prompting (quite apart from general handwringing and soul searching) a flurry of economic studies by business, academic and governmental groups attempting to assess the impact of the steep downturn and offer some perspective on what lies beyond the next one or two budget cycles.

It's not that such studies didn't exist before, but rather that none of the state's policy players and certainly none of the public felt much need to pay attention to them. Now that the economists and deep thinkers have our collective attention,

> "The value of a 25 year economic forecast is its use at the retirement roast of the person whso wrote it." — Fred Silva, executive secretary, California Constitutional Revision Commission

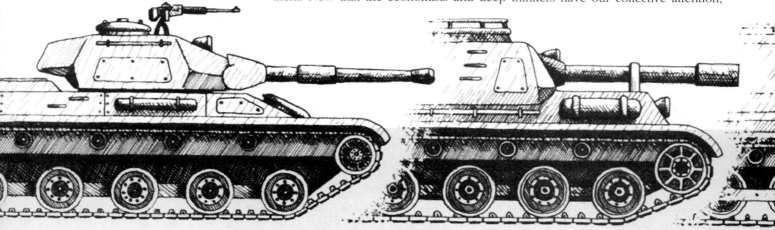

however, the question is whether their redefinitions of the past and their unsettling visions of the future lead us to any answers about how to plan for the next quarter century while simultaneously dealing with the very real problems of the here and now.

Certainly, it would be easier to set store in what the economists say about where California is going in the long term if their studies agreed on where the state has been in the recent past. That, alas, is asking too much.

What the studies do offer is a useful cataloging of the key variables that will shape California over the next decade or so and four somewhat distinct scenarios — each partly dependent on short-term policy choices — of what the state will look like in the early part of the next century.

But first, just a little history. Californians like to view the state's ups and downs in the most extreme fashion. In the case of this recession, however, our tendency toward melodrama has some justification.

What happened here in 1990 was a confluence of forces that had been building for more than a decade. Apart from the most obvious ones, such as the end of the great real estate boom and the dramatic drop in military spending, the state began to feel the negative effects of population growth, lack of investment in infrastructure, fiscal policy reforms directed by the initiative process that decreased money available for education and other public services, and regulatory policies that made California less attractive to new businesses.

Despite their disagreement on the precise depth, scope and duration of the recession, the economists and policy analysts who have weighed in on the subject do agree that California has experienced something more fundamental than a cyclical downturn. To any lay observer, that hardly seems a startling revelation. But in the policy community, it put to rest the myth that the state's economic base was sufficiently diverse to withstand major cutbacks in national defense spending.

Among economists, the steep recession and the apparent divergence of California from national trends also forced a more serious attempt to distinguish short-term, or cyclical impacts from permanent or structural changes in the state's economy. In a report prepared last summer for the California Business-Higher Education Forum, Larry Kimbell, director of the UCLA Business Forecasting Project, pointed to a rough consensus among forecasters about which were which. He parsed it this way:

• Jobs lost from defense cuts are permanent, with no reasonable prospect for recovery of those jobs in the next decade.

• Jobs lost to corporate downsizing are permanent, hitting once-secure middle-management and white-collar jobs particularly hard both in California and the country as a whole. Kimbell estimated that 400,000 of the 600,000 jobs lost in California during the recession occured in downsizing industries, which include not only defense and aerospace, but also retail trade, commercial construction, finance, transportation and telecommunications.

• California's housing and construction industries, while suffering the longest and most depressed downturn in postwar history, will eventually join in the national recovery of these sectors, and may get an additional boost by the need for earthquake rebuilding and seismic retrofitting. New and existing home prices, which soared in the 1980s, will stabilize for a few years and then begin to rise in line with general inflation.

• Foreign trade will be one of the most important sources of long-term growth for California, picking up in the Far East as the Japanese economy recovers and accelerating with Mexico because of the North American Free Trade Agreement (NAFTA). Although Kimbell's analysis was done before the recent Peso crisis, economists at the Business Forecasting Project said the current situation does not alter their long-term outlook.

Part of the reason economists have such difficulty reaching consensus forecasts, especially for the long term, is their annoying refusal to settle upon what to measure and how to measure it. In other words, a cautionary note to the lay analyst trying to compare forecasts: even the variables are infinitely variable.

It helps a little to divide recent studies on California's economy into two broad categories — those based upon historical notions of trade, comparative advantage and market forces; and, with appropriate apology to the practitioners, those based upon an extensive collection of empirical data, which then is turned into equations and cranked through econometric models.

In the former category, again with apologies for oversimplification, put the Palo Alto-based Center for the Continuing Study of the California Economy, the Berkeley Roundtable on the International Economy, the Denver-based Center for the New West, and assorted business and trade associations whose studies reflect the concerns and priorities of their members. In the latter category put the UCLA Business Forecasting Project, the state Department of Finance, the Legislative Analyst's Office, and the state's major banks.

*Illustration by Rob Wilson*

Obviously, the categories overlap, and some of the recent economic studies by academic and political or civic interest groups draw from both types of analyses.

That said, the big variables look something like this:

• **Geography:** Assuming the next major earthquake does not move the Pacific coastline eastward to Arizona, California's location at the edge of the continent and on the border of two major trading nations remains a positive for the state's long-term future. J. Ian Morrison, president of the Menlo Park-based Institute for the Future, takes geographic advantage a step further. He argues that climate, specifically a true Mediterranean climate in portions of the state, will continue to make California a magnet for "the smart, rich and hopeful."

• **Population:** This is a complicated variable to estimate because it depends not just on birth and death rates, but also on assumptions about domestic migration to California, which in turn are based on assumptions about job growth in the state. Some economists are more optimistic than others. In its 1994 report, the Center for the Continuing Study of the California Economy, for instance, was quite emphatic about the long-term trend: "Given the substantial projected growth in population and jobs in the nation, there is no doubt about the finding that California will grow significantly in terms of total jobs, population and households." The report estimated that the United States would add 30 million residents between 1993 and 2005, and another 100 million in the years after 2005. "The question of California reaching a population of 40, 45 or even 50 million is more a matter of when than whether," the CCSE study concluded.

• **Demography:** This obviously is intertwined with population, but there is general agreement among economists who study the state that aging of the baby-boom generation is a fundamental driving force behind many of the changes projected between now and 2020. Those changes include not just the obvious — such as reconfiguration of the workforce, increased demands for health-care services that may not get satisfied, and strains on the Social Security and other retirement systems — but also more subtle political and social effects. What happens to the gentrified urban areas that flourished in the 1980s as boomers abandon them in search of safer and more distant suburbs, and what new political pressures emerge as boomer children reach college age and find the state's public university system more costly and seriously overcrowded?

• **Diversity and immigration:** There continues to be disagreement among and between economists and politicians about which income and service-seeking population groups are leaving or coming to California, and how much of the movement is strictly a function of the recession. What is clear, regardless of the direction national immigration policies may take in the next few years, is that sometime in the next century, all groups in California — white, African American, Latino or Asian — are going to be minorities. And if nothing else, that implies a new level of social and political tension in California as traditional alliances and antagonisms among the population groups break down and reform.

Wither California in the next 25 years?

As always in economics, there is a scenario with a statistical back-up to suit almost any vision. Stephen Levy, of the Center for the Continuing Study of California, whose forecast appears on page 61, is traditionally an optimist. But many of his prognosticating colleagues are less sanguine given what they regard as a set for fairly limited, and ultimately painful, policy choices. (Why do you think they call economics "the dismal science"?)

The following scenarios are by no means fully wrought forecasts but rather a rough categorization of views from the recent studies of the state's economy.

• **Blade Runner:** This is futurist J. Ian Morrison's grimmest vision of the path California, specifically Southern California, will take. As in the movie by the same name, it assumes "an executive high-tech city where the well-off live in a fortress environment, and beneath them, literally and metaphorically, is a multiethnic polyglot gong show which is both unsafe and unpleasant," Morrison says. Morrison has a variation on this theme in which he describes "white and cranky" baby boomers sitting in nursing homes singing "I Got You, Babe" to each other and demanding that a young multiethnic population pay for them to live in comparative luxury.

• **Texification:** This is University of California, Berkeley, Public Policy Professor John Ellwood's description of how the political and fiscal policy choices California has already made — as well as those that voters seem likely to make in the near future — turn the Golden State into a sort of Texas on the Pacific. Ellwood notes that through the mid-1960s California's rapid economic growth and high per-capita income allowed it to be a high-tax, high public-service state that invested more per capita on public projects (including schools) than the national average. Today, he says, in a view widely shared by economists, California is a moderate tax, moderate public-service state. "What we're headed to is Texas," he says. "Small government, low investment, low wages and a greater gap between rich and poor."

• **Pittsburgh:** This is the coinage of economist Eugene Smolensky, Ellwood's colleague and dean of the Graduate School of Public Policy at UC Berkeley. It embodies a bit of the "Blade Runner" and "Texas" scenarios by assuming that Los Angeles becomes so congested and unlivable that large numbers of people leave to seek better jobs and better conditions elsewhere. The optimistic result, for those who remain, is Pittsburgh after the collapse of the steel industry — a less-polluted and less-congested city with a well-developed infrastructure and an economy based on banking and finance. In other words, a new equilibrium.

• **Convergence:** For proud Californians, who glory in being, well, different, this is perhaps the least appealing view of the future. It may also be the most realistic. David Hensley, who used to be at the UCLA Forecasting Center and now works for Salomon Brothers, notes that contrary to early wisdom on the differences between California's recession and the one experienced by the rest of the country, the state is actually looking more and more like the United States as a whole. In other words, California's historical uniqueness, in economic terms, is precisely that — history.

"We've been looking at the industry and economic structure of states, and what we're finding is that rather than states cleaving toward what they do best, over the past 30 years they are overwhelmingly converging to a national norm," he says. "This is true of California, too; now more than ever and certainly more than Californians ever believed, the state is a true microcosm." 🏛

---

*Susan F. Rasky was an award-winning journalist for* The New York Times *before coming West to head the California News Service, a project of the University of California, Berkeley, Graduate School of Journalism.*

# THE JUSTICE SYSTEM

The judiciary may be the most powerful of the three branches of state government because the Constitution is so detailed and because the Supreme Court has the power to strike down acts of the Legislature or initiatives that conflict with the state and federal constitutions. The court also uses its power to void acts of the executive branch that violate either a statute or the Constitution.

Under a series of forceful chief justices — among them Phil Gibson, Roger Traynor and Donald Wright — the state's highest tribunal often led the way for the United States Supreme Court. The California Supreme Court built a reputation for activism and independence with decisions that struck down the death penalty (People v. Anderson, 1972), outlawed the state's system of financing public education (Serrano v. Priest, 1971) and invalidated an anti-fair housing initiative approved by the electorate (Mulkey v. Reitman, 1966).

An activist Supreme Court has often been viewed as a second Legislature — more powerful than the first. Governor Ronald Reagan sought to reduce the activism of the court through his appointments, but one of the big disappointments of his eight years as governor was that his appointee for chief justice, Donald Wright, turned out to be another activist.

In 1977, Democratic Governor Edmund G. Brown Jr. had an opportunity to recast the court and by 1981 his appointees comprised a majority on the court. He appointed the court's first woman, Chief Justice Rose Elizabeth Bird; first black, the late Wiley W. Manuel; and first Latino, Cruz Reynoso. Bird was a highly controversial figure when she was appointed and throughout her tenure on the court. While there were many criticisms of the Bird court by conservatives, the most critical was the court's failure to allow any executions during her tenure as Chief Justice. (Polls indicate that over 80 percent of California citizens favored the death penalty.)

In November 1986, in an unprecedented election, three of the Brown-appointed liberals, Justices Bird, Reynoso and Joseph Grodin lost their confirmation elections. This enabled Governor George Deukmejian to appoint three new conservatives to the high court. These three combined with two previous appointments gave the court a conservative majority which it has retained to date.

## Lower and appellate courts

The Supreme Court sits at the apex of the California judicial system. There are three lower levels — the municipal courts, the superior courts, and the district courts of appeal. Members of the Supreme Court and the district courts of appeal are appointed by the governor subject to confirmation by the Commission on Judicial Appointments (consisting of the chief justice, the attorney general and one appeals-court justice). In recent years, the commission has called for public hearings on controversial appointees. Bird was approved by a 2-1 vote following a heated public debate. Incumbent judges' names appear on the ballot at the first general election following their appointment and again at the end of each 12-year term. If the incumbent receives a majority of "yes" votes for retention, he or she has another 12-year term.

• *Municipal courts.* These local courts hear misdemeanor cases, preliminary hearings on some felony charges, small-claims actions and civil cases involving relatively small amounts of money (less than $25,000 in both municipal and justice courts).

• *Superior courts.* These countywide courts hear juvenile criminal cases, felonies, appeals from justice and municipal court decisions, and civil cases that cannot be tried in the municipal courts.

• *Courts of appeal.* These are divided into six districts (based in San Francisco, Los Angeles, Sacramento, San Diego, Fresno, and San Jose). Each division within each court contains three or four justices, with three justices normally sitting on each appeal. The court has jurisdiction over appeals from superior-court actions and decisions of quasi-judicial state boards.

• *The Supreme Court.* The state's highest court handles appeals from the district courts of appeal, although some cases can be taken directly from the trial court to the Supreme Court. In death-penalty cases, for example, appeals automatically go from the superior court to the Supreme Court. The high court also reviews orders of the Public Utilities Commission and has some appointive powers.

Judges of the municipal and superior courts are elected by the people for six-year terms. The governor fills vacancies on the municipal and superior courts. On occasion, there is a wide-open race for a judgeship, but usually the post is filled by appointment and the incumbent retains the judgeship at the ensuing election. District courts of appeal and state supreme court judges are confirmed (they face no actual opponent) in a yes or no vote of the people to twelve year terms. They also must stand for confirmation in the first state election after their appointment.

A judge may be removed or otherwise disciplined by the Supreme Court — but only upon recommendation of the Commission on Judicial Performance. Judges are also subject to impeachment and recall, but the more common disciplinary procedure is through an investigation by the commission and action by the high court.

The state Judicial Council is a 21-member board charged with the overall administration of the court system. It is headed by the chief justice, who in turn appoints most of the members. The Administrative Office of the California Courts is the staff agency charged with carrying out the council's policies and conducting research for the council.

California uses the standard jury system. Grand juries (19 citizens in most counties, 23 in Los Angeles) investigate public agencies and have the power to hand down criminal indictments. However, the state Supreme Court ruled in 1978 that preliminary (probable-cause) hearings must be held, whether or not a suspect is indicted. Trial juries usually consist of 12 registered voters, but both sides in a case can agree to a smaller panel or waive a jury and submit the case to a judge. A unanimous vote is needed for acquittal or conviction in a criminal case. 🏛

# CALIFORNIA'S COURT SYSTEM

## U.S. SUPREME COURT

## CALIFORNIA SUPREME COURT

Original jurisdiction; habeas corpus, mandamus, certiorari, prohibition

## DISTRICT COURTS OF APPEAL

| First District | Second District | Third District | Fourth District | Fifth District | Sixth District |
|---|---|---|---|---|---|
| San Francisco | Los Angeles | Sacramento | San Bernardino San Diego | Fresno | San Jose |

Original jurisdiction; writs of mandamus, prohibition, habeas corpus, ceritorari

## SUPERIOR COURTS
### ONE IN EACH COUNTY

Original jurisdiction; Civil-amount in controversy exceeds $15,000, mandamus, habeas corpus, equitqable relief, probate, family law and juvenile court matters. Criminal-felonies.

## MUNICIPAL COURTS

### ONE IN EACH DISTRICT OF MORE THAN 40,000

Civil jurisdiction; amount in controversy, $15,000 or less. Criminal: lesser misdemeanors, preliminary hearings for felonies, infractions

## MUNICIPAL COURTS

### ONE IN EACH DISTRICT OF 40,000 OR LESS

Civil jurisdiction; amount in controversy, $15,000 or less. Criminal: misdemeanors, preliminary hearings for felonies, infractions

## JUDICIAL COUNCIL

Makes rules on judicial procedure; surveys and expedites judicial business.

COMPOSITION:
Chief Justice
Fourteen judge appointees of chief justice
Four elected by State Bar
One Assembly
One Senate

## COMMISSION ON JUDICIAL NOMINEE EVALUATION

Evaluates the Governor's prospective judge candidates.

COMPOSITION:
Nineteen elected by State Bar
Six appointed by governor

## COMMISSION ON JUDICIAL APPOINTMENTS

Confirms or rejects appointees of Governor to Supreme Court and Courts of Appeal

COMPOSITION:
Chief Justice
Attorney General
Senior Justice on Court of Appeals

## COMMISSION ON JUDICIAL PERFORMANCE

Recommends to Supreme Court censure, removal or retirement of judges

COMPOSITION:
Three judges appointed by the Supreme Court
Two lawyers elected by State Bar
Six public members—two each appointed by the governor, Assembly speaker and Senate president pro tem.

RECOMMENDATIONS, ADVICE CONFIRMATION

LINES OF APPEAL OR REVIEW

# THE LUCAS COURT

**Since Rose Bird's departure, the California Supreme Court has been less controversial, and less diverse**

## By Bob Egelko

*Bob Egelko covers the state Supreme Court for the Associated Press.*

Reprinted from *California Journal*, June 1994

**P**eople who have lost track of the state Supreme Court might not remember why California has no campaign funding limits for public financing of legislative elections this year. It isn't because of legislative or public opposition; in fact, 53 percent of the public voted for those changes in a 1988 initiative.

No, the reason is that the court extinguished that initiative in a 4-3 ruling last December, saying voters would have preferred the remnants of a rival measure that already had been gutted by federal courts.

Another question. "Why aren't Proposition 103 rate rollbacks moving ahead, six years after that initiative passed and three years after Insurance Commissioner John Garamendi adopted regulations and ordered hearings?"

Responsibility might be assigned to the state bureaucracy, the insurance industry or flaws in Proposition 103 itself. But the most immediate reason is that the court agreed a year ago to review the legality of the regulations, but hasn't scheduled a hearing yet or allowed Garamendi to implement rollbacks in the meantime.

Finally, why aren't new jails and courthouses being built in San Diego County with the money from a sales tax increase that was approved by a majority of the voters, under a financing system that the court seemed to have endorsed in 1982?

The reason is that a new court majority took another look in 1991 at the two-thirds vote required by Proposition 13 in 1978 for "special taxes," interpreted the requirement more broadly and struck down the San Diego measure.

Good or bad, these decisions, and the court that issued them, deserve more attention than they're getting.

Largely by upholding death sentences, the court headed by Chief Justice Malcolm Lucas for the last several years has managed to avoid the prominence and controversy that surrounded the Rose Bird court in the years leading up to the 1986 elections, when Bird and two colleagues were voted out of office. A return to a lower profile was probably healthy for the court and certainly welcomed by the justices. But the Lucas court is an important force in the state, and it's hard to understand its near-invisibility.

For example, although Justice Edward Panelli retired January 31, more than four months after announcing his plans, Governor Pete Wilson left the vacancy unfilled for months, with no criticism from his rivals. Meanwhile, the seventh seat at monthly oral arguments was occupied by a succession of appellate justices, including some Democrats.

In a year of obsession with crime and punishment, the court wasn't even mentioned during the primary elections for governor. The only candidates who seemed interested were two Democratic hopefuls for insurance commissioner, state Senator Art Torres and Assemblyman Burt Margolin; they joined some consumer groups this March in an unsuccessful request to the Deukmejian-appointed majority on the court to withdraw from an insurance case in which the former governor represented an insurance company.

The last time many legislators seem to have taken notice of the court was in 1991, when Lucas, in a ruling upholding a term-limits initiative, belittled the effect of a 38 percent cut in the Legislature's operating budget. Legislative committees rushed to propose a 38 percent reduction in the court's budget before cooler heads prevailed.

The court's funding could suffer if the governorship were won by a Democrat, who presumably would feel less affinity for the 6-1 majority of Republican appointees. But there isn't much a new governor could do about the current majority, which, barring personal tragedies or a major scandal, should be with us into the next century.

The three 1987 Deukmejian appointees who swung the court to the right — Justices John Arguelles, Marcus Kaufman and David Eagleson — all retired in less than four years, after becoming eligible for maximum retirement benefits. Their successors — Joyce Kennard, Armand Arabian and Marvin Baxter — are younger and have many years to go on the pension ladder, as does Wilson's first appointee, Ronald George, who succeeded the retiring Justice Allen Broussard in 1991.

Justice Stanley Mosk, at 81 a 30-year veteran and the only Democrat on the court, floated enough retirement rumors before the 1986 election to keep his potential opposition off balance, avoided the purge of his fellow liberals and has shown few signs of slowing down. He is the

---

UPDATE:

After serving eight years as its leader, on May 1, 1996, Chief Justice Malcolm Lucas retired from the California Supreme Court. Governor Pete Wilson selected Supreme Court Associate Justice Ronald George to serve as the new Chief Justice.

Earlier, Judge Armand Arabian retired from the Court on February 29, 1996. Wilson appointed Chinese American Court of Appeals Justice Ming W. Chin to replace Justice Arabian. In addition, Governor Wilson nominated African American Court of Appeals Justice Janice Rogers Brown to the vacant position on the Court created by George's elevation. Brown had previously served as Wilson's Legal Affairs Secretary prior to her appointment to the Appeals Court. The Commission on Judicial Nominee Evaluation rated Judge Brown as "not qualified" because she had only one year's prior judicial experience. Brown is the first person selected to the State Supreme Court in its entire judicial history who has received this lowest rank from the Commission. Despite this "judicial experience" issue Governor Wilson nominated her to the bench, and she was confirmed by the Commission on Judicial Appointments.

leading dissenter on the court, slightly ahead of Kennard, who established herself as the least predictable justice soon after her appointment in 1989.

As for Lucas, the 67-year-old chief justice remains the leader of the court's controlling bloc, though he no longer writes the most opinions, as he did for several years after his elevation by ex-law partner Deukmejian in 1987. He has a few years left before maximum pension eligibility, shows no obvious ill effects from a 1987 colon cancer operation, and hasn't dropped a hint about leaving.

Lucas also seems to have withstood the embarrassment of a *San Francisco Chronicle* account last November of his frequent out-of-state travels. The article disclosed that a Lloyds of London subsidiary, which had cases before Lucas' court, paid for two of his trips to overseas conferences, raising concerns about judicial ethics. Saying the trips were part of his job, Lucas asked for an investigation by the Commission on Judicial Performance, whose nine members include five judges appointed by the Supreme Court. The commission cleared him two months later, saying the unique nature of the chief justice's job should have dispelled any suggestion of illicit influence or appearance of impropriety.

Probably the harshest public evaluation of the court was another *Chronicle* article in November, concluding that the court had sunk into mediocrity since its trailblazing years of the 1950s to mid-'70s, based on interviews with scholars and assorted legal observers. Assessments like those are beyond the scope of the present article or the capability of its author, who wishes to observe only that objective standards are elusive, and it's probably more useful to examine the justices and their work in their own time.

The current court can be divided roughly into two phases. In the first three or four years, the court defined itself largely by deciding how far to go in discarding or narrowing the doctrines of the Bird court and its predecessors. Conservatives were firmly in control, but the presence of Mosk, Broussard, and later Kennard kept debate brisk and dissents relatively frequent.

Some of the biggest plums fell quickly. In 1987 the court, under the surprising authorship of Mosk, ruled that a death sentence could be imposed without proof of intent to kill, overturning the key decision in the Bird court's death-penalty reversals. The next year, majorities led by Lucas barred suits by third parties against insurance companies for mishandling or delaying claims — overruling a 1979 decision detested by insurers — and severely limited damages for wrongful firings.

As expected, the court also started giving generous readings to initiatives that the Bird court had interpreted more narrowly. The 1991 ruling in the San Diego County case, strengthening Proposition 13's clout against local taxes, was the culmination of a trend of several years. Prosecutors won longer sentences and broader rules on confessions under a 1982 crime initiative known as the Victims' Bill of Rights. The court's sympathetic view of initiatives may have saved consumer-sponsored Proposition 103 in 1989 when the justices decided to rewrite rather than discard its rollback of insurance rates.

In civil rights, where previous courts had expanded the reach of anti-discrimination laws, the Lucas court displayed its empathy for businesses and its distrust of regulatory agencies in a series of rulings by Panelli, starting in 1987, that trimmed the powers of the state Fair Employment and Housing Commission. In 1990 the court barred suits against businesses for discriminating against the poor but said it would allow other claims of arbitrary bias recognized by the Bird court. Lower courts have had trouble deciphering that ruling, and it's likely to be refined in a future case.

The first phase contained a few surprises — the rejection of a "sub-minimum" wage for workers receiving tips, the upholding of a one-house legislative veto of Deukmejian's nomination of Dan Lungren as state treasurer — and one outright stunner: Over the repeated dissents of Lucas and Panelli, the remaining appointees of anti-abortion Governor Deukmejian joined their colleagues in refusing to reconsider a Bird court ruling continuing state funding for Medi-Cal abortions.

Attempts to curtail the funding were later dropped by Wilson, but the abortion issue may soon be back before the court in the form of a never-enforced state law requiring parental consent or a judge's approval for an unmarried minor's abortion. The court finally addressed the underlying privacy issue this January in a ruling upholding drug testing of college athletes; Lucas' majority opinion, a masterpiece of ambiguity, contained much talk of core values and balancing tests, but few clues about the court's approach to abortion or other privacy disputes.

The court entered its second phase around 1991, when the majority was solidified by the appointment of George, a bright and ambitious former state death-penalty lawyer, to succeed Broussard — Jerry Brown's last remaining appointee. Its task of culling the casebooks for undesirable precedents largely complete, the court enjoyed a friendly legal landscape and political security, and could set its own agenda.

At times, this included bursts of activism usually associated with more liberal courts. After a legislative attempt to declare surrogate-motherhood contracts legal and regulate them was vetoed by Wilson, the court declared one type of surrogacy legal without regulation last year. Dismissing suggestions that a contract to bear another's child for pay exploited poor women, Panelli's opinion coolly observed that poverty often induces women to take bad jobs. Kennard, dissenting from the all-male majority, said the court was devaluing the role of the birth mother.

More often, the court has stayed true to its creed of judicial restraint, deferring to the decisions of legislators, voters and trial judges. But the court has encountered some unforeseen problems in the last few years, often as the consequences of its own earlier decisions.

First and foremost was the death penalty, the downfall of the Bird court and the top priority of the Lucas court. The repeal of the intent-to-kill requirement cleared the way for a dramatic turnaround of the affirmance rate — from 6 percent under Bird to more than 90 percent in the last four years, the highest in the nation. Critical of the previous court's second-guessing of trial judges, the new majority relied on the doctrine of "harmless error," regularly concluding that mistaken rulings could not have influenced the jury's death verdict. The concept was

ers, not by victims' damage suits against landowners for faulty security. Another maxim was that firm lines had to be drawn around liability, at the price of occasional harshness to individuals. So a mother who heard neighbors scream, and ran outside to see her child lying in the street, couldn't sue a hit-and-run driver for emotional distress because she didn't see the accident. And someone who saw a lover die in a car crash caused by a drunken driver couldn't sue unless the couple was married.

This approach has the advantage of clarity and doesn't have to sacrifice an understanding of human problems. One of the court's most acclaimed and influential rulings was a 1990 case balancing the rights of patients and the interests of medical re-

sometimes carried to great lengths, excusing a judge's improper refusal to let a murderer tell jurors why he deserved to live, and another judge's erroneous decision to allow evidence of a gruesome wine-bottle rape.

The court also tore into the case backlog, deciding 56 capital appeals in a single year, 12 fewer than the Bird court had resolved in seven years. To promote efficiency and discourage repeated appeals, the court adopted time limits and other procedural restrictions, in a 1992 ruling modeled on a U.S. Supreme Court decision.

But the backlog refused to disappear, and instead changed shape: The number of Death Row inmates without lawyers rose above 100, and the average waiting period for a lawyer reached three years, as a combination of limited pay and bleak prospects discouraged experienced attorneys from accepting capital appeals. That meant cases were taking longer to reach the court, and potential new grounds for future appeals were being created. Meanwhile, the court's efforts to dismiss new claims on procedural grounds without a hearing were meeting a chilly reception when the cases arrived before federal judges, increasing the likelihood that death sentences would be reversed and cases returned to state courts for new trials.

The length and arduousness of capital cases also took time away from civil cases, held down the court's statistical output and may have spurred some justices toward retirement. A commission appointed by Lucas in 1987 had recommended shifting some of the death-penalty workload to state appeals courts, but Lucas never endorsed the idea and it's scarcely been mentioned since.

Another area that has proven more complicated than it first appeared is torts, the broad field of liability for physical, mental and financial injuries. Decisions of the early years seemed to yield some simple rules. Tort suits were not to be the primary instrument of public protection or social policy; thus, foot-dragging by insurers was to be deterred by regulators, not by private lawsuits, and crime was to be controlled by police and lawmak-

searchers. A man sued doctors after an organ, removed during a life-saving operation, was tested and found to contain a cell pattern that was a potential source of new medical products. The court rejected the patient's claim of a violation of property rights, which could have entitled him to a share of the profits; but Panelli's majority opinion let him sue the doctor on more limited grounds, for failing to inform the patient of the research plans or obtain his consent. The ruling provided guidance to doctors and patients, left research unimpeded and discouraged the exploitation of unknowing patients.

But not all problems can be resolved so neatly. The court's tendency to create rigid categories, and its inclination to limit damage suits, have led it at times to try to pound square pegs into round holes. A glaring example involved assumption of risk, the doctrine that denies all damages to a person who engages in a dangerous activity and is injured by someone else's negligence. Most state courts have treated the concept as outdated since a 1975 state Supreme Court ruling that allowed damages when both parties were negligent, with the award reduced by the proportion of the victim's fault. But the Lucas court signaled in 1990 that it might revive the prohibition on damages, and granted review of about a dozen cases. Two years later, the court produced a fragmented and bewildering ruling.

In the case of a woman injured during a company football game, three justices, led by George, said sports participants had no duty to act carefully, and could be sued only for reckless or intentional harm. Three others, led by Kennard, said a suit should be allowed only if injuries resulted from activities that were more dangerous than the victim anticipated. The seventh justice, Mosk, said assumption of risk was outmoded, but agreed with George that no duty had been breached. Even the court couldn't figure out which of those standards to apply to the next case that raised the issue. The result, apparently, was that the approach of letting juries weigh the fault of each side had been discarded for dangerous activities, without any clearly defined policy to put in its place.

Further trouble lay ahead in a more significant case, involving suits for fear of disease caused by pollution. In the case of Salinas-area residents who learned their water wells had been contaminated with carcinogens, lower courts found their fears of cancer reasonable and awarded damages against the polluting company. But the Supreme Court, urged by businesses to prohibit all such suits and leery of "speculative fears," devised a new rule last December; In normal cases, damages would be awarded only if plaintiffs could prove they were more likely than not to become ill. But apparently unwilling to throw the Salinas residents out of court, the majority, led by Baxter, created an alternate test: They would have to prove only a significant risk of disease, because the polluter (according to the court) had disregarded a known risk of harm. The decision left the many interested parties on both sides neither satisfied nor enlightened. The new standards seemed arbitrary and the boundary lines murky. Underlying the decision may have been the court's unstated view that fears, like other emotions, are too intangible to be trusted as the basis of a lawsuit.

A similar approach outside the tort field resulted in perhaps the court's most awkward ruling in recent years — the December 1993 decision denying enforcement of Proposition 68, a 1988 campaign finance initiative.

Voters approved two political reform measures on the same ballot. Proposition 68, which included contribution limits as well as partial public financing for legislative candidates who limited their spending, got 53 percent of the vote. Proposition 73, which contained a different system of contribu-

tive, said the four-member majority. Lucas' opinion said voters would have passed that provision by itself, even if they'd known in advance that the rest of the measure was invalid. What was left of Proposition 73 was still a competing regulatory scheme, and there was no room for Proposition 68, the court said.

The result was cheered by legislators and major contributors, but was hard to square with the court's professed reverence for the people's will. Two initiatives, both approved by a majority of the voters, had added up to zero reform. The ruling didn't even end the case; Proposition 73's legislative authors were soon back before the justices, asking for a new ruling that would rewrite their measure and cure its legal flaws.

The last few years have shown some weaknesses in the Lucas court, but the court is not without its strengths. It retains the support of much of the bench and bar, quickly mobilized behind Lucas when his travels came under scrutiny. It is also accepted by most of the public, which handily approved the current justices when they've appeared on the ballot, and is likely to do so again this fall. Despite a decline in the number of rulings, due largely to the increase in death penalty cases, the court is as hard-working as any of its predecessors. Lucas takes his leadership role seriously and has appointed productive task forces on racial and gender bias, technology, and the future of the court system. Mosk has been one of the nation's highest-regarded state judges for many years; the lesser-known Kennard and George appear to be extremely capable jurists with much untapped potential.

tion limits and several other provisions, including a ban on public financing, got 58 percent. The state Constitution says the ballot measure with the most votes prevails, but an appeals court, following some earlier appellate rulings, decided to allow enforcement of the parts of Proposition 68 that didn't conflict with Proposition 73. The Supreme Court disagreed and announced a new rule in 1990: When two ballot measure contain competing regulatory schemes, the measure with fewer voters is entirely unenforceable.

However, federal courts were already in the process of dismantling Proposition 73, and soon ruled that its core provision, the contribution limits, unconstitutionally favored incumbents. Proposition 68 had no such defect, so its sponsor, Common Cause, asked the state Supreme Court to revive the measure, since its rival had been effectively nullified. But the Supreme Court refused, and declared that Proposition 73 wasn't entirely dead; one previously obscure provision, broadening an existing ban on publicly financed mass political mailings, was unaffected by the federal rulings and was actually part of the essential purpose of the initia-

But the court, like a medieval royal family, suffers from inbreeding. For 12 years, two governors with a common agenda have promoted a succession of mostly like-minded justices from the appellate courts, with similar backgrounds as business or government lawyers, while stocking the lower courts with ex-prosecutors. When the high court justices sit around the conference table, there are no former poverty lawyers, civil-rights lawyers, labor lawyers, public defenders or academics, and probably few who have ever represented or have ever been, a poor person. That's not a formula for healthy debate. When the court hits a dead end in its thinking, it needs new ideas and new perspectives to find a way out.

Oddly enough, a possible prototype for change is sitting in the governor's office. When Wilson was a U.S. senator recommending candidates for federal judgeships, his picks were fairly diverse, sexually, racially, professionally and even ideologically. His appointments as governor have fit a different mold, but whoever is elected this November could strengthen the court by following Senator Wilson's model. 🏛

# Three strikes one year later

## Proponents claim that the three-strikes law has lowered the crime rate without swamping state prisons. But county law-enforcement officials say they are awash in defendants — a river of human criminals that promises to flow into prisons soon enough.

### By John Borland

Reprinted from *California Journal*, October 1995

**H**ad the brutal kidnapping and murder of Petaluma's Polly Klaas by a paroled felon happened 150 years ago, odds are there would have been a lynching. California may be more measured than that today, but outraged citizens still needed something to assuage their fear and anger. They got a law.

In the wake of the Klaas affair, the idea of putting repeat offenders behind bars for life swept the state, embodied in a concept called "three strikes and you're out." A law to that effect passed both houses of the Legislature in 1994, and appeared on the 1994 ballot as Proposition 184. It was a sign of the times that a three-strikes bill carried by Assemblyman Richard Rainey (R-Walnut Creek), a former sheriff supported by the District Attorney's Association, failed because it applied only to violent acts and thus was labeled insufficiently "tough on crime." The successful version, authored by then-Assemblymen Jim Costa (D-Fresno) and Bill Jones (R-Fresno), put criminals behind bars for 25-years-to-life for *any* felony, provided the perpetrator had two prior violent or serious convictions. Governor Pete Wilson, then anchoring his nascent re-election campaign with square-jawed crime credentials, signed it into law.

Nearly lost in the acclaim were cries that the law would boost the prison population to a level far beyond what the state could afford. Based on Department of Corrections figures, the Legislative Analyst's Office estimated that 25 new prisons would be needed to hold the 80,000 new prisoners projected to enter the system by 1999, just to maintain current levels of overcrowding. But the prison population has not skyrocketed as quickly as expected. The LAO has downgraded its estimation of prison construction to a

> We do have ... periods of time when we have to borrow a few civil judges.
>
> — Judge Joan Weber

mere 15 new prisons over the next five years — surely no easy task but marginally less Herculean than the original charge.

Attorney General Dan Lungren's office trumpets a significant reduction in the California Crime Index, the measure of reported crimes committed in the state over the course of a year. "There were 57,000 crimes prevented in the first year," says Fresno photographer Mike Reynolds, the guiding spirit behind the three-strikes proposal. Reynolds' adult daughter was slain by a repeat offender during an attempted purse-snatching, prompting her father to make three-strikes a personal crusade. "That's with no cost of incarceration, no prosecuting costs, and most of all, no victims." Reynolds, along with Wilson and Lungren, publicly attributes the drop almost entirely to the preventive effect of three strikes, an assertion questioned by professional criminologists.

But if prisons have not yet borne the brunt of the law, it may be due largely to logjams at the county level. Trial courts around the state are accumulating a towering backlog of cases. In some areas, civil courts have had to be commandeered in order to fulfill defendants' constitutional rights to a speedy trial. Jails are filling with three-strike suspects waiting for their trials, leaving little room for those charged with lesser offenses. The county-level justice systems that serve as the gateway to state prisons are staggering underneath the burdens of the three-strike caseload.

When Westwood attorney Tom Dempsey received a court date last May, he expected that the case, on behalf of a client who had bitten into a sharp piece of metal hidden in a salad, would come up soon. He was wrong. He waited for six weeks as his scheduled courtrooms and jurors were continually shunted towards "strike" cases. The waiting eventually became too expensive, and Dempsey and his client settled. "It was a very good case," Dempsey says. "We just couldn't get started."

Stories like Dempsey's are growing in number across Los Angeles County, according to presiding Superior Court Judge Gary Klausner. Branch courtrooms in Pomona, Long Beach and Torrance have stopped hearing civil cases altogether. The downtown Los Angeles civil courthouse, equipped with only minimal security provisions, has had to take on hundreds of cases involving third-strike, gang-related, or otherwise potentially violent defendants.

The problem is this: Before the passage of the three-strikes law, less than 5 percent of felony cases went to trial, mostly because defendants were willing to plea bargain a lesser sentence. But facing life in prison, nearly 75 percent of third-strike defendants, and 50 percent of first- and second-strike defendants are demanding full jury trials. About 3100

third-strike cases had been filed in Los Angeles by the end of August, along with more than 20,000 second- and first-strikes. In the law's first year of operation, these strike cases made up only 23 percent of felony cases filed, but soaked up nearly 80 percent of Los Angeles' felony trials, according to the county Bench-Bar Coalition. Add in the fact that strike cases tend to take slightly longer to try than ordinary jury cases, Klausner says, and the county's criminal-court system becomes hopelessly overwhelmed. "We need an additional 30 judges just to stay even," he says.

While the situation is far worse in Los Angeles than in other parts of the state, other courts report similar symptoms. Santa Clara County has reassigned three judges from split duty to solely criminal cases as a result of their strike load. San Diego is keeping up with its caseload, according to presiding criminal Judge Joan Weber, but the county has brought in a number of retired judges to help and has assigned three judges to work full time on three-strike cases. Even with these measures in place, Weber says, "we do have ... periods of time when we have to borrow a few civil judges."

The rise in caseloads comes at a time when judicial resources are already strained. County money appropriated by the state in recent budget agreements was supposed to be partially returned through state funding of 75 percent of trial-court costs. That level remains stuck in the mid-30s. Several years ago, the state Judicial Council recommended that 61 new judges be added statewide to keep up with growth in the population and crime rates. There have been no such additions.

"We're here ... to carry out the will of the people," Klausner says. "If the people and the state want three strikes, then we say that's fine, but they have to realize that we need 'x' number of resources." Without those resources, he says, courts will begin to fail those who need civil justice: small businesses, tenants and landlords, spouses seeking restraining orders and more. "What worries me is when people begin to feel they don't have access to the courts, that they have to go to [private alternatives]. If you're rich, fine; if not, tough, go to the streets." Three strikes can work, Klausner says, but only if there is more support for the courts. "Don't give me a hammer and tell me to build a house."

Predictably, the backup in the courts is washing upstream into county jails. Originally envisioned as little more than holding pens for nonviolent offenders sentenced to less than a year of imprisonment, jails have gradually come to look more like their prison cousins. Part of this change is simple population pressure: Even though 28 of the state's county jails are under court-ordered population caps, the three-strikes influx has slightly speeded the rate of increase in the total number of prisoners, according to a January survey of jails taken by the Sheriffs' Association and the state Board of Corrections. Only a few counties have had the funds to add jail space recently; more common, as found in Los Angeles, is space unused due to the inability to fund operating costs.

Even more significant, many sheriffs say, is the changing nature of the people behind jail bars. The January survey found that the percentage of inmates awaiting trial, as opposed to those already sentenced, had risen from a historical average of 50 percent to more than 60 percent. That ratio is now close to 80 percent in some county jails, and shows no sign of leveling off. Many jails are no longer accepting suspects charged with misdemeanors, are releasing virtually anyone who is not a violent felon, or are telling police to simply skip arresting low-level offenders. "If it continues to grow," says Merced County Sheriff Tom Sawyer, the chairman of a statewide panel examining the effect of three strikes on county jails, "the easiest way to get out of jail is going to be to get sentenced."

As with the courts, the problem seems to be worse in Los Angeles County, where Sheriff Sherman Block recently drafted regulations barring almost all new misdemeanants from the jails. Block has also had to close several jail facilities due to county budget cutbacks, further curtailing available space. "We predict that very soon we will have an all-felon jail," he says. Even with some budgetary relief, he adds, the pre-trial population of three-strikes offenders will continue to force releases of sentenced prisoners long before their time is up. "The people who used to be in the county jail are on the streets," Block says. "The people who used to be in state prison are in the county jail. And the people in state prison — you have the worst of the worst there."

The gradual rise in violent offenders has pushed jails to increase security measures. "We're getting individuals in for their second or third strike that essentially have nothing to lose," says Imperial County Chief Deputy Sheriff Michael Hackett. "Why should they worry about following internal rules? They ask, 'What are you going to do, send us to prison for life?' The only way to maintain order, Hackett says, is to "run a less kinder and gentler jail than in the past."

Closely related to the level of court and jail crowding is the way in which county district attorneys treat the policy of wiping prior offenses from the records of the accused. The law says this is to be done only rarely. Counties like Los Angeles, which takes this dictum very literally, thus wind up with a heavy stream of defendants lacking any incentive to plea bargain and speed their cases through the system. Counties such as Alameda, where the district attorney is more liberal in wiping priors, manage to resolve more cases and have substantially lower backlogs in the jails and courts.

Rainey is now carrying several bills that would modify the three strikes law, one of which would standardize district attorneys' decisions on when to ignore prior offenses. He hopes this will reduce some of the pressure on the overburdened county systems. But unless this passes, or until more money is put into the system, judges and sheriffs see little hope of relief. "Right now, it's just like being in a river coming out of the mountains," Sawyer says. "And there's a lot of runoff." 🏛

If it continues to grow, the easiest way to get out of jail is going to be to get sentenced.
—Merced Sheriff Tom Sawyer

# The Arming of California

## By John Borland

Reprinted from *California Journal*, October 1995

In tiny Isleton, set quietly in the southwest corner of Sacramento County, Police Chief Eugene Byrd has found a sure-fire way to put his town's name on the map and the town's books closer to the black. In most portions of the county it is difficult to procure a license to carry a concealable weapon. The permits must be issued by a local police chief or sheriff, who often raise such arduous barriers as proving a need to have such a license. Some jurisdictions add requirements such as costly liability insurance or make applicants undergo psychological tests at their own expense.

Not in Isleton. Chief Byrd has made it known that he will issue permits to just about anybody who is honest, who isn't a felon, and who lives in the county. He has a waiting list for the permits of close to 6000 people, more than six times the population of the city. And close to a third of Isleton's projected 1995-1996 budget is supported by Byrd's prediction that he will issue around 700 permits this year, at $150 a pop.

"The Second Amendment says that there's a right to have, not that you need to have," Byrd says. "I don't see that [it] has been repealed." He has never had a problem with the law-abiding citizens who are legally issued weapons permits, he says, and he staunchly defends their right to defend themselves, at home or on the streets, with a gun. "When you take firearms away from honest citizens," he says, "there's going to be crime."

It may not come as a surprise that Sacramento County Sheriff Glenn Craig is upset about Byrd's actions. "I'm concerned that a lot of people not able to get a permit from us are going to him," Craig says. He cites one case in which a suspect in a county burglary case, who had three drunk-driving arrests, was denied a permit by the county, went to Isleton, and was approved there. "[Byrd] has at most 1000 people in his community," Craig says. "And he's decided that he knows what's best for all of Sacramento County. I don't think that's ethical conduct."

On one level, this is little more than a turf war between Byrd and Craig. But the two voice opposing sides of what is shaping up to be one of the biggest firearms legislative battles of the next few years. The National Rifle Association has identified the push for "right-to-carry" concealed weapons laws as its highest priority, seeking to join California with the 29 states where law-enforcement agencies must show why an applicant *shouldn't* be able to carry a gun, rather than the other way around. "This is moving across the country," says National Rifle Association California liaison Steve Helsley. "It's here now."

The battle also showcases an even broader war over gun control in California as the state approaches a crucial point in its history of gun laws. If the generally firearms-friendly Republican Party now controlling Congress and the state Assembly also takes over the state Senate, it will usher in a political climate more sympathetic to the arguments of the NRA than to the gun-control lobby. If the GOP fails in the Senate, the state is likely to stay deadlocked, or perhaps slip slowly back into the control-oriented climate of past decades. But until both houses of the Legislature are controlled by one party or the other, any piece of even marginally controversial firearms legislation will be stuck in a holding pattern around the Capitol dome. "The last session has been, 'They throw one out, we kill it, we throw one out, they kill it,'" says Sandy Cooney, western regional director of Handgun Control Inc.

Most of the heavy skirmishes now center on handguns, which were used in more than 60 percent of California's 3700 homicides last year. The good news is that the total number of such killings dropped slightly in 1994, according to state Department of Justice statistics. But this must be put in context: Handgun homicides nearly doubled, from 1332 to more than 2600 between 1988 and 1993 — a considerably higher rate of growth than for murders overall. "Homicide rates among most groups didn't go up," says University of California, Berkeley, law professor Frank Zimring. "But for kids [18 to 25 years old] it went through the roof." The rate of gun homicide in this particular group tripled, he explained.

This disturbing fact has produced two predictable results: Pro-gun people want greater access to guns for defense, and gun-control advocates want stricter control. Firearms advocacy groups estimate that nearly half of California households already contain at least one gun. "It isn't a matter of people getting guns anymore. People have guns," says former state Senator H.L. Richardson (R-Arcadia), founder and chairman of the board of directors of the Gun Owners of California. "In the last few months, the gun market has ground to a halt. The market is saturated."

This slowdown, however, comes shortly after what amounted to a nationwide gun-buying spree after the debate and passage of the federal Brady bill, which requires that handguns be registered and that buyers wait five days before claiming their purchase, and the Clinton/Feinstein assault-weapon ban. "[President Bill] Clinton has been the best thing in the world for gun sales," the NRA's Helsley says. The debate over the dangers of having assault weapons on the street scared people into buying guns for protection, aside from the push of gun enthusiasts to buy what they wanted before the laws passed, he says.

Ironically, it seems that neither the Brady bill, since it is less strict than pre-existing California law, nor the assault-weapons ban are having much effect in this state. The federal ban, like the 1989 Roberti-Roos state ban before it, leaves loopholes enough that the banned guns or their near-likenesses remain easily available. "All of these guns are still for sale. They never stopped being for sale," Helsley says. A quick look into a gun catalog or gun store backs up his assertion. Magazines may hold fewer bullets, and there may be fewer options — such as flash suppressors, grenade launchers or bayonet holders — but the basic semi-automatic guns are still for sale.

But Handgun Control's Cooney vigorously defends the federal laws, pointing out that 45,000 people in states without waiting periods or background checks have been stopped from buying guns. He also notes that the price of pre-ban assault weapons has gone up three-fold. "No one ever said it was a panacea," he says. "No law is perfect."

On the state level, most of the current session's gun-control measures have come from urban Democrats, largely from Los Angeles. The most prominent of these was an attempt by Senator Richard Polanco (D-Los Angeles) to ban the manufacture of "Saturday Night Specials," a category he defined as cheap, poorly made handguns disproportionately used in the commission of crimes. The bill died in the Assembly Public Safety Committee after the failure to gain last-minute support from Assemblyman Richard Rainey (R-Walnut Creek), a moderate former sheriff. "It really took into consideration a lot of guns, not just Saturday Night Specials," Rainey says, explaining his eventual opposition. "It even banned the gun I used to carry."

The primary legislation for pro-gun forces was "right-to-carry" bills, the most successful of which was authored by conservative Assemblyman Pete Knight (R-Palmdale). "I want to see ... a level playing field across the state," Knight says. "Sheriffs and chiefs have not been issuing these permits in a reasonable manner. I believe those permits should be issued unless there is a reason for not issuing them."

One bewildering constant in these debates is the use of law-enforcement testimonials by both sides. The California Police Chiefs' Association, in particular, appears to have aligned itself with gun-control advocates. The NRA claims support from "rank-and-file" cops, but a monolithic, uniform opinion at any rank proves difficult to find. "What we're interested in is reasonable laws related to control of [guns'] use in society," says Sheriff Craig of Sacramento. "That doesn't mean there is an opinion of law enforcement."

At the heart of the debate lies the Second Amendment to the United States Constitution, which reads: "A well regulated militia being necessary to the security of a free state, the right of the people to bear arms shall not be infringed."

It is a troublesome string of phrases, both grammatically and legally. The NRA and other pro-gun groups argue that the latter half of the amendment proves the framers envisioned a virtually unlimited individual right to own and carry weapons without government interference. "Past practices of the country would indicate that it is an individual right," Helsley says.

California is one of the few states in the country that does not include a right-to-bear-arms provision into its own constitution. What it has done since the late 1960s is reserve to the state government the bulk of the authority to write firearms legislation. Richardson, who carried the 1969 preemption law as a state senator, believes his law reserves all gun-related regulation rights to the state. "That's what was intended, that's what was debated, that's what we had in mind," he says. The point, he explains, by explicitly occupying the total field of firearms legislation, was to "keep kooky cities like San Francisco" from creating a statewide patchwork of contradictory local gun laws.

But Erik Gorovitz, a San Francisco-based attorney working with the Legal Community Against Violence, disagrees with Richardson's interpretation. Gorovitz, in the final stages of a project researching state pre-emption law, believes that Richardson's law actually leaves significant space to pass local legislation on gun-related issues. "There has been a sort of chilling of local regulation because of the fear of protracted legal challenges," Gorovitz says. "In fact, there is plenty of room to be creative."

A few communities around the state already are heeding Gorovitz's advice. Pasadena has passed a city ordinance requiring the registration of ammunition. Lafayette, in Contra Costa County, has imposed strict and costly security requirements on gun dealers in an effort to discourage unmonitored "kitchen-table" dealers selling from their homes. Several municipalities around the state have already passed or are working on efforts to trace and regulate local gun dealers.

And in late August, Vice-Mayor Trixie Johnson of San Jose proposed a package of gun-control measures in front of her City Council, some already a part of city law and some — such as the requirement that all guns be sold with a trigger lock preventing accidental firing — new.

The response of the NRA and other gun owners' groups to such efforts is simple: They will try to take away the offending politicians' jobs. The 1994 recall campaign against then-Senate President pro Tempore David Roberti (D-Van Nuys) exemplified this approach. Richardson's group is still proud of that effort, despite its failure. "He's no longer around, is he?" Richardson says, noting that the money and time Roberti spent on the recall probably sunk his subsequent primary campaign for state treasurer. "We sent a big message to the Legislature with that one."

Richardson's group and the NRA also contribute money and volunteers to ordinary campaigns. "There's a lot of candidates that feel they won" because of NRA volunteers and dollars, Helsley says. Gun-control advocates would be the last to challenge this. "Sacramento has been bought by the gun lobby," says a frustrated Cooney.

Both pro-gun and gun-control groups tout their expanding grass-roots operations. The 1996 elections will be a key test for both, potentially providing the impetus to end the current stalemate. Until then, there will be emotional speeches on both sides, but little movement.

Richardson at least is confident. "Sometimes we feel it necessary to go in and scar people up," he says. This year, "there will be some surprises." 🏛

# THE LEGISLATURE

California's Legislature is not much different from Congress and legislative bodies in other states in overall power and structure. It is, simply stated, the policy-making arm of government, restricted only by the federal and state constitutions and the governor's veto. Like Congress, it can also conduct investigations into almost any issue of public concern and impeach public officials. The Senate must ratify top-level, non-judicial appointments of the governor, while both houses have the opportunity to reject the executive's nominations for any vacancy among the state's constitutional offices. It also can ratify amendments to the United States Constitution. In recent years, there has been a trend toward the Legislature's appropriating for itself some of the appointive power traditionally given to the executive. Thus, it is not uncommon now to have a commission consist of both gubernatorial and legislative appointees.

Seats in both the 40-member Senate and 80-member Assembly are apportioned on the basis of population and under the 1991 reapportionment for the first time the court joined two adjacent assembly districts into one senate district throughout the state. (Until 1966, the Senate was apportioned by geography, like the United States Senate.) Assembly members serve two-year terms; Senate terms are for four years, with half the terms expiring every two years. Under the provisions of Prop. 140 of November 1990, term limits are now imposed on state legislators (3 terms, 6 years in the Assembly; 2 terms, 8 years in the Senate). The Senate and Assembly are organized differently, with power diffused in a committee of the upper house but centered in the office of speaker in the Assembly.

## The Senate

The lieutenant governor is the president of the Senate, but this official has virtually no power. The lieutenant governor is entitled to cast a vote to break a 20-20 tie, but this is very rare. If the Senate can be said to have a single leader it is the president pro tempore, who is elected by a simple majority of his colleagues. The pro tem is charged with overall administration of the house, but the real power — committee appointments and assignment of bills to committee — rests with the five-member Rules Committee. The president pro tempore is chairman, and the other four seats are traditionally divided between the two major parties. In the past rural vs. urban, north vs. south or personal animosities created conflict. In recent years the divisions in the Senate have tended to be along party lines. David Roberti provided stable leadership to the Senate from 1980 (when Willie Brown was elected speaker) to 1994 when Roberti was forced to leave the Senate because of term limits, the first state legislator in the nation to be forced out of office. The current President pro Tempore is Senator Bill Lockyer.

Aside from the Rules Committee, the two most important panels in the Senate are the Appropriations and Budget and Fiscal Review committees. The Budget and Fiscal Review Committee handles the budget. The Appropriations Committee hears any other bills with direct or implied state cost. Thus it can kill almost any major bill.

## The Assembly

Until 1995 the Assembly had a form of government that might be called self-inflicted dictatorship. The speaker was elected by at least 41 votes (a simple majority) and thereafter wielded tremendous power; this officer appointed all committee chairs and named all committee members except for the Rules Committee. Control over committees amounted to the power to kill any bill. A bill defeated in committee could be brought to the floor by a majority vote of the full assembly, but this occured very infrequently. A vote to withdraw a bill from committee would be tantamount to a vote of no-confidence for the speaker. The speaker's control over legislation made whoever holds this office the second-most-powerful official in state government next to the governor. However, on occasion, the speaker had difficulty leading. Battles within majority Democratic ranks in 1979-80 between then-Speaker Leo McCarthy and challenger Howard Berman, each with his own faction, led to legislative paralysis in the lower house. In 1988 the "Gang of Five" (anti-leadership Democrats) openly feuded with Democratic Speaker Willie Brown over legislative matters in the Assembly. Though the five were punished by Speaker Brown (losing chairmanships, committee assignments, staff and office space) they refused to back down. For a time, the "Five" combined with the Republican caucus had a majority in the Assembly. However after the November 1988 elections, Democrats had 42 seats plus the rebellious "Gang of Five" who were no longer needed for a majority. The "Five" returned to the Democratic fold, and their transgressions forgiven.

However, a combination of term-limits-fomented-bailouts of veteran Democractic assembly members, the court-designed reapportionment of 1991, and a nationwide Republican surge provided the necessary ingredients for substantial Republican gains and corresponding Democratic losses in the Assembly in the 1994 general election. After the dust settled, 41 Republicans and 39 Democrats were elected to the Assembly. Many pundits began writing Willie Brown's epitaph as speaker. It appeared that Brown would lose his speakership and that Republican leader Jim Brulte would replace him. However, it didn't happen—then. Rumors of Willie Brown's political death were exaggerated: Brown had an ace up his sleeve. Republican Assembly member Paul Horcher switched from Republican ranks to independent in early December 1994. On the floor he surprised his GOP brethren by voting for Willie Brown as speaker. This created a 40-40 tie and meant there was no immediate resolution of the leadership issue for the time being. Horcher said he left Republican ranks because Republican assembly leadership had become too conservative (and had shunned him for being to cooperative with the Democrats).

In January, Democrats and Horcher moved to oust Republican Richard Mountjoy from the Assembly. Mountjoy had been elected simultaneously to the Assembly and to the Senate in a special election in the 1994 election. Although Mountjoy fought to stay in the Assembly so that he could continue to vote for Brulte, he was removed in mid-January 1995 on a 40-39 vote. (Of course, if he had resigned from his Senate seat, he could have remained in the Assembly.) With

Mountjoy gone, Willie Brown was elected as speaker 40-39 (not with the customary 41-vote margin). And, Speaker Brown agreed to share power with Republicans. Of the 26 standing committees, 13 were chaired by Republicans and 13 were chaired by Democrats.

Angered by Horcher's defection, Republican Assembly leaders went on to recall him from office and elect a new Republican loyalist, Gary Miller, to the seat. In June 1995 Brown announced he would be running for Mayor of San Francisco (he won), and Democrats united behind maverick Republican Doris Allen electing her as the new speaker. Immediately Republican leaders sought to recall Allen, and several months later she resigned from the speakership. Allen, in turn, voted for her one Republican ally, Brian Setencich to replace her as speaker, again with Democratic caucus support. Republicans successfully recalled Doris Allen and she was replaced by Scott Baugh as assemblymember from the district. Brown's departure from the Assembly and Miller's and Baugh's election to the chamber, allowed Republicans to depose Brian Setencich as speaker and elect their leader, Curt Pringle as speaker and Rules Chair. Speaker Pringle quickly "Brownized" Democrats by selecting Republicans to chair all committees (with one exception, Reform party member Dominic Cortese) and gave each solid Republican majorities.

In any case, instability and turmoil will likely be the pattern in the Assembly for the forseeable future. Every two years a fresh new wave of 30-35 rookie legislators will be elected. The grizzled veterans will be members who have served for a term or two. One thing is certain however: the immense power speakers such as Willie Brown once held is a relic of the past. Post-Brown speakers may retain the traditional legislative powers of the speaker, but will not be able to exert the all-encompassing influence of the past in the new term limits era.

Much of Willie Brown's power hinged on continuity (he's now in his 15th year as speaker and 31st as Assembly member.); his ability to maintain the Democratic majority; and his success in wheedling large campaign donations from special interests (concerned about what passed or what was killed in the Assembly) and then divvying them out to Democratic Assembly members for their campaigns. This is gone. In the new term-limits era the Assembly Rules Committee may become more important in the Assembly in performing its various housekeeping duties: assigning bills to committee, setting salaries for legislative employees, determining offices for members and purchasing supplies. The Senate is likely to become the more influential legislative house because the upper house will have more experienced members. After all, most new senators have previously served in the Assembly. In the new term limits era, it is also possible that some term-limited senators may be able to continue their political careers by running for the Assembly (if they haven't already served six years there after 1990).

## Legislation

There are three basic types of legislation: bills, constitutional amendments and resolutions. These measures can only be introduced by legislators. The governor cannot introduce a bill, but he can ask a friendly member to put it in the hopper. Even the governor's budget carries the name of a lawmaker. In fact, however, very few bills are the direct inspiration of a legislator. Most bills come from interest groups, staff members, constituents, government officials, or a variety of other sources.

A bill is simply a proposed statute. It can be enacted by a simple majority vote in both houses unless it is an urgency measure or carries an appropriation, in which case a two-thirds vote of approval is required. Constitutional amendments are proposed changes to the state Constitution; a two-thirds vote of each house will place one of these measures on the ballot for voter consideration. Resolutions are merely statements of legislative viewpoint. They may be addressed to other governmental agencies, describe state general policy, or commend or memorialize someone. They are normally passed by voice vote. Constitutional amendments and resolutions, unlike bills, are not subject to gubernatorial veto.

## Legislative process

When a member introduces a bill, its title is read and it is printed. Then it is assigned to a committee by the Assembly or Senate Rules Committee. The committee hearing is the most crucial stage in the legislative process, for it is at this point — not on the floor — that the fate of most legislation is determined. Following public hearing, the committee can kill the measure or send it to another committee (usually the fiscal committee) or to the floor as is or with recommended amendments. When it reaches the floor, the bill's title is read a second time, amendments are often made, and the legislation is placed on the agenda for debate. After debate, a roll call is taken. If the bill is passed, it is sent to the other house, where the same process takes place. If the bill is amended in the second house, it must return to the house of origin for acceptance or rejection of the amendments. If approved at this point, the bill goes to the governor for signature or veto. If the amendments are rejected, a conference committee of three members of each house is formed to compromise differences. This procedure is always followed on the budget and often used at the end of a session to speed the last-minute rush of bills (because a conference committee report can be produced more rapidly than a revised printed version of a bill).

A bill goes to the governor if both houses approve a conference committee recommendation.

In the Senate, roll calls are taken orally by the secretary of the Senate and aides. Once a roll call is concluded, members may not change their votes, and absent members cannot add their votes. The Assembly uses an electronic vote counter. Members push switches, and lights shine on a board — green reflecting aye; red, no. With the unanimous consent of the membership, members are allowed to change their votes the same day or add their votes if their actions do not alter the outcome.

## Legislative modernization

Until 1966, the Legislature met for general sessions in odd-numbered years and for short budget sessions in even-numbered years. Legislators then received $6,000 a year, and their elective positions were not considered to be full-time occupations. In 1966, the voters approved Proposition 1a making each year's session unlimited, raising the pay to $16,000 and allowing lawmakers to give themselves cost-of-living increases of five percent a year. In the June 1990 primary election voters approved Prop. 112. While some of the provisions of this constitutional amendment established new ethics regulations, perhaps its key feature was the creation of a new Citizens' Compensation Commission. The reason this amendment was proposed was because the Legislature angered many votes when they voted to increase their salaries.

To deflect this criticism the commission was established. In December 1991 the new commission raised salaries of state legislators from $40,816 a year to $52,500. In addition, legislative leaders received extra compensation. Current salaries established by the commission are: legislator, $75,600; Speaker and President pro Tem, $90,720, and floor leaders, $83,160.

In 1972, the people approved another constitutional amendment. This one put the Legislature on the same two-year schedule as Congress, with bills remaining alive for two years. The Legislature now is in session year-round, with breaks for Easter, Christmas, part of the summer and during statewide elections. In addition to their salaries, legislators receive $109 a day for expenses and have use of leased automobiles, credit cards and district offices.

In addition to the standing committees, which consider the merits of bills, the Legislature also establishes two-house joint committees and one-house select committees to study specific problems (often of special concern to only one legislator, who becomes chairman of the committee). These committees can submit recommendations to the Legislature but have no direct power over legislation. Many of these select committees have been eliminated under the new budget strictures of Proposition 140.

## Legislative staff

Each member of the Legislature has a personal staff plus the assistance of specialists assigned to committees and to the party caucuses. There are also three major independent bureaus with significant influence on the legislative process— the legislative counsel, the legislative analyst, and the auditor general.

• *Legislative counsel*, Bion Gregory, has a large staff of attorneys to provide legal advice to lawmakers and draft their bills and proposed amendments.

• *Legislative analyst*, Elizabeth Hill, provides advice to the Legislature on anything with a fiscal implication, which can cover virtually every major bill. The analyst annually publishes a detailed analysis of the governor's budget, which becomes the basis for legislative hearings on the fiscal program.

• *Auditor general*, Kurt R. Sjoberg, conducts investigations of state agencies to determine whether they can be run more economically and efficiently, he reports directly to the Joint Audit Committee and to the Legislature as a whole.

In all, a staff of some 2,000 served the Legislature until the passage of Prop. 140 in November 1990 which mandated term limits for members and budget reductions for the Legislature. The Legislature's staff has been reduced to comply with the measure. In addition to the analyst, auditor general, and counsel, there are sergeants-at-arms, secretaries, political aides, and committee consultants. The consultants are the most important element of the staff; they provide specialized knowledge for committees, gather information and provide independent evaluation of information obtained from interest groups, the governor and others.

## Reapportionment

Almost nothing stirs the juices of a legislator — either at the state or federal level — as much as the prospect of his or her district being reapportioned. Redistricting takes place every decade and has the potential of throwing many legislators out of office. Every congressional, Senate and Assembly district in California must be redrawn after each census to ensure districts are equal in population.

California's Assembly districts have always been apportioned by population, but the state Senate has been apportioned under two systems. Prior to 1926, the Senate was also apportioned by population, but in that year the voters approved a "federal plan" devised by Northern Californians to keep control of the Senate from rapidly growing Southern California. This plan provided that no county could have more than one senator and that one senator could represent no more than three counties. As a result, the senator from Los Angeles at one time represented 440 times more people than the senator from Alpine, Inyo and Mono counties. This was the most severe apportionment imbalance in the nation. Such discrepancies were eradicated in 1966, when the U.S. Supreme Court's "one-man, one-vote" edict went into effect.

Redistricting can be simple if both houses of a legislature and the governor are of the same political party. The party in power merely divides the state to suit itself and gives the opposition party the scraps. The usual procedure is to offer some members of the opposition good deals so that a nominally bipartisan reapportionment bill can be passed. Actually, it is impossible to create good districts for one party without fashioning some just as good for the other. But the legislators doing the redistricting can usually pick and choose whom to favor among members of the opposition. In the 1980's reapportionment, although Democrat Jerry Brown was governor and Democrats had solid majorities in both houses, Republicans stymied the majority party's reapportionment plans by qualifying three separate referenda for the June 1982 ballot. Voters voted "no" against the three Democratic sponsored bills and forced the Democrats to make some adjustments to the district lines.

Under the state Constitution, the Legislature is empowered to reapportion all seats (52 in Congress, 40 Senate and 80 Assembly districts), subject only to a gubernatorial veto. Thus, when a governor is of a different party than the Legislature's leadership an impasse is apt to develop. In this case, either a bi-partisan plan is drawn favoring the incumbents of both parties, maintaining the status quo, or the matter ends up in the courts.

Republicans tried repeatedly in the 1980s to modify the reapportioning process. Their objective was to shift the decision making away from Democratic legislative leaders:

1) In 1982 Republicans joined with Common Cause and qualified Prop. 14 to establish an independent districting commission to do the reapportioning. Voters defeated the proposal.

2) In 1983 then Assemblyman Don Sebastiani qualified a new initiative which provided, he claimed, "fairer" districts than the one the Democrats had devised. This initiative was declared unconstitutional by the state Supreme Court prior to its being voted upon. The court ruled that reapportioning could take place only once each decade.

3) In 1984 Governor Deukmejian authored an initiative to have reapportioning handled by a panel of retired appellate judges. Voters rejected this proposal.

The 1991 reapportionment plans passed by the Democratic-controlled Legislature were vetoed by Republican Governor Pete Wilson. Because of the impasse, districts were drawn by the state Supreme Court with the help of "special masters." 🏛

# CALIFORNIA LEGISLATIVE PROCESS

## INITIAL STEPS BY AUTHOR

### IDEA

Sources of bills: legislators, legislative committees, governor, state and local governmental agencies, business firms, lobbyists, citizens.

### DRAFTING

Formal copy of bill and "layman's digest" prepared by Legislative Counsel.

### INTRODUCTION

Bill submitted by senator or Assembly member. Numbered and read first time. Referred to policy committee by Assembly or Senate Rules Committee. Printed.

## ACTION IN HOUSE OF ORIGIN

### COMMITTEE

Testimony taken from author, proponents and opponents. Typical actions: Do pass; amend and do pass; no action; hold in committee (kill); amend and re-refer to same committee; refer to another committee; send to interim study. Committee actions are reported to the floor. Bills with any fiscal implications, if approved by policy committee, are re-referred to Appropriations Committee.

### SECOND READING

Bills given do-pass recommendations are read the second time on the floor and placed on the daily file (agenda) for debate on a subsequent day.

### FLOOR DEBATE AND VOTE

Bills are read the third time and debated. A roll-call vote follows. For ordinary bills, 21 votes are needed in the Senate and 41 in the Assembly. For urgency bills and most appropriations measures, 27 and 54 votes are required. If these numbers are not reached, the bill is defeated. Any member may seek reconsideration and a second vote. If passed or passed with amendments, the bill is sent to the second house.

## ACTION IN SECOND HOUSE

### READING

Bill is read the first time and referred to committee by the Assembly or Senate Rules Committee.

### COMMITTEE

Procedures and possible actions are nearly identical to those in the first house.

### SECOND READING

If cleared by committee, the bill is read a second time and placed on the daily file (agenda) for debate and vote.

### FLOOR DEBATE AND VOTE

The procedure is identical to the first house. If a bill is passed without having been amended in the second house, it is sent to the governor's desk. (Resolutions are sent to the secretary of state's office.) If amended in the second house and passed, the measure returns to the house of origin for consideration of amendments.

## RESOLUTION OF TWO-HOUSE DIFFERENCES (IF NECESSARY)

### CONCURRENCE

The house of origin decides whether to accept the second-house amendments. If the amendments are approved, the bill is sent to the governor. If the amendments are rejected, the bill is placed in the hands of a two-house conference committee composed of three senators and three Assembly members.

### CONFERENCE

If the conferees present a recommendation for compromise (conference report), both houses vote on the report. If the report is adopted by both, the bill goes to the governor. If the conferees fail to agree, or if either house rejects the report, a second (and even a third) conference committee may be formed.

## THE GOVERNOR

### SIGN OR VETO?

Within 12 days after receiving a bill, the governor may sign it into law, allow it to become law without his signature or veto it. Bill is sent to Secretary of State's office and given a chapter number. A vetoed bill returns to the house of origin for possible vote on overriding the veto. It requires a two-thirds majority of both houses to override. Urgency measures may become effective immediately after signing. Others usually take effect the following January 1st.

# Imbalance of power

## The Senate is quietly becoming the Legislature's dominant house

### by Steve Scott

Reprinted from *California Journal*, August 1995

There are few institutions which more accurately reflect the extremes in decorum and philosophy which have come to characterize American society in the '90s than the California Assembly. These days, Assembly sessions find Republicans and Democrats literally shouting across the aisle at one another, with personal invective — and the odd obscene gesture — substituting for the fine art of debate. If the Assembly were a hockey game, the penalty box would be S.R.O.

By comparison, the state Senate seems like the Assembly on Valium. Although the issues and ideologies are just as heartfelt, everything and everyone moves more slowly in the Senate. With a few exceptions, members are almost irritatingly polite to one another, and the excruciatingly long speeches and roll-call voting make it seem like nothing will ever get done. Visitors to the Capitol might be tempted to bypass the Senate and spend their time in the more entertaining Assembly. To do so, however, would mean passing up the house which is emerging as the place where the real work of lawmaking is taking place.

When it comes to the fine art of legislating, the Senate is increasingly where the action is.

The signs pointing to the Senate's importance are everywhere. For the first time in recent memory, more legislation is being introduced and passed in the 40-member Senate than in the 80-member Assembly. Key Assembly staffers, including one of its top budget analysts, have migrated to the Senate. Lobbyists, advocates and administration officials looking to build consensus for their legislation are increasingly focusing their efforts on the upper house. Perhaps most tellingly, some campaign contributors have, at least for the moment, held back on contributions to Assembly leadership PACs, while continuing to give to those in the Senate.

"There's no question that the policy work is being done in the Senate," says Jerry Haleva, a former Senate staffer-turned-lobbyist. "You have two things working for you [in the Senate]: stability and history."

The Senate has always been viewed as the less explosive and more deliberative of the two houses. Its smaller membership, coupled with an institutional demeanor that stresses collegiality, has created an air of bipartisan cooperation. During a protracted 64-day budget stalemate in 1992, the Senate had achieved a two-thirds majority on legislation that would have ended the impasse before it began, and its budget ultimately became the framework for the final deal. Still, despite its emphasis on cooperation and compromise, the Senate has spent much of the last three decades in the long shadows cast by powerful Assembly speakers, such as Jesse Unruh and Willie Brown.

All that changed last November, when Republicans achieved a majority for the first time since 1970, setting in motion a sequence of events leading to Brown's exit from the speakership. While the long-term impact of Brown's tactical maneuvering will be left for historians to decipher, the short-term effect is indisputable: chaos. Evenly-divided committees in the Assembly have locked up both Democratic and Republican policy initiatives, leaving only those issues about which there is relatively little opposition or disagreement. Brown's role in engineering the election of Republican Doris Allen as speaker led to the unusual spectacle of GOP lawmakers conspiring against the first speaker of their party in a quarter-century.

With the Assembly unsettled, the Senate has become the place to take bills you hope to get passed. Compromises on such thorny questions as state-local realignment and re-writing the state's Environmental Protection Act have gained most of their momentum in the Senate. One Wilson administration official concedes the Assembly unrest is what prompted them to pursue a major new student-testing proposal through the Senate.

The most visible sign of the power shift has been this year's budget fight, still unresolved as of early July. Evenly divided Assembly subcommittees wrangled endlessly, and unproductively, about philosophical issues — that is, when they were able to achieve a quorum at all. The expanded two-house conference committee dithered for weeks, failing to reach compromise on anything really substantive, thanks to the deadlock among Assembly conferees. Meanwhile, Senate budget conferees worked among themselves to find common ground, and there are indications Senate leaders might try, as they did in 1992, to craft their own bipartisan solution.

"Because of the policy vacuum in the Assembly, there is inevitably a shift of power to the Senate," says Tim Hodson, director of the Sacramento-based Center for California Studies.

Assembly members, both Democrat and Republican, deny that any great shift of power has taken place and argue that what shift there has been is temporary. Assembly Republican Caucus Leader Jim Brulte (R-Rancho Cucamonga) believes the narrow majority makes the Assembly a better avenue for creative policy.

"We now have policy fights that are legitimate policy fights," says Brulte. "On any given day any member can introduce any bill or motion, and it can pass or fail."

If there has been a shift in policy influence from the Assembly to the Senate, one of its primary beneficiaries is Senate President pro Tempore Bill Lockyer (D-Hayward). For one thing, Lockyer is the only legislative leader whose position within his caucus is relatively secure. The struggles between Allen and Brulte have Assembly Republicans tied in knots. Brown has one foot out the door as he campaigns to become mayor of San Francisco. In the Senate, the rise of Senator Rob Hurtt (R-Garden Grove) as the chief election strategist has eroded the influence of Senate GOP Leader Ken Maddy (R-Fresno). Maddy survived a 1993 challenge from Hurtt, but only after putting his rival in charge of the caucus' campaign effort. Since then, new arrivals to the Senate have been more ideologically and temperamentally compatible with Hurtt's in-your-face conservatism than Maddy's more low-key moderate politics.

"The degree to which Senator Maddy controls that caucus these days is questionable," says one lobbyist. "Clearly, Hurtt has a great deal of influence, as does [San Bernardino GOP Senator] Bill Leonard."

Maddy and Hurtt both maintain their differences have been set aside for the greater goal of achieving a majority. "There's no open friction," says Leonard, who has been something of an intermediary between the two. "If nothing else, what's happened to the Assembly Republicans reinforces our common goal to take over the Senate, and that our personal disagreements ought to be secondary." Hurtt seems less concerned about Maddy's commitment than that of some of the rest of his colleagues. "Ken is doing a lot of things that are helping us," he says, "but we also need some help from some of our other troops, too."

For his part, Maddy insists he's not in immediate danger, but he has no illusions about how long that will last. "If we win in '96, and I'm down to my last couple of years, there's going to be a great deal of activity regarding who's in leadership," he says.

In addition to his relative security as a legislative leader, few will deny that Lockyer has eclipsed Brown as the most influential Democrat in the state. While the former speaker was losing his majority in the Assembly, Lockyer retained his, leaving him as the only protection for his party's policy priorities and political constituencies. Lockyer concedes his position places more responsibility on him to keep Wilson and the Assembly Republicans in check.

"Environmental law, tax policy, labor law, and consumer protection ... are the principal areas where our constituencies and philosophies will be at great risk," he says. "There's a hope that we will be successful in preventing serious harm to those perspectives."

As the Democratic seawall blocking the "Republican wave," Lockyer is positioned to scarf up contributions from traditional Democratic donors, such as public employee unions, trial lawyers, and the education community. "Democrat money is more likely to gravitate to Lockyer, because he's seen as the plug that's holding everything up," says GOP political consultant Wayne Johnson. Traditionally conservative business donors also will likely gravitate toward Lockyer, since they no longer will feel compelled to give to Brown, the lame-duck leader of a minority party.

Is it happening? Well, Lockyer says he recently had "a $500,000 week" in his money-raising efforts. By way of comparison, Brulte claims to have raised $1 million since November, and still carries an outstanding debt from the 1994 elections. Lockyer says he doesn't use the Assembly turmoil as a selling point, but only because he doesn't have to. "Routinely, [contributors] say to me, 'The Assembly is a mess ... it looks like a high school food fight,'" he says. Hurtt also reports increased interest in his GOP effort as a result of the Assembly unrest. "Some of the 'third house' people [lobbyists] have been saying, 'Hurtt, get your presentation together,'" he says. "We shall respond to the call."

"I'm sure there are lobbyists getting migraines trying to figure out who to give to," jokes Hodson. "Who's in charge? Who do you suck up to?"

While there is disagreement about whether the Senate is more powerful now, few dispute the contention that the Senate's influence will expand considerably when term limits take full

*Continued on page 45*

# Fade from Brown

Curt Pringle, the first "legitimate" Republican speaker since 1970, faces the difficult task of finding enough common ground with Democrats to enact some of the GOP agenda while at the same time remaining true to his conservative principles.

by John Borland

Reprinted from *California Journal*, April 1996

Curt Pringle, recently elected Republican speaker of the California Assembly, stood at a luncheon podium, addressing a group of journalists and public-relations officers, warming up the crowd with a story about his children's science fair projects. A square-spectacled man whose boyish face broke into a nervous smile at his own jokes, Pringle, who hails from Orange County, was still struggling against the ghost of Willie Brown Jr., the flamboyant San Francisco Democrat who had held both the office and the press corps' rapt attention for 15 years.

Pringle's story was drifting out of control — a fact made clear by the color of his face, which turns a habitual red when he is angry or embarrassed, and by the uncertain laughs drifting up from the audience, many of whom were learning far more about the reproductive organs of sharks than they had ever expected to know. After discussing the number and location of the pickled shark's ovaries, Pringle revealed that the specimen had been pregnant, and with obvious relief rushed too quickly through the story's punch line: "... So this shark literally had eight babies, and as a pro-life legislator we had the opportunity to dissect nine sharks that all qualified..."

There was little audience reaction, and Pringle quickly moved forward to more comfortable ground — a discussion of the Assembly Republican Caucus' legislative agenda. And here he gained his stride, able to do battle with Brown's shade from a position of strength. Curt Pringle is a policy man, a deeply conservative political technician skilled at selling his ideas to his allies and at moving as much of his agenda as practically possible from point A to point B. He is not the natural charismatic diplomat that was Willie Brown; when leaving the world of legislative and electoral details, his shark stories, for instance, swim somewhat astray. What he does share with Brown is a single-minded dedication to keeping power in his hands and in those of like-minded lawmakers. His relentless pursuit of the Assembly's top seat has finally won the GOP uncontested control over the Assembly's agenda for the first time in 25 years.

Pringle was born in western Iowa and grew up in Orange County, bookends of American conservatism. His family moved to Southern California in 1968 to launch a chain of dry-cleaning outlets. Pringle and his family now are in the vertical-blind business, a late 1980s change prompted in part by the strict government regulation facing dry cleaners. Pringle's political focus began early, stemming from involvement in the Boy Scouts and also linked to what he perceived as the burdens imposed on the family business by government. As a teenager, he dropped in on a city council session, returned for several more, and was hooked. "He attended more meetings than some of the council members for a while," remembers his father, Larry Pringle.

Pringle first ran for the city council at age 20. He lost, but the race inched him into the local political establishment. Over the next several years, while working for his father's business, he served on several local boards and volunteered substantial time on behalf of the county GOP organization. He moved up quickly in the party hierarchy, putting himself in position for an Assembly bid in 1988 at age 29.

The opportunity to run for the position proved something of a harbinger of both his ambition and success. The seat's GOP incumbent — the late Richard Longshore — died the day after the primary, allowing the county party organization to select a replacement. Ten people applied for the spot, Pringle says, including Congressman Bob Dornan's chief of staff, the wife of the deceased nominee, a local representative of then-U.S. Senator Pete Wilson, and a Santa Ana city councilman. But the honor went to Pringle, then a vice-chairman of the county party. "I knew that the people I needed to talk to to gather those votes were the membership of the central committee," Pringle says. "I was in a strong position to obtain the necessary votes."

The general election campaign against Democrat Rick Thierbach itself was messy and expensive, but it was Election Day that seared Pringle's name into the minds of political observers statewide, and nearly doomed him to one nondescript term in Sacramento. The GOP county central committee, claiming to be worried about Democrats busing in noncitizens to vote, hired a group of uniformed security guards and stationed them at the district's most Democratic precincts. The guards allegedly approached Latino voters, asking if they were citizens. Pringle won by a scant 800 votes, and Democrats erupted, calling for an investigation into the hiring of the guards.

Pringle says he did not know about the decision until Election Day but offers no apology. "There was a lot of concern ... that some of the Democratic precincts in that district had had a surprising increase in Democratic registration towards the very end," he says, noting that a Democratic staffer in the area was later indicted on multiple counts of voter fraud. "Those happened to be 20 precincts down in Santa Ana that happened to be the most unsafe areas in the district," he adds.

"That was a single effort by a campaign manager," says Orange County GOP Chairman Tom Fuentes, whose organization was responsible for funding the guards. "Curt was maligned, and he showed what a good man he is by sustaining himself and our cause though that contrivance." A federal lawsuit filed against the county party was eventually settled out of court for $400,000, to be paid by the party's insurance.

The controversy helped to turn Pringle's first Assembly term into an exercise in legislative futility. He chalks it up simply to the fact that his swing district made him a target from day one; but whatever the cause, his first-year influence extended little beyond his ability to cast floor votes in support of the minority GOP caucus. "I have a very strong knowledge and history of how the command and control of this place operated under the former regime," Pringle says. "Willie Brown selected an office for me, created the sixth floor office for me. ...They put us onto the worst committees, gave us the smallest budget, and virtually every bill that I introduced that somebody liked, they took it from me."

The freshman legislator lost to Democrat Tom Umberg in an expensive 1990 campaign, and returned to his father's business. But in 1992, he ran in a substantially more Republican Assembly district, easily beat two moderate primary challengers, and walked over his Democratic opponent. He returned to the house with some seniority in place and quickly rose through the leadership ranks, serving as whip and assistant caucus leader. And when then-Minority Leader Jim Brulte (R-Rancho Cucamonga) stepped down from the post last summer, Pringle was positioned to replace him.

For a year after the sweeping 1994 GOP election wins in the Assembly, Brown stymied Republican efforts to elect their own speaker, (see *CJ*, December 1995). In January of this year, Pringle finally accomplished with a political battering ram what Brulte never could, keeping all but one of the house's Republican votes — Setencich's own — behind him in his bid for the top spot. There is no small irony in the fact that it finally took Brown's own departure, to become mayor of San Francisco, for Republicans to break down the gates.

But Brown's exit was only one of two events needed to set the stage for Pringle's ascension. The first was the recall and replacement of Allen with a GOP loyalist — a campaign that brought another round of ethical questions close to Pringle's doorstep. While Allen's district was overwhelmingly Republican, there were initially several competitive GOP candidates seeking to replace her, and some observers feared a split vote could allow a Democrat to slip into the seat. Conveniently enough, two Democrats also graced the ballot, one of them an unknown legal secretary named Laurie Campbell. Her candidacy was challenged in court by Orange County Democrats, who alleged that she was a GOP plant put on the ballot to diffuse the Democratic vote. A Sacramento judge, while not addressing Campbell's Democratic credentials, nonetheless tossed her out of the election because she had not personally gathered the signatures needed to put her on the ballot despite signing an affidavit to that fact. Only later was it revealed that Campbell was a friend of the eventual, Pringle-backed winner, now-Assemblyman Scott Baugh, and that a Pringle staffer and a staffer of GOP Congressman Dana Rohrabacher had been among those helping to gather Campbell's signatures.

Pringle himself denies any involvement in or foreknowledge of the Campbell project. "What my staffer did was one day. He was called by someone without my knowledge. He went with them, and he collected signatures, according to what I have determined, on one day," he says. "That's the extent of what I know of his involvement... I did not know of that on that one day."

Given the apparent Republican involvement in the signature-gathering effort, Pringle says it probably is not surprising that the people involved would have called his office, but insists he was not informed until considerably afterward. As to the offending staffer? "He was reprimanded for violating the internal policies of this office, and [put] back to work," Pringle says. The aide later resigned after pleading guilty to misdemeanor charges of election fraud.

Meanwhile, to become speaker, Pringle had to oust then-Speaker Setencich, who could hold the job by enticing one Republican vote away from Pringle. Setencich spent the winter break traveling the state, promising to turn committee majorities and control over resources back to the GOP caucus. Pringle responded with repeated admonitions that Republicans must be allowed to choose their own leader — i.e., Pringle. Several weeks before the resumption of session in January, Assemblyman Trice Harvey (R-Bakersfield) announced he would support Setencich's speakership if a few conditions were met.

But Pringle brought Harvey back into line by marshalling some big GOP guns and having them fire salvos across Harvey's bow. "I am a realist," Pringle now says. "I knew that it was a difficult task, and I never ever assumed that I could do it alone." The GOP leader's reinforcements began to assemble midway through the winter break, when Assembly Republicans received a letter from the state GOP asking them to sign a pledge promising to support the caucus majority's choice for speaker. Around the same time, Governor Pete Wilson began to pressure Republicans viewed as possible Setencich supporters, forcefully arguing Pringle's case. And when Harvey appeared ready to go south, word filtered down from national GOP congressional campaign circles that support for Harvey's forthcoming bid for Congress just might hinge on his support for Pringle.

"I solicited help from anyone that was willing," Pringle says. "The issue of control of the state Assembly affects all Republicans, all Californians, and for that matter has national implications... I am not bashful, I asked for help." Harvey snapped under the pressure, and Pringle had the job.

Pringle moved quickly to establish his own identity, selling the former speaker's state-owned Cadillacs and replacing them with a more prosaic sedan, closing some of the more suspicious outlying Majority Services offices, and promising a wide-ranging audit of house operations. But he also quickly consolidated power as Brown might have, giving Republicans supermajorities on the vital fiscal, rules, and other "juice" committees.

Despite this early show of confidence, Pringle's narrow victory in an incomplete house gives him a tenuous grasp on the reins of power. He has the respect and loyalty of most of the Republican caucus, and once Brulte leaves, he will be its senior member. "In choosing a speaker, we couldn't have done a better job," says fellow Orange County Assemblyman Mickey Conroy (R-Orange).

But the speaker cannot afford to lose the support of a single Republican, a situation that ties Pringle's hands in the guidance of his caucus. "One thing Willie Brown always did — he had a lot of screwballs and crazies in the Democratic caucus, but he was always able to keep them on a short leash," says Tony Quinn, a former legislative staffer and GOP analyst, noting that Pringle lacks the two- or three-member cushion to be able to act similarly.

This was evident in January's final days, when the GOP caucus finally managed to pull its economic agenda — a myriad of tax cuts, tort-reform bills, regulation roll-backs, and welfare restructurings — out of committee and pass the bills in a rapid-fire series of sessions. But at the same time,

the press and much public attention fixed on a few social bills: a roll-back of motorcycle helmet laws, an ultimately unsuccessful bill for paddling graffiti vandals, a ban on same-sex marriages. In the days since, Pringle has been single-minded in his explication of the economic issues, but says he had no power or desire to stop members from pushing their own bills.

"There is absolutely no question that there are 41 intelligent Assembly Republicans here that have many ideas and they will introduce bills on their own," Pringle said. "In terms of what our agenda is, that doesn't mean that we will not ever vote on anything else, that we won't consider and debate other important things that affect our lives."

Which is not to say that Pringle — and Brulte, who the caucus still looks up to as the political whiz who fashioned its new-found majority during the 1994 elections — won't sometimes give pointed advice. "Pringle and Brulte are right in tune with each other," Conroy says. "We do debate the issues, but they usually win, because their arguments are better."

The realities of the job may have served to moderate Pringle's tone in the house. One of the most staunchly social and economically conservative legislators in the caucus, Pringle now has the difficult task of getting as much of the conservative agenda through the house as possible, and still trying to work out enough compromises with the Democrat-led state Senate to pass some significant legislation.

"There are people here on both sides that I consider 100 percenters," Pringle says. "They want to get all or nothing. I don't necessarily view the legislative process that way." He and Senate President pro Tempore Bill Lockyer (D-Hayward) have set up a conference committee structure to examine the GOP Assembly bills for points of compromise. But new dangers will arise when budget time rolls around, and Pringle will likely have to win over even the "100-percenter" pro-life members of his own caucus, some of whom have never supported a budget, before Assembly Democrats will provide enough votes to muster the 54-vote requirement.

Democrats view the new speaker with suspicion. "Unlike some of his [caucus]... he does see a role for government," says Assembly Minority Leader Richard Katz (D-Sepulveda). But "it's not clear to what extent he can rein in some of the more extreme elements of the caucus," he adds.

It will be the 1996 campaigns that ultimately decide Pringle's future. As leader of the GOP Assembly election team, he needs to hold his razor-thin majority in order to retain his speakership, and desperately wants to pick up a small safety margin. But storm clouds are gathering on November's horizon. Quinn underlines the fact that Pringle's best-laid strategies could thus be caught in an electoral riptide. "I think has fate is determined by factors beyond his control," Quinn says. "Just like 1994 was beyond Brown's control." 🏛

*Continued from page 41*

effect in 1996. "Long-term, with term limits, there's a power shift to the Senate," concedes Brulte, who will himself be running for Senate next year. The migration of staff from one side to the other is only one factor leading to this prediction. A larger factor will be the concomitant migration of people like Brulte, making the transition from one house to the other.

"We'll have greater expertise because we'll have people who serve a few years in the Assembly, then migrate to the Senate," says Lockyer. "We'll benefit from their expertise."

Of course, some of the people moving over from the Assembly will be the same impatient, term-limited hotheads currently churning the waters in the lower house. UC-San Diego political science professor Gary Jacobson, who studies term limits, says the Senate's eight-year terms are "still pretty short," and there's no inherent reason why the Senate will be all that much more stable. "They're still going to be worried about their futures," says Jacobson. "You're still going to see them running for Congress or other offices." Concerns about their career track may also increase the temptation of some to break through the somnolent decorum of the Senate and turn it into "Assembly, Part Deux."

"You've got so many new people ... who ran on platforms of not getting along," says former Democratic Senator Barry Keene, now a political science lecturer at CSU-Sacramento. "It's going to take an enormous effort to absorb this group of belligerents and I don't know if it's possible."

Lockyer believes it is possible, but only by continuing to work on keeping the Senate's "institutional culture" intact. He has earned praise from friend and foe alike for his accessibility and skill in organizing the house. Once a bomb-thrower himself, Lockyer has also earned credit for, as one lobbyist put

it, "exercising control over some of his previous instincts."

Whether Lockyer's discipline results in better policy decisions depends, of course, on how one views the outcomes. While the Senate may be a more pleasant place to do business, the Democratic majority still means that Democrats win most of the battles, and Republicans lose most of them. "With Democratic majorities on all the committees, the results are pretty much pre-ordained," notes Brulte. On the other hand, there is no systemic reason why the Assembly couldn't be just as disciplined, if one party or the other was capable of achieving a clear majority.

"We [Senate Democrats] count very much on Republicans to divide among themselves," says Senator Tom Hayden (D-Santa Monica), a veteran of both houses. "If they start up the hill with 41, straight at us, I don't know what will happen."

Even if the Assembly is never able to fully contain its infighting, it will never be irrelevant so long as legislation must clear both houses in order to become law. Lockyer believes the Assembly will become "the house of advocacy," while the Senate serves as the "social glue that forges compromises and has a more balanced product." The cohesiveness of that glue, however, will depend in large measure on who's applying it.

"With all the turnover, there's going to be an even higher premium on the particular talents of particular legislators," says Assemblyman Wally Knox (D-Los Angeles). "That's going to be the dominant factor over the long haul." 🏛

# TRANSITIONAL PRO TEM?

## Bill Lockyer leads the Senate into the era of term limits

## by Steve Scott

Reprinted from *California Journal*, November 1994

**E**arlier this year, as the state budget debate was approaching its end game, Bill Lockyer (D-Hayward) found himself in a familiar position: He was surrounded by reporters after a floor session. The rookie pro tem had just spent a fair bit of energy and time tamping down a fire that had erupted in the tension of the budget denouement. The battle was not the budget itself. Rather, it was an ugly public spat between Senators Dan McCorquodale (D-Modesto) and Steve Peace (D-Chula Vista). At one point, Peace, the Senate's loosest cannon, yelled across the floor that McCorquodale was "a nut case." When a reporter asked about the flap, Lockyer responded with a roll of the eyes that recalled similar expressions of exasperation one might have seen from his predecessor, David Roberti.

"When tensions arise in the Capitol," Lockyer shrugged, "these little blisters tend to arise."

There was a time in California political history when having both Peace and Lockyer in the same house would have been viewed as a sign of the coming Apocalypse. For much of his early career, Bill Lockyer didn't soothe blisters, he caused them. But times have changed, so much so that the 53-year-old Hayward Democrat has become only the third person in two decades to hold the post of president pro tempore of the Senate.

Lockyer's ascension comes at a time of great upheaval in the Legislature, and he faces challenges unimaginable to any of his predecessors. Term limits are likely to accelerate the arrival of bomb-throwers like Peace from the Assembly, where fiery partisanship is practically in the job description. Pressure will be on Lockyer to maintain the customary deliberativeness of the Senate while at the same time mollifying the more partisan members of his own caucus. Lockyer must also manage the surge of power and influence that most believe will flow into the Senate as a result of term limits, since the upper house will likely become the repository of the Legislature's institutional memory. On top of all that, Lockyer must also keep a check on his own partisan impulses, while at the same time following through on the one clear charge he's been given by his caucus: Keep the Democrats in power.

"David Roberti had a luxury Bill Lockyer will never have," observes Assembly Republican Leader Jim Brulte (R-Rancho Cucamonga). "Roberti had significant majorities to work with. Locker's strength or weaknesses will not be relational to his own abilities. It will relate to the solidification of his majority."

To the extent that Brulte is wrong, and ability is a factor,

the new pro tem certainly has the qualifications for leadership. For Lockyer, politics and the California Legislature has been, and remains, his life's work. Born in East Oakland in 1941, Lockyer grew up in the area he now represents, attending San Leandro High School. He earned a political science degree from UC-Berkeley, but his political activism was born not in the classroom, although as a participant in the Berkeley "Free Speech Movement" of the 1960s.

Already an activist in local Democratic circles, Lockyer worked for seven years as an aide to Assemblyman Robert Crown, and when Crown died in 1973, won the special election to replace him, using what were, at the time, unusual techniques. "At that time, a massive lawn-sign campaign, and campaigning to the reduced universe of likely voters were revolutionary ideas," he recalls. Lockyer quickly established himself as a young man in a hurry, but when the speakership beckoned ambitious lawmakers in 1979, Lockyer was content to wait his turn.

"From my observation of the speakership, it seems that half of the time is taken up handling the egos of the place," he said at the time. "Up to now, I've been one of the ones that's needed a temper calmed."

When he moved over to the Senate in 1982, Lockyer found himself serving on, and eventually chairing, the

**Lockyer taking oath of office**

**Lockyer with Ken Maddy**

the "First Amendment scumbags" in the media, and a 1990 scuffle with a trial lawyer lobbyist whom he said threw "a girlie punch" at him. While still in the Assembly, Lockyer was threatened with arrest by Senator Alfred Alquist (D-San Jose) when he refused to leave a hearing room after Alquist had snubbed one of his bills.

Although he concedes this reputation is "part of my baggage," Lockyer insists such behavior is in the past, and that his detractors have to go back several years to find truly erratic behavior. "I think he has worked hard to get [his temper] under control," said Senator Robert Presley (D-Riverside). "It's a moot concern if you get it under control."

A "kinder and gentler" Lockyer was well positioned to step into leadership, and when the term-limited Roberti let it be known that he was going to run for statewide office, Lockyer immediately began lining up the votes to become pro tem. By getting out ahead of the curve, Lockyer insists he was able to get the votes he needed without making cutting individual deals for chairmanships or staff. Still, his mere acceptance of the job implied one huge promise to his Democratic colleagues: Don't lose control of the Senate.

After he took over for Roberti in late January, Lockyer moved to assuage early concerns that his leadership would be more partisan than Roberti's. Senate Minority Leader Ken Maddy (R-Fresno), who had been one of the early skeptics about Lockyer's ability to tone down the partisanship, says he was satisfied with Lockyer's even-handedness in his first session. "He has tried very hard to accommodate everyone in the Senate, particularly the minority party," concedes Maddy. "He has attempted to keep most things status quo." Lockyer's handling of his first budget negotiations earned him points for being tough, but practical, and his more mercurial tendencies remained firmly in remission.

"He has been in total control of himself since the word go," says Senator Leroy Greene (D-Sacramento). "It was a relief to some of us who thought 'well, he's OK now, but what happens if he blows?' He didn't blow."

Keeping the Senate's traditional decorum intact didn't mean, however, that Lockyer had turned the house over to the GOP. As Roberti had during his first session as pro tem, Lockyer used the Senate's confirmation authority as a tool to establish his political *bona fides*. Two of Governor Pete Wilson's appointments — one to the UC Regents, the other to the CSU Board of Trustees — were shot down by Lockyer through his position as the chairman of the Senate Rules Committee. It was the first time in 111 years that a UC Regent appointment had been rejected by the Senate. While he kept

powerful Judiciary Committee, even though he was still attending law school at night. When he took his bar exam, there was, he recalls, "considerable press interest: 'Will the chair of Judiciary pass the bar?'" He did, and established himself as a master at the insider game. Lockyer was one of those who negotiated the infamous "napkin deal" altering the state's liability laws, which was worked out among lawmakers and lobbyists at Frank Fat's restaurant two days before the end of the 1987 session. Lockyer, in fact, displayed the napkin on the floor of the Senate the night the bill was passed.

While working his way up the legislative ladder, Lockyer's policy reputation was of someone who liked to push big ideas. In the Assembly, Lockyer introduced the first legislation to promote the concept of "comparable worth" for traditionally female occupations. Four years before it became a political litmus test, Lockyer introduced the first three-strikes-you're-out law for serious felonies. He wrote the first "Lemon Law" protecting automobile purchasers, and was an early advocate of legislation to keep large companies from filing harassing lawsuits against citizens. Lockyer's policy direction is informed by what he calls his "philosophical and temperamental sympathy for the rebellion in life," but he hastens to add that he does not share what he considers the more naive aspects of classical liberalism. "I'm much more sensitive to matters of history, tradition, and community."

Still, this rebellious spirit may have played a role in the development of Lockyer's more widely-known reputation — the one for temperamental instability. Stories of Lockyer's emotional outbursts are the stuff of Capitol legend. Tales include criticizing Senator Diane Watson (D-Los Angeles) during a committee hearing for "mindless blather," a pass he made at a UPI reporter which was followed by an attack on

the Senate from dissolving into a circus during the budget, Lockyer did engineer a show vote on an extension of a 1991 tax hike on the wealthy, and he says he was the only one of the "Big Five" who didn't want to "just get through the year."

Although he didn't make any wholesale changes, Lockyer is taking steps to put his own stamp on the administration of the house. His most controversial administrative step to date has been his decision to appoint the next session's committee chairs on the last day of this year's session. Lockyer moved some existing chairs into new roles, and elevated a number of less-tenured members into prominence. He also proposed creation of a separate Criminal Procedure Committee, comparable to the Assembly's Public Safety Committee, to take some of Judiciary's crime load.

Republicans charged that the committee assignments, and the decision to announce them early, point the way toward more partisanship from Lockyer in the future. "A lot of us were taken aback by it," says Senator Bill Leonard (R-Redlands). "He seemed like he was trying to solidify his leadership by keeping all parties in his caucus as happy as can be." Leonard says the appointment of Senator Tom Hayden (D-Santa Monica), an ardent environmentalist, to chair Natural Resources puts the Democrats "squarely at the far left end of the discussion" on environmental issues. For his part, Lockyer insists the move was simply aimed at insuring a smooth transition by giving prospective chairs a head start on organizing for the new session.

"The debate for me was simply one of whether to wait for January," says Lockyer. "Theoretically, you'd enhance your position [politically] by keeping everyone guessing."

Whatever Lockyer may have done for the organization and policy direction of the Senate so far, his biggest challenge as pro tem began in earnest when the session ended last month. Fourteen of the 20 seats up for grabs in the November election began the campaign in Democratic hands. Several have been, to varying degrees, contested. With the Democrats sitting at 22 by session's end, a loss of two seats could force him to cut deals with independents Quentin Kopp and Lucy Killea in order to retain power next year. "He's been handed a challenge that is almost overwhelming, with the number of races, the number of campaigns, the Republican surge, and the decline in voting by the Democratic base," says Hayden.

Lockyer began tackling that particular challenge even before he officially took over as pro tem. Throughout the 1993 interim, Lockyer worked six days a week on fund raising. When making his pitch in person, Lockyer brought along a stack of charts, *a la* Ross Perot, laying out the case for his party's continued control of the Senate. His chief target in these presentations was what he calls the "theocratic right," as personified by conservative GOP Senator Rob Hurtt (R-Garden Grove) and his Allied Business PAC. Lockyer has also made it his business to reverse what he sees as a tendency for contributors to favor the more flamboyant and well-connected Willie Brown's Assembly leadership caucus. "They develop some history with Willie, so it's almost autopilot," he says. "If they are going to contribute to Democratic races ... the Senate is entitled to equal treatment."

Even with all this effort, Lockyer faced an uphill climb to keep his numbers steady. Republicans say the narrow margin makes Lockyer's leadership tenuous at best. Any further narrowing of the margin would, according to Maddy "suggest all kinds of things for potential coalitions. There's

a group of Democrats that don't like Lockyer." Democrats insist Lockyer won't be weakened, even in the wake of possible election setbacks. "As long as Democrats and the independents control, he's fine," says Hayden.

"Serving as leader when so many Democrats are exposed is a particularly thankless job," adds Senator Pat Johnston (D-Stockton). "It's not credible to suggest that [Lockyer] was anything less than totally committed and quite successful in supporting our candidates."

Assuming Lockyer's still exercising functional power come next year, he faces an even more uncertain task: guiding the Senate into the term-limit era. "The power of the pro tem is probably going to be enhanced somewhat, and the power of the speaker will be reduced," offered professor Larry Berg, who directs USC's Unruh Institute on Politics. Berg's suggestion echoes an assessment shared by most in the Legislature, many of whom suggest the only thing keeping the Senate from rolling over the Assembly now is the experience and savvy of Willie Brown.

"The Senate will probably be the center of political stability and innovation in California," Lockyer says. "I have to, in collaboration with my colleagues, create a new, more dynamic Senate." That, in Lockyer's view, means taking steps to modernize the Senate technologically, keeping hold of the Senate's more experienced staffers, and doing a better job of controlling the flow of legislation. An early indication of how he will do might have come the last night of session: The Senate adjourned an unheard-of four hours *before* the midnight deadline rather than the more-typical four hours after.

Lockyer's Democratic colleagues see him as an excellent person to handle the transition to the new order. "He's indefatigable," says Hayden. "Those who've watched him for awhile know that he likes doing this. He'll go the extra mile." Greene says Lockyer's experience in both houses and as a player in policy issues give him the experience base to insure maintenance of an institutional memory. Johnston says Lockyer brings not only a good balance of policy and political skills, but also what he described as a "refreshing candor and directness" to the job.

Republicans offer a less flattering vision of the future. "The one thing that's more possible with Lockyer than with Roberti is an all-out war situation," says Maddy. "He's always volatile. You never know when he's going to blow up." Leonard says that, as long as the margin remains narrow, he sees coalitions in which the GOP teams with different sets of Democrats on different issues. "His [Lockyer's] will wind up being more of an administrative leadership," says Leonard.

Outside observers say it's still too early to predict how a Lockyer leadership will ultimately pan out, because the full impact of term limits likely won't be felt until 1996, when Willie Brown leaves the Assembly. Berg suggests Lockyer's ability to balance the conflicting impulses of stability and partisanship will say much about how the Senate moves into its new era.

"In leadership politics, the personality and skills of the individual may will be the critical factor," says Berg. "Bill Lockyer has a basic idea where he wants the institution to go. That is extremely important." If his words are any indication, Lockyer understands his role in shaping the future of the Legislative branch.

"I'm a transitional pro tem between the old Senate and what will eventually emerge as the new Senate," he says. "I think I have the appropriate combination of political and policy skills for that time." 🏛

# LOBBYING & INTEREST GROUPS

The Political Reform Act of 1974 helped reshape relations between lobbyists and legislators. Prior to enactment of this proposition, legislative advocates spent a great deal of time and money entertaining lawmakers and thus winning their favor (and their votes). But the 1974 act prohibited a legislator from taking more than $10 a month from a lobbyist, barred lobbyists from "arranging" for campaign contributions from their clients (this provision has since been invalidated by the courts), established extensive and detailed expense and income reporting requirements, and established the Fair Political Practices Commission to implement the law. The measure has been reasonably successful in cutting the entertainment tie between legislators and advocates and began modifying the way of life in the Capitol. Actually, the system had started to change in 1966 when the Legislature became a full-time body. Many lawmakers and lobbyists brought their families to Sacramento, reducing time available for socializing. In addition under the terms of the ethics measure, Proposition 112 of June 1990 members are: 1) barred from accepting honoraria (payments for speeches), 2) prohibited from receiving compensation for appearing before a state board or agency, 3) limited in the acceptance of gifts from special interests, 4) prohibited from accepting any compensation from lobbyists, 5) required to wait one year after leaving legislative sevrvice before filing as a lobbyist, 6) required to attend ethics training at the begining of each legislative session. In addition, the measure established the California Citizens Compensation Commission to set salaries for elected officals.

The system today is a far cry from the 1930's and 40's when the late Artie Samish boasted: "To hell with the Governor of California! I'm the Governor of the Legislature." And the state's archetypical lobbyist then was probably right. In his long reign, hardly a bill passed the Legislature without Samish's approval. He raised about $1 million over a six-year period from a nickel-a-barrel levy on beer provided by his biggest client and spent it getting legislators "elected and unelected," as he liked to put it. Until 1953 when he was convicted for income-tax evasion, Samish dominated Sacramento; other lobbyists were virtually powerless by comparison. Samish's downfall began when he was interviewed for Collier's magazine and posed with a ventriloquist's dummy he called "Mr. Legislature." The resulting embarrassment prodded the Legislature to pass a mild "reform act" regulating "legislative advocates" in Sacramento. But if the activities of lobbyists are not as blatant as in Samish's day, their power continues unabated. Indeed, the increasing costs of running for election — campaigning for a hotly contested Assembly seat can cost more than $1 million — has made lobbyists and the firms that employ them more important than ever. Moreover, the Legislature in recent years has been plagued with a new round of scandals set off by a "sting" operation run by the FBI and the U.S. Attorney's office. Four Senators were convicted for taking money to help secure passage of the FBI's phony legislative proposal, a bill that would have subsidized a shrimp-packing plant on the Sacramento River.

One Assembly member, a major lobbyist and several staff members were also convicted or pled guilty by mid-1994.

## Types of lobbyists

The corps of advocates includes almost every interest group in the state. In 1996, 1092 individual lobbyists were registered. They fall into several categories:

• *Contract lobbyists.* These advocates will work for almost any client willing to pay their fee. The most successful of them charge high prices, make substantial campaign contributions and get results.

• *Corporation and trade association lobbyists.* These advocates work for one company and represent only the interests of their firms, although they often work in tandem with other lobbyists trying to reach the same goal.

• *Public agency lobbyists.* Aside from the associations representing public agencies, numerous cities, counties and special districts maintain their own representatives in Sacramento. And most state agencies have "legislative liaisons," though they are not required to register.

• *"Brown-bag" lobbyists.* These advocates represent interests seeking reforms in a variety of so-called public-interest fields. They include numerous organizations with budgets sufficient only for bag lunches.

## Lobbying process

Lobbyists operate in several ways. They provide information and arguments on pending legislation in an attempt to win legislators to their point of view. This information function is a legitimate part of the Legislature's work as it helps define issues. Lobbyists also: have their memberships apply pressure; establish friendships with legislators and wine and dine them; and contribute sometimes substantial amounts to campaigns. Lobbyists also lobby the governor, the bureaucracy, regulatory commissions, the courts and the public.

Lobbyists succeed because there are a great many bills considered each year about which lawmakers have relatively little knowledge or interest, and a word from a lobbyist may tip the balance. A smart lobbyist knows he or she is wasting time trying to persuade a legislator who has a firm philosophical commitment to one side or another on an issue, and so focuses on the uncommitted lawmaker. All legislators are susceptible to persuasion by representatives of interest groups. But some are more attuned, for example, to corporate spokesmen, while others are more apt to go along with a representative of an environmental organization.

In the term limits era at the capitol it will be much harder for lobbyists to develop friendships with the turnstile-members. More of the lobby focus will likely shift to grassroots lobbying: letter writing or fax campaigns, plugging local members into candidates' campaign staffs, and bringing the membership to the capitol for meetings with elected officials and/or rallies and demonstrations. However, rookie legislators may need to look to veteran, savvy lobbyists for help. After all, there are no term limits for lobbyists. 🏛

# "Astroturf lobbying"

## Powerful (and not-always-popular) special interests influence the Legislature from behind the shield of others

## By Bill Ainsworth

Reprinted from California Journal, November 1994

When state Senator Leroy Greene's (D-Carmichael) office received a barrage of calls this past April from senior citizens supporting a bill backed by oil companies, his staff wondered why so many Sacramentans were interested in such an obscure issue. But as the calls started tying up his phone lines, a seething Greene realized he was on the receiving end of an elaborate — and he says deceptive — public-relations blitz.

The lobbying campaign is one front in a war that oil companies are waging against California regulations requiring auto companies to sell electric cars. The industry spent hundreds of thousands of dollars to generate phone calls and postcards from ordinary citizens to create the illusion of grass-roots support for the bill.

The bill itself would have made it more difficult for utilities to service electric cars. But instead of broadcasting its own support for the legislation, the oil industry enlisted the help of a respected consumer group, Toward Utility Rate Normalization. TURN, which believed the legislation would prevent utility bills from going up, lent its name to a mass mailing that the oil companies quietly bankrolled. The bill itself quietly died before the end of the legislative session.

The oil industry's effort is just the latest example of an increasingly popular lobbying technique — termed "astroturf" by critics because the "grass-roots" are artificial. Three years ago the insurance industry spent $1.5 million encouraging citizens to write and call legislators to express support for no-fault auto insurance. During the past year, Philip Morris has spent hundreds of thousands of dollars to drum up small-business opposition to smoking

restrictions. These efforts allow unpopular special interests to hide behind "white hat" groups — such as consumer activists, environmentalists, senior citizens and small business owners — whose motives are considered above suspicion. In some cases the public-relations firms hired by special interests actually create "grass-roots" groups.

As part of "astroturf" campaigns, the businesses fund phone banks, petition drives and mass mailings — methods refined by citizens' groups.

"Big business tries to make it look like they have a bunch of citizen support," says Ruth Holton, executive director of California Common Cause. "It's extremely deceptive." Such campaigns, Holton says, undermine efforts by genuine citizen activists. "How is a legislator going to tell the difference between a big business effort and a genuine effort?"

Assemblyman Terry Friedman (D-Los Angeles) first encountered "astroturf" campaigns while sponsoring anti-smoking legislation. His AB 13 banned smoking in all indoor restaurants and nearly all workplaces. Tobacco industry lobbyists decided that a lobbying campaign led by tobacco barons might not impress lawmakers. Instead, they decided to find ordinary, salt-of-the-earth citizens who also opposed the restrictions. The industry's high-powered, high-priced public-relations firm organized "grass-roots" small business owners and ferried some of them to Sacramento.

Meanwhile, Philip Morris already had experience creating and sustaining "grass-roots" groups. Three years ago, the tobacco giant hired the Dolphin Group, a Los Angeles public-relations

firm, to form the California Business and Restaurant Alliance. Friedman calls it a front group for the tobacco industry. Located in the Dolphin Group offices, the alliance has recruited witnesses, published newsletters, and commissioned economic studies against local smoking restrictions.

Last year, when Friedman threatened statewide restrictions, the alliance turned its attention to Sacramento. Alliance members testified eloquently against AB 13 at a Senate Judiciary Committee hearing in April. Their opposition was especially helpful because the established restaurant group, the California Restaurant Association, supported the bill. One witness, Maurice Prince, told the committee that the anti-smoking bill would drive customers away from her popular Los Angeles eatery, Maurice's Snack & Chat. "I hate for you to tell me what I can do with my restaurant," she said. "I have worked day and night for my restaurant." Prince, who was later whisked from the hearing by a tobacco industry driver, said she was recruited into the effort by the Dolphin Group.

Tobacco lobbyists had shrewdly arranged for witnesses from key senators' districts. Prince, for example, owns a restaurant in Senator Diane Watson's (D-Los Angeles) district, while Rudy Martinez, another witness, owns a restaurant in Senator Art Torres' (D-Los Angeles) district. Both lawmakers are sensitive to problems faced by minority business owners.

After the testimony, Torres and another Los Angeles-area Democrat, Charles Calderon, moved to gut AB 13 by allowing smoking in restaurants

---

*Bill Ainsworth is a Sacramento reporter for the* San Francisco Recorder.

and wiping out tough local ordinances. Both senators said they were responding to the testimony by "grass-roots" opponents. "I'm concerned about [Martinez'] restaurant because that's in my district," said Torres at the hearing.

Torres later changed his mind and dropped his amendments after Friedman threw a fit. A candidate for insurance commissioner, he had been stung by criticism that he was hiding behind "grass-roots" opposition while actually doing the bidding of the tobacco industry.

Dolphin Group President Lee Stitzenberger, however, denied that his firm was running an "astroturf" campaign. "These aren't people made out of whole cloth. They are concerned business people who oppose smoking restrictions."

Friedman's bill eventually passed the Legislature and was signed into law by Governor Pete Wilson. It would be overturned, however, by the passage this month of Proposition 188, also sponsored in large measure by Philip Morris. The campaign to pass the initiative is being run by The Dolphin Group.

In its campaign against Friedman's anti-smoking bill, the tobacco industry created a new "grass-roots" opposition group. In another recent astroturf campaign, the oil industry exploited its alliance with an existing citizens' group — TURN. Earlier this year, TURN, which fights to keep utility bills low, sponsored legislation to make it more difficult for utilities to invest $600 million in the equipment needed to service electric cars. Under California anti-pollution regulations, by the year 1998, electric cars must make up 2 percent of the sales of major automakers. TURN argues that the investments are so speculative that utility company shareholders, not ratepayers, should bear any risk associated with them. Utilities and their environmentalist allies disagree, contending that the investments will help them manage their electricity more efficiently and eventually lead to lower rates.

Oil companies quickly realized that the bill had important implications for the future of electric cars. Without a large investment in charging facilities, electric cars cannot be driven conveniently. The Western States Petroleum Association, the oil industry trade group, wrote a letter to senators on the energy committee, arguing that the investments amount to an unfair subsidy to a competitor.

But the association's public-relations firm, Burlingame-based Woodward & McDowell, did not bring oil-company executives to Sacramento to testify for the bill in public. Instead, it organized "Californians Against Utility Company Abuses," a coalition including TURN, the California Manufacturers Association and other large energy users. Next, the firm sent 200,000 letters to taxpayers, urging them to stop a plan "cooked up" by utilities to "increase your gas and electric rates by $600 million to subsidize their profit-making ventures."

Warning that "powerful utility company lobbyists are already working behind the scenes to defeat these consumer-protection bills," the letter urged citizens to return postcards supporting TURN's legislation. It was signed by Audrie Krause, executive director of TURN, and Howard Owens, director of the Congress of California Seniors. The citizens who received the letter were not told that it had been written by the oil industry's public-relations firm and paid for by the industry.

Provoked by the alarming letter, 50,000 people returned postcards to Woodward & McDowell, which then forwarded the cards to legislators' offices. The firm then organized phone banks. It called citizens who had returned the postcards, and patched them in directly to the offices of their lawmakers. The phone banks targeted the 11 members of the Senate energy committee, which planned hearings on Senate Bill 1819. In this case, however, the campaign may have been too elaborate for its own good. Many citizens were confused by the calls from the phone bank. When they were patched in to government offices, some did not know whether they opposed or supported the bill.

Senator Greene said his district and Capitol offices took calls for two days from constituents who believed that his office was calling them. His staff members grew increasingly irritated. At the hearing, Greene and other senators were so angry that they forced the bill's author, Senator David Kelly (R-Hemet), to put it on hold.

Senator Steve Peace (D-Chula Vista) called the campaign a "sleazy tactic" because the mailing failed to mention oil-company funding. "You ought to make a public apology to every member of the Legislature," Peace told oil lobbyists.

Senator Tom Hayden (D-Santa Monica) said TURN's alliance with the oil industry had tainted the consumer group. "I find it to be the end of the independence of TURN," he said. Krause insisted that her group's association with the oil industry does not compromise its independence. She and oil industry representative Scott Macdonald of Woodward & McDowell defended their effort, arguing that it was a coalition, not an "astroturf" campaign.

"These are concerned citizens responding to an issue that is important to them," said Macdonald.

Both the tobacco and oil industry campaigns demonstrate the increasing sophistication of statehouse lobbying. It used to be enough for tobacco and oil lobbyists to strut around the Capitol, whispering in lawmakers' ears and making strategic donations. Now, however, these and other industries have found that their chances of success increase if they build coalitions with citizens' groups — even if they have to invent their own group. Critics charge, however, that the special interests are not only building coalitions with grass-roots groups, but using them — and hiding behind them — for their own selfish purposes.

"These guys should have built the Stealth bomber," said one supporter of Friedman's anti-smoking bill. "They are so good at disguising themselves."

Common Cause supported a bill by Terry Friedman this year that would have required more complete financial disclosure of astroturf and other lobbying campaigns. Under its provisions, clients of lobbyists would have had to itemize the money they spend on activities like economic studies, phone banks and public-relations campaigns.

"They shouldn't be able to hide their activities," Friedman said. "This is a sunshine bill."

At the end of the 1993-94 session, the California Manufacturers Association helped defeat Friedman's bill, arguing that it would have imposed burdensome record-keeping requirements. Although Friedman himself is leaving the Legislature to become a Los Angeles judge, Common Cause's Ruth Holton plans to seek a new author next year. She expects to see lobbyists rely more on public-relations experts to mobilize support for their clients' positions because term limits will weaken their relationships with lawmakers.

# Third House Rising

In the ever-changing world of the term-limited Legislature, lobbyists, too, must change. No longer able to rely on long-term relationships, they may be called upon to spoon-feed institutional memory to neophyte lawmakers.

## By John Borland

Reprinted from *California Journal*, February 1996

t's a campaign reformer's nightmare: A reporter calls a legislator's office with a question about a bill and is told to wait. The voice that replaces the staff member and answers questions is friendly and helpful enough. But it turns out to be that of a lobbyist working the bill, who just happened to be in the office when the phone rang.

This gaffe was only one particularly clumsy demonstration of the widening gap between lobbyists' and lawmakers' experience. By next year, nearly 75 percent of Assembly members will have served two years or less. New lawmakers will have at most 16 years in a state legislative career before being ushered out by term limits, and many observers fear that this rapid-rotation system is draining vital legislative knowledge out of Capitol offices — potentially dangerous in an environment where a good spin on the facts approaches the value of spun gold.

Proponents of term limits and some legislators downplay this diminution of institutional memory, saying it is more important for a lawmaker to be a quick study than to have first hand memories of a 10-year-old legislative fight.

"What I've found in one year is that most everything is learnable," says first-term Assemblywoman Sheila Kuehl (D-Los Angeles), noting that most new members bring some of relevant experience with them. "It's not like we're coming straight out of high school."

But others argue that unexperienced legislators' lack of history will lead them to accept and rely on biased information spoon-fed by lobbyists and the executive branch. "The reality is that if I know the policy area and you don't, I'm going to be able to influence you ... even if I play it completely straight," says Tim Hodson, director of the Center for California Studies at California State University-Sacramento and a former Senate staffer. "If the only information you're getting is from biased sources, how do you assess it?"

Lobbyists have no term limits, other than those imposed by a bad reputation or a poor sales pitch. But the now-perpetual legislative turnover nevertheless is forcing change in the third house. The friendships cultivated by long time advocates are disappearing with the legislative old guard. Lobbyists who founded lucrative careers on their access to powerful ears are being forced to rebuild their relationships with each new class of lawmakers.

"Those old relationships that were the mainstay of lobbyists are going to [disappear]," says Jack Gualco, head of the Gualco Group. "You've got to start new every two years."

The new working conditions are changing some of the third house's faces and tactics. "Some of the older lobbyists are saying, 'I don't know if I'm going to be comfortable in this new environment,'" Gualco says. "The big clean-out will be when the Senate really turns over."

While there has been no mass exodus from the profession, some older lobbyists may be thinking about speeding up their departure.

"I see a lot of veteran lobbyists who work on the basis of cultivated relationships having a hard time adjusting," says Barry Brokaw, a former Senate staffer who now lobbies for Sacramento Advocates. "You're seeing a lot of senior members of the third house retire in the last three to five years."

At the beginning of the career line, the ranks of lobbyists are growing, swelled increasingly by staffers disturbed by shifting legislative sands. "I've gotten calls from a lot of [staffers] looking for jobs," says one longtime contract lobbyist. "There's no stability over there."

Gene Erbin, now an employee with Nielsen, Merksamer, Parrinello, Mueller and Naylor, left his position as Democratic Assemblyman Phil Isenberg's (D-Sacramento) chief counsel earlier this year. "It was a combination of instability, restlessness and a good offer in my case," he said. "[The Capitol] is a different place than when I had worked there initially ... Are there other people who are growing frustrated and are anxious to change their position? Probably."

The number of lobbyists has been growing steadily since members of the corps first were required to register in 1974. But the rate of growth has jumped in the last decade, leaping from about 740 individuals in 1985 to nearly 1100 today. In 1975, by comparison, 616 lobbyists registered with the state.

Lobbyist spending, tracked quarterly by the Secretary of State's Office, also has risen sharply over the years. In 1975, companies and special interests spent $19 million to lobby state government. That figure rose to $74 million in 1985, and to $122 million in 1994, the last year for which totals are available. Even after adjusting for inflation, this is a 22 percent increase in the last decade, and a 150 increase in lobbyist spending over the last 20 years.

Faces and dollars aside, the rules in the advocacy game are essentially the same as always: Talk to the member and explain as best you can, as clearly as you can, why he or she should vote in the interests of your client. But the revolving slate of new members has made this task more complicated than in past years.

A lobbyist needs to win the trust of members and staffers in order to stand out as something more than a vaguely suspect face in a vaguely suspect crowd. This becomes more difficult because the size of the crowd is growing, even as opportunities to talk to the increasing number of new members become less frequent. "There is less personal contact," notes George Steffes, a one-time aide to Governor Ronald Reagan who has lobbied since 1972. "The old backslapping days are definitely going. ...There's more substance involved, but only because there is less personal contact involved."

Lobbyists say it is more essential than ever to know their issues and to be able to explain quickly and clearly why the member should feel a certain way, or care at all about the issue. "I don't have the time or [energy] for them to be too subtle," notes freshman Assemblyman Steve Kuykendall (R-Rancho Palos Verdes). "I need them to be specific, to put it into a big picture... Sometimes they become so ingrained in the process ... that they fail to do the fundamental sell on why we should do it at all."

"This does force us more and more into the sales ranks," Gualco says. The newer, more technically oriented generation of lobbyists "may be more marketing-savvy than people who have been around for a long time," he adds.

The relative scarcity of personal contact and relationships boosts the importance of other lobbying avenues. "Lobbyists will have to use a whole lot of other tools than the good-old-boy network," notes William Rutland, who works with Steffes' firm. These include talking to staff, preparing position papers for members and the media, forming coalitions with other interested parties, and eliciting vocal support for an issue from inside a member's district.

This latter "grass-roots" approach has generated a spate of publicity in recent years as public-relations firms have turned their attention — and the content of their pitches to clients — toward building constituent support. The idea is a persuasive one, especially to interests leery of becoming too identified with under-the-dome shenanigans: If constituents, who the legislator ultimately represents, can be persuaded to contact their representative, their voices will be more persuasive than that of lobbyists paid to represent a position.

Many long time lobbyists say this long has been a piece of their arsenal,

depending on the receptivity of the individual legislator. "I've always felt that the way to have a successful lobbying project is to do a number of things," Steffes says. Legislators always listen to people in their districts, he says, and the trick for a good lobbyist is to develop ways to communicate with those constituents. "The organizations that have large memberships in every district" — such as doctors, optometrists or trial lawyers — "are going to be better off than those that just have one company or factory."

Nevertheless, most note that this kind of constituent communication is no substitute for a face-to-face chat with the member.

"It has to be done in conjunction with a visit to the member here," says Beverly Hansen, a former assemblywoman now employed by Lang/Mansfield Governmental Relations. "Most people who visit the member in the district for the grass-roots ... don't explain the legislative process."

Lobbyists view their emerging position as the in-house repository of memory with mixed feelings. Some admit there are advantages to being the only ones who know what is going on. "On the dark side, there are tricks that would be laughed out of the building now, that can be dusted off and used again five years from now," says John Quimby, a former assemblyman and veteran county lobbyist. "It will be like a comedian working a new crowd in a new town."

But many bemoan the necessity of starting lobbying campaigns practically from the beginning with each new class. "It's going to be an absolute disaster," says Bill Bagley, the former legislator and current University of California regent who lobbies for the firm of Nossaman, Guthner, Knox, and Elliot. He cites work on the Freedom of Information Act, which took half a decade or more to reach the point of passage. "What you do is hammer away, achieve consensus.... With a six-year limit, it will be impossible to have legislative initiative."

"There is a flood of things headed our way with [federal] devolution," notes John White, a representative of several environmental groups. "If you add up all the talent that's leaving, and look at the flood of responsibility coming to the state, I wonder if we're going to be able to handle it." 🏛

# The centering of the environmental movement

## Are environmental groups, long considered bastions of liberalism, being forced into a compromising position in an environmentally hostile political atmosphere?

### By Keena Lipsitz

Reprinted from *California Journal*, January 1996

A particularly astute military strategist once said that nothing unifies like being shot at. As proof of this axiom, people are pointing to environmental groups' nimble bullet-dodging in this year's state and federal revamping of environmental laws and regulations. In the recent tug-of-war over sacred "green" cows, like the Endangered Species Act (ESA) and the California Environmental Quality Act (CEQA), environmentalists have managed to hold their ground. But even as the attack forced them to unite, it also exacerbated behind-the-scenes tensions over strategy. Groups that have historically been on the more progressive end of the environmental spectrum have been digging in their ideological heels and watching in horror as some colleagues have been trying to sit down with the "enemy" to make deals. Stretched taut by low funds and too many battle fronts, the more grass-roots oriented organizations have been forced to allow their politically savvy brethren to do the talking, particularly in Sacramento. Many say the results for environmental protection could be disastrous over the long haul.

Tensions over strategy in the environmental community are nothing new, but the 1994 elections lurched the country and the state to the right. And this has meant that crucial environmental battles are taking place between those who seek to protect all current environmental laws and those who feel that government has gone too far to protect the environment at the expense of jobs and the economy. As anti-regulatory forces in Congress moved to restrict the authority of the Environmental Protection Agency and gut the Endangered Species Act, Republicans in the state Legislature, infused with fresh blood of freshman conservatives, set to work on dismantling the California Environmental Quality Act (CEQA), California's Clean Drinking Water Act, and a host of other environmental laws and regulations. One signal of the coming battle was the appointment of freshman property rights advocates Keith Olberg (R-Victorville) and Bruce Thompson (R-Fallbrook) to the Assembly Natural Resources Committee, making the "green" movement's traditional hold on that key committee more tenuous.

At the same time, prominent groups like Greenpeace, the Wilderness Society and the Sierra Club were reporting declining membership, revenue and influence. In April of last year, instead of celebrating the 25th anniversary of Earth Day, environmentalists were asking whether anyone still cared about the environment. According to John White, a Sierra Club lobbyist, historically, environmental groups in California are not used to losing. "Our hubris left us unprepared for the economic downturn. ...The early 1990s gave us a sobering understanding of just how fast things can turn."

The flurry of activity following the 1994 elections sent a wake-up call to California's environmental groups. They quickly mobilized, often forming coalitions with interested parties to hammer out solutions — as in the case of the December 1994 Bay Delta Agreement where environmentalists joined with agricultural and urban interests to try and resolve a decades-long battle over the San Francisco Bay Delta. But as 1995 came to a close, some environmentalists began to question not only the cost of compromise, but whether environmentalists actually were participating in such talks of their own accord. While some interpret the coalition as a new era of cooperation and a sign that traditionally hostile business interests are willing to accept some regulation, others see environmentalists being forced to the table by the environmentally hostile political atmosphere.

Observers point to the Bay Delta Agreement as one instance of where the latter might have occurred because the negotiations took place at the same time as an attempt to gut the Endangered Species Act in Congress, thus threatening one of the "green" movement's most effective weapons. Zeke Grader, executive director of the Pacific Coast Federation of Fisherman's Associations, crashed the Bay Delta negotiations when he discovered that the agreement would not adequately protect certain runs of salmon in the Delta. Regarding environmentalists' signatures on the agreement, Grader says, "Some of them felt it was the best they were going to get. ...A lot of them are just tired of fighting."

Ann Notthoff, senior planner for the Natural Resources Defense Council, sits on the Bay Delta Advisory Commission, which is responsible for implementing the agreement. Notthoff says the negotiations may not have been worth the effort for environmentalists, if other parties in the negotiations continue to "undermine" the agreement in Washington, D.C. Specifically, she cites attempts by Central Valley agricultural interests to amend the Central Valley Project Improvement Act of 1992, which set aside 800,000 acre feet of water a year for the anadromous fish population, as well as a recent measure by Representative Richard Pombo (R-Stockton), which would amend the Endangered Species Act to prohibit the regulation of water to protect species.

More recently, environmentalists split over an overhaul of California's endangered species act. In the final days of the 1995 legislative session, the Planning and Conservation League (PCL), the National Audubon Society, and the Native Plant Society parted ways with other environmental groups by supporting reforms endorsed by the Wilson administration, developers and agricultural interests. These would have loosened the restrictions for destroying protected species in exchange for encouraging landowners to set aside habitat. The deal fell through when a companion bill sponsored by Senator Jack O'Connell (D-Carpinteria), which would have offered landowners an incentive for handing over land by giving them millions of dollars a year in tax credits for their donations, became stuck in committee.

Senator Tom Hayden (D-Santa Monica), chairman of the Senate Natural Resources and Wildlife Committee, lambasted PCL, the more outspoken of the measure's environmental supporters, for pushing what he saw as a weakening of the ESA.

"You don't need environmentalists to do the compromising. You need environmentalists to paint the big picture, to attack the status quo, and to project the vision," he said in a December 1995 interview with the *San Francisco Chronicle*.

But Jerry Meral, executive director of the Planning and Conservation League, argues that the only way environmentalists can prevent the Legislature from dismantling the ESA is through calculated compromise. "[Hayden] has no control over his own committee. He's dreaming if he thinks his committee can preserve the ESA. We're only one or two votes away from complete repeal of the ESA."

This type of panic over legislation has not reached some corners of California's environmental movement. Gary Ball, co-director of the Mendocino Environmental Center, a community-based organization, says that his group is concerned about what is happening in Sacramento, but, "Being a small environmental group, there's only so much [we] can do ... whatever they do in Sacramento, we'll just have to respond to it."

But according to Capitol insiders, if environmentalists are not more proactive, environmental protections may be dragged back decades in environmental gains. Legislative staffers have commented that the few environmental groups with hired lobbyists in Sacramento have been utterly overwhelmed by the deluge of anti-environmental legislation. This has given other interests with more money a distinct advantage. According to one staff member, in past battles, like the 1992 timber wars and the effort to get the gnatcatcher listed as an endangered species, environmentalists had the upper hand.

But times have changed.

Although environmentalists in California managed to hold off the worst of the anti-environmental onslaught this year, they watched Wilson sign a bill which will place a measure on the March primary ballot enabling voters to decide whether they want mountain lions more strictly managed. They also saw the repeal of a bill that established environmental advertising standards.

More important, there were a number of near misses that promise to re-emerge in 1996. Capitol insiders say efforts to reform the ESA will undoubtedly continue, as well as attempts to rewrite the California Environmental Quality Act. Environmentalists are also keeping an eye on a bill sponsored by Senator Charles Calderon (D-Whittier) which they claim will lower the quality of drinking water in the state.

The battle promises to be fierce because the Republican window of opportunity may be closing. As opinion polls indicate that the public isn't happy with this recent assault on environmental protection, moderate Republicans in Washington, D.C., are joining Democrats to protect the authority of the Environmental Protection Agency and the Endangered Species Act. While this might bode well for the long run, it means that conservative Republicans may be fighting like a cornered cougar in the meantime.

In the coming year, Capitol insiders have warned that, among environmentalists, the left hand needs to carefully watch what the right hand is doing. In other words, they need to coordinate their activities and not be susceptible to a divide-and-conquer strategy. With resources ever tighter and new battle fronts popping up overnight this may prove to be an impossible task. 🏛

# PARTIES, POLITICS & ELECTIONS

## Political Parties

By both design and tradition, political parties in California are exceptionally weak — especially when compared to the machine politics prevalent in some eastern states. The weakening of the party structure was engineered by Hiram Johnson and the Progressives starting in 1911 as a reaction to the machine politics of the railroad interests and San Francisco boss Abe Ruef. Parties were explicitly forbidden from endorsing in non-partisan contests and implicitly from making pre-primary endorsements in partisan contests for much of this century. All local offices and judgeships were made nonpartisan, and a unique method of running, called cross-filing, was instituted. Numerous provisions were written into the law for the express purpose of reducing party power, and many of these restrictions remain in the law today. An independent spirit was fostered in California, and even now there are parts of the state where the electorate pays very little attention to a candidate's party. It is these areas — notably the San Joaquin Valley and the rural districts that can hold the balance of power in state elections.

Under cross-filing, which lasted from 1914 to 1959, a candidate could file for the nomination of not only his or her own party but other parties as well (and until 1952, without any indication of party affiliation). This had the effect of weakening party structure and making pressure groups and the press more important. It also led to the election of popular candidates in the primary, when they won both the Republican and Democratic nominations. Generally, cross-filing helped Republicans more than Democrats, and it is probably significant that Democrats have done much better in elections since the system was eliminated in favor of traditional primaries.

California now has six official parties — Democratic, Republican, Libertarian, Peace and Freedom, American Independent, and the Green Party. A party can win official status by getting the signatures of one percent of the registered voters or by obtaining a petition signed by a number of voters equal to ten percent of the votes cast for governor in the previous election. To remain official, a party must get two percent of the vote for a statewide candidate and retain one-15th of one percent of registered voters. Loss of official status means that a party can run candidates by write-in only, a difficult assignment in an era of electronic voting.

### Party organization

The party structure is spelled out in detail in state law, although some minor variations are allowed for Democrats and Republicans. These are the basic official elements of party structure:

• *National committee members.* These are elected by the delegation to the national convention and serve as the state party's representatives on the national committee of each party.

• *Delegates to national conventions.* Slates are developed by supporters of each primary candidate, and winning delegates — with alterations and additions — cast the state's votes at the quadrennial convention. The winner-take-all primary is used by California Republicans. State Democrats use a proportional representation system of delegates elected from congressional districts. California's primary and presidential primary will be moved ahead on the calendar to the fourth Tuesday in March 1996 to give California voters a greater opportunity to influence presidential nomination politics.

• *County central committees.* These committees, elected directly by the voters, are charged with directing party affairs in each county. In fact, however, these committees are weak, and the real power is held by the office-holders in each county.

• *State central committee.* This committee is comprised of about 1400 members in the GOP and 2500 to 3000 members in the Democratic Party. This committee is charged with electing party officials, managing and operating the party, and selecting presidential electors. An executive committee of the state central committee handles the day-to-day operation of the party.

• *State chairs.* In theory, the chair speaks for the party and develops election strategy in conjunction with the executive committee. With rare exception, however, the main leaders are the major officeholders of both parties.

As noted, Progressive reforms weakened party organization in the state. However, several developments may serve to strengthen California parties in the 1990s:

1) Because of court rulings in the 1980s, parties may now make endorsements in partisan primaries and in nonpartisan contests. Democrats have established detailed regulations for their party on their endorsing rules and format. Republicans have decided, because of potential divisions, not to endorse. Since 1988, (the first year that endorsing went into effect), endorsing has not been a major factor influencing the nomination or election politics of the Democratic Party, but it could evolve into a significant factor in the years ahead because of term limits and many open (no incumbent) districts.

2) Parties have democratized selection to State Central Committees. There are fewer appointments by office-holders, and more elections from the counties. Democrats have created Assembly District Caucuses in the 80 districts to choose 12 delegates per district.

3) Lastly, election by Democrats of Jerry Brown (former governor and ambitious elective office seeker) symbolized the growing importance of the state chair's position. Current state chairs are Bill Press for the Democrats and John Herrington for the Republicans.

# POLITICAL PARTY ORGANIZATION

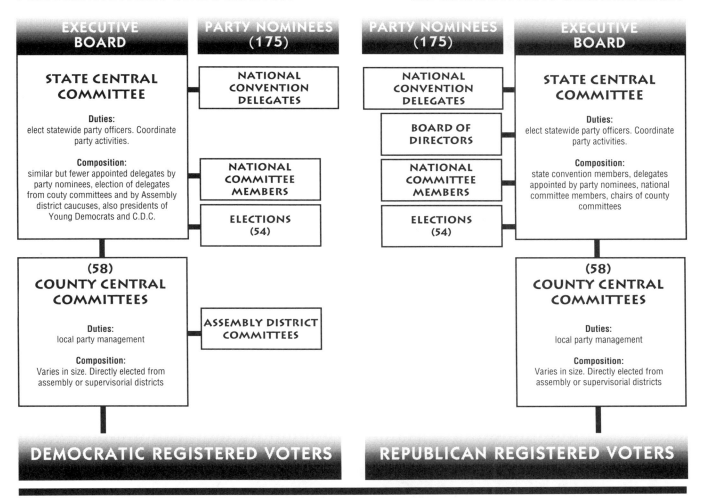

**DEMOCRATIC PARTY ORGANIZATION**

**EXECUTIVE BOARD**

**STATE CENTRAL COMMITTEE**

**Duties:**
elect statewide party officers. Coordinate party activities.

**Composition:**
similar but fewer appointed delegates by party nominees, election of delegates from couty committees and by Assembly district caucuses, also presidents of Young Democrats and C.D.C.

**(58) COUNTY CENTRAL COMMITTEES**

**Duties:**
local party management

**Composition:**
Varies in size. Directly elected from assembly or supervisorial districts

**PARTY NOMINEES (175)**

NATIONAL CONVENTION DELEGATES

NATIONAL COMMITTEE MEMBERS

ELECTIONS (54)

ASSEMBLY DISTRICT COMMITTEES

**DEMOCRATIC REGISTERED VOTERS**

**REPUBLICAN PARTY ORGANIZATION**

**PARTY NOMINEES (175)**

NATIONAL CONVENTION DELEGATES

BOARD OF DIRECTORS

NATIONAL COMMITTEE MEMBERS

ELECTIONS (54)

**EXECUTIVE BOARD**

**STATE CENTRAL COMMITTEE**

**Duties:**
elect statewide party officers. Coordinate party activities.

**Composition:**
state convention members, delegates appointed by party nominees, national committee members, chairs of county committees

**(58) COUNTY CENTRAL COMMITTEES**

**Duties:**
local party management

**Composition:**
Varies in size. Directly elected from assembly or supervisorial districts

**REPUBLICAN REGISTERED VOTERS**

## Elections

A person may register to vote in California who is 18, a citizen of the United States and a resident of the county of registration for at least 30 days prior to the election (and who is otherwise not disqualified, such as in the case of certain felons). There are several types of elections in California:

• *State primaries.* These take place the first Tuesday after the first Monday in June of even-numbered years. At these elections, nominees for national, state and some local offices are selected. Usually, there are a number of propositions also on the ballot.

• *State general elections.* These take place on the first Tuesday after the first Monday in November of even-numbered years, and voters make their selections from among the nominees chosen in the primaries. The ballot usually contains more propositions.

• *Special elections.* These rarely take place on a state-wide basis because of high cost, although there was one in November 1973 when Governor Ronald Reagan put his tax-limitation initiative to a vote (it lost). Special elections are more often held locally to fill vacancies in Congress and the state Legislature. These are different from most other elections in that the voters are given a list of candidates of all parties. If no one candidate receives a simple majority, a runoff is held four weeks later among the top vote-getters in each party. In some cases, this means that candidates far down the list make the runoff while the candidate who finished second in number of votes does not.

• *Local elections.* Often, elections for local city council and special district-director posts are not consolidated with the primary and general elections and are held at various times during the year.

# Political History

During the early years of state history, there were rapid political swings based on economics. When things went well, the big-business interests were in control. During a depression period in the 1870s, the Workingmen's Party under Denis Kearney of San Francisco came to power and managed to get much of its program enacted. When prosperity returned, the party disappeared. Economic and political power went into the hands of the "Big Four" — railroad magnates Charles Crocker, Mark Hopkins, Collis P. Huntington and Leland Stanford. Southern Pacific dominated California politics from the 1880s until the advent of the Progressives more than 25 years later.

## The Progressives

Republican newspaper editors started in the first decade of this century to drum up opposition to the railroads and the boss of San Francisco, Abe Ruef. Disgruntled Republicans started the Lincoln-Roosevelt league, and graft-fighter Hiram Johnson became the group's candidate for governor. He pledged to kick Southern Pacific out of the Republican Party and out of California government. He won easily and immediately started enacting reforms such as the initiative, referendum, recall, cross-filing, civil service, and a multitude of other programs. Johnson went to the United States Senate in 1916 and was succeeded by another progressive, William D. Stephens. The movement lost its force in the 1920s as postwar prosperity produced political apathy. Until the next depression, the regular Republicans maintained control of state government.

The Great Depression resulted in the 1934 gubernatorial candidacy of muckraking author Upton Sinclair (his slogan: "End Poverty in California") with his radical plan for reforming the economic system. Republican Frank Merriam defeated Sinclair by about a quarter of a million votes. With the Democrats riding high nationally under President Franklin D. Roosevelt, the Republicans finally lost the governorship in 1938 to state Senator Culbert Olson.

Four years later, a new progressive era began under Earl Warren. Aided by cross-filing, the former Alameda County district attorney and state attorney general portrayed himself as a non-partisan official — an image he embroidered later as an activist Chief Justice of the United States. Warren's personal popularity was unprecedented in California political history. He was able to push most of his programs through the Legislature (with a compulsory health-insurance plan the notable exception). Warren was the Republican vice-presidential nominee in 1948 (with Thomas Dewey) and perhaps could have remained governor indefinitely. After 10 years as the state's chief executive, he was named U.S. Chief justice by President Eisenhower in 1953.

The new governor was Goodwin J. Knight, who was reelected in his own right in 1954 but was unable to establish himself as leader of the Republican Party because he had to contend with two other major figures, then-Vice-President Richard Nixon and U.S. Senator William Knowland. In 1958, Knowland decided that for political and personal reasons —

he thought being governor was a better stepping stone to the presidency — he would leave his safe Senate seat to run for governor. Knight was pushed aside and virtually forced to run for Knowland's seat. Knowland embraced a right-to-work initiative, setting the stage for a massive Democratic victory led by the gubernatorial candidate, Edmund G. (Pat) Brown. Nixon, defeated in a 1960 run for president against John F. Kennedy, tried an unsuccessful comeback by running against Brown in 1962.

In his second term, Brown became embroiled in a bitter intra-party fight with the powerful speaker of the Assembly, Jesse M. Unruh, and elected to seek a third term rather than give his arch-rival a clear shot at his job. In the primary election, Brown's forces concentrated on shooting down the moderate Republican candidate, former San Francisco Mayor George Christopher, preferring to run against the conservative Ronald Reagan, a former actor. Somebody goofed: Reagan crushed Brown in the general by a million votes.

Democratic nominee Unruh tried to unseat Reagan four years later. Although plagued by limited financial resources, Unruh cut Reagan's victory margin in half. Reagan kept his 1966 pledge not to seek a third term in 1974, leaving the gates wide open. Twenty-nine candidates ran in the primary, with Brown's son, Jerry, and Houston I. Flournoy emerging from the pack to represent the Democratic and Republican parties in November. Brown won by only 179,000 votes, almost blowing his big early lead. Four years later, he rebounded with a 1.3-million-vote victory over the GOP attorney general, Evelle J. Younger.

In 1982 Jerry Brown continued the two-term limit tradition and ran for U.S. Senator (he lost to San Diego Mayor Pete Wilson, a Republican). Attorney General George Deukmejian won a tough primary against Lieutenant Governor Mike Curb for the Republican party nomination and squeaked past the Democratic candidate, Los Angeles Mayor Tom Bradley, in November.

In a repeat in 1986, Deukmejian trounced Bradley, winning by over a million and a half votes. Alan Cranston won re-election to a fourth term in the U.S. Senate, defeating Republican Rep. Ed Zschau.

Pete Wilson maintained Republican control of the state's chief executive position with his victory over Democrat Dianne Feinstein in November 1990. Wilson's non-ideological, pragmatic philosophy is more in the Warren, not Reagan, mold.

For the first time this century both U.S. Senate seats were up for election in 1992, the extra seat as a result of Pete Wilson's resignation from the Senate, and for the first time in the nation's history two women, Democrats Dianne Feinstein and Barbara Boxer, were elected the the U.S. Senate.

In 1994 Kathleen Brown, Pat's daughter and Jerry's sister, won the Democratic nomination for Governor. She was soundly defeated by Pete Wilson in November after leading by more than 20 points in the polls a year earlier. Feinstein was re-elected to the U.S. Senate after defeating Rep. Michael Huffington by a whisker in the most expensive election in U.S. history. 🏛

# Bye-bye, GOP. Ta-ta, Dems.

## California voters flee traditional parties

Reprinted from *California Journal*, November 1993

Illustration by Chris Van Overloop

## By Chris Collett

A favorite topic of debate among political pundits, pollsters and politicians over the last few years has been the question of whether California is more Republican or Democratic in its partisan beliefs. Without much question, it is agreed that the 1970s wasthe decade of the Democrats. In the fallout from Watergate, Jerry Brown was swept in for two terms as governor, and the Democrats built staggering majorities in both houses of the Legislature.

The 1980s, many then argued, belonged to Republicans. Bolstered by the California-based presidency of Ronald Reagan, a two-term governor in George Deukmejian and seat gains in the Assembly, the GOP overtook the Democrats in partisan identification for the first time in 1986. Presumably, as its supporters and some non-partisans have strongly argued, the only thing that kept Republicans from winning majorities in the Legislature and in the state's congressional

---

*Chris Collet is a PhD candidate in political science at the University of California, Irvine.*

delegation was gerrymandered districts. By 1987, Secretary of State March Fong Eu had warned her fellow Democrats that "California had become a Republican state."

With this in mind, it seems natural to ask, "To whom does California belong in the 1990s?" Recent election results suggest that the Democrats have re-emerged. Victories in two crucial U.S. Senate races in 1992, and stunning gains in congressional and Assembly seats despite districts more favorable to Republicans suggest that the Democrats, indeed, may be regaining the strength they enjoyed before the Reagan Revolution.

But the answer to the question, surprisingly, is that the decade of the 1990s seems to belong to neither Republicans or Democrats. The '90s, rather, are poised to be the decade of independents, decline-to-states and an assortment of third parties. Beginning in 1968, California steadily drifted from the two major parties, to the point where, in November 1992 (see Graph 1), nearly 14 percent of its voters were registered either as decline-to-state or with one of the state's minor parties. In terms of raw numbers, decline-to-state and minor-party registation have grown at whopping rates of 566 percent and 145 percent respectively since 1968. By comparison, Republican registration has grown at 62 percent and Democratic at 58 percent over the same time period.

**S**ome would argue that in the candidate-centered age of politics, party registration means very little. In fact, recent research by Ed Constantini and Charles Dannehl at the University of California, Davis, has underscored this, by showing the decline in the relationship between Democratic registration and Democratic vote share in California. Furthermore, reg-

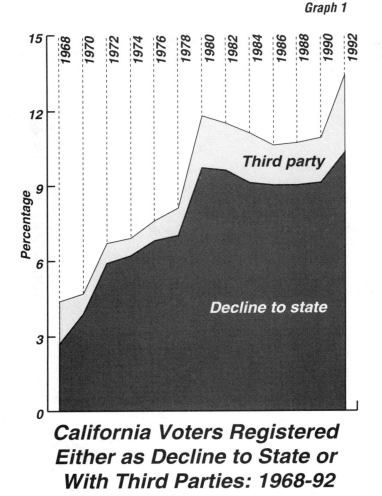

**Graph 1**

## California Voters Registered Either as Decline to State or With Third Parties: 1968-92

source: Secretary of State, Report of Registration 1968-1992

istration data have been considered suspect because it is thought that one to two million voters still on the rolls are "deadwood" — those who have either moved or are deceased.

But the gradual movement away from the two major parties in the last 25 years is evident in the more trusted party identification data as well. Since 1966, *The Field Poll* essentially has asked respondents: "Generally speaking, do you think of yourself as a Republican, or Democrat, or what?" As Graph 2 shows (see page 33), the increase in those who give responses other than "Democrat" or "Republican" has steadily increased from 4.4 percent in 1966 to 33.7 percent in 1992. Like minor-party and decline-to-state registration, this trend reached its peak in last year's election.

While arguing that some sort of

enduring shift in partisan loyalties took place in California in the mid-1980s in the direction of Republicans, scholars of California politics such as Constantini, Kay Lawson of California State University, San Francisco, and James Fay of CSU, Hayward, have acknowledged this turn toward independence as manifested by shifts in registration data. But often, as noted above, survey data regarding party identification are cited to support the Republican cause, and indeed the data do support this case. Republicans have made considerable gains. But if party identification data are looked at in terms of the number of voters supporting neither major party rather than in terms of Republicans versus Democrats (Graph 2) we see a trend much more long term and dramatic than any recent shifts in partisanship.

Because California voters have become increasingly independent, such drastic shifts from Republicans in the late 1980s to Democrats in 1992 are not only possible but very likely to reoccur. Since independents — who again comprise anywhere from 15 to 33 percent of the vote depending on how one looks at it — are more susceptible to short-term electoral factors such as economic conditions, campaigns, and advertisements which influence the vote, elections may boil down solely to which campaign spends the most, has the most potent message, and makes the fewest mistakes. Democratic and Republican labels, even in legislative elections, have clearly diminished in value. "Coattails" have become non-existent.

**C**alifornia's move away from Republicans and Democrats is perhaps most apparent by recent trends in voting for

# The independent voter

### Percentage of California Voters Identifying with Neither Republicans nor Democrats

Graph 2

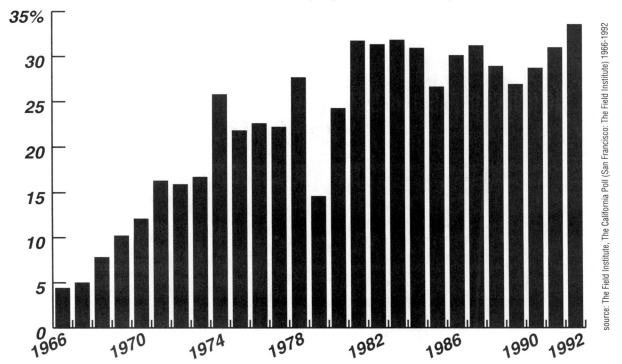

source: The Field Institute, The California Poll (San Francisco: The Field Institute) 1966-1992

third parties. In 1968, when the American Independent and Peace and Freedom parties emerged as the right- and left-wing alternatives to centrist politics during the Vietnam War, voters in California gave minor party candidates for the Legislature and Congress an average of just under 3 percent of the vote. This increated to nearly 6 percent in 1980, when the Libertarian Party first qualified for the ballot and fielded an entire slate of candidates. By 1990 the average share given to third parties had mushroomed to nearly 7 percent, and passed this mark in Assembly and State Senate races in 1992.

**V**oting for third-party candidates in statewide elections has also increased substantially. In last year's U.S. Senate races, all third-party votes combined accounted for 7.8 percent in the race between Democrat Dianne Feinstein and Republican John Seymour and 9 percent in the dust-up between Democrat Barbara Boxer and Republican Bruce Herschensohn.

In the presidential race, gadfly independent Ross Perot gained 21.2 percent in the Golden State, which was above his national average.

The question, of course, is whether this increased share of the vote is enough to affect an election. While third parties still are not likely to win any legislative or congressional seats, they still may have an impact on given races. And in recent years, they have definitely impacted several incumbent and aspiring California politicians, including:

• Doug Bosco, a four-term Democratic member of Congress representing the North Coast, who was defeated 43 percent to 42 percent in 1990 by Republican Frank Riggs. Considered by many to be the upset of the year, it was widely held that the Peace and Freedom candidate, Darlene Comingore, who won 15 percent, split the left vote and kept Bosco form retaining his seat.

• Sunny Mojonnier, a four-term Assembly Republican from the San Diego area, who lost by 5 percent to Democrat Dede Alpert in 1990 in a

predominant Republican district. While ethics problems and campaign gaffes cost the once popular Mojonnier, Libertarian candidate John Murphy took 11 percent of the vote, and perhaps a close re-election from the Republicans.

• Jeff Marston, another San Diego Republican, lost what was considered a potential Republican seat to Democrat Mike Gotch. In a race that separated Marston from Gotch by 617 votes, Libertarian candidate Ed McWilliams garnered over 5000 votes, or 6 percent;

• Democratic Congressman Richard Lehman, who narrowly retained his seat in 1992 after being challenged by Republican Tal Cloud. In a race that was decided by less than 1000 votes, Peace and Freedom candidate Dorothy Wells received 12 percent, or over 12,000 votes;

• Republican Phil Hawkins who in 1992 challenged incumbent Democratic Assemblyman Bob Epple in the 56th District in Cerritos. Losing to Epple by 1 percent, Hawkins saw Libertarian candidate Richard Gard receive 5 percent of the vote.

• Senator Bill Craven, a Republican who has served in the Legislature since 1973. Running for re-election in 1990 free from a Democratic challenge, Craven still saw over 33 percent of the total votes go to the Peace and Freedom and Libertarian candidates.

In the fall of 1983, John Simon wrote in the *California Journal* that "in only a few cases, does one [of the third parties] hold a balance of power in a legislative or congressional district." But clearly, times have changed. An average of 7 percent — again, the average share given to third parties — was greater than the margin of difference between Republicans and Democrats in 13 legislative and congressional races in 1990, and 18 races in 1992. In total, these 31 seats were distributed nearly evenly to both parties, with Democrats winning 16 and Republicans 15. Thus, if third parties fielded candidates in these competitive, "swing" districts, they could now play a significant role in who wins the seat, and ultimately in determining which party controls each house of the Legislature and the congressional delegation. Because third-party candidates in Assembly races attract a slightly higher average vote share than do their counterparts in state Senate and congressional elections, their impact would likely be the greatest.

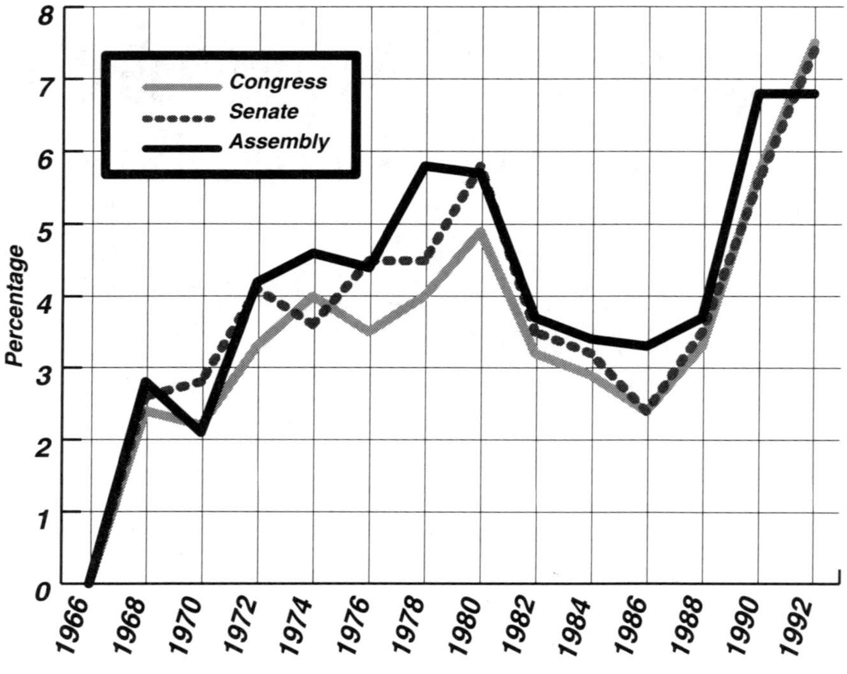

**W**hatever their impact on elections, third parties provide a constant receptacle for disgruntled Californians to cast protest votes. This may be an apt metaphor as a ballot cast for a third party candidacy is often consid-

ered a "wasted" or "throwaway" vote. But with an unpopular governor and Legislature — combined with increasing anxiety about the economy, education and immigration — the third-party phenomenon in California may

be the latest channel of revolt for the politically disgusted. Call it the next chapter in an evolving California story that began in 1978 with Proposition 13 and continued through 1990 and 1992 with stringent term limits and cutbacks in legislative perks, services and salaries.

Equally plausible, however, is that third parties will become a fixture, if not a force, in California politics. No one is suggesting that there will be any Green members of Congress anytime soon, or any Libertarian members of the Assembly. But as long as the aforementioned conditions persist — weak party identification, sluggish economy, dissatisfacation with a government run by both parties — third-party

candidates will continue to attract many voters looking for alternatives. This creates an unpredictable scenario in many districts, especially in north coast areas where the Peace and Freedom Party and Greens have done well, and in Orange and San Diego counties where the Libertarians have prospered. Furthermore, given the trends in state-wide party identification and registration and the current electoral climate, it wouldn't be that farfetched to see a Ross Perot or other independent slate of candidates emerge in California politics.

A small path along that route already has been forged by two members of the state Senate — Quentin Kopp of San Francisco and Lucy Killea of San Diego. Both are independents, with Kopp having originally run for the Legislature as an independent and Killea having left the Democratic Party in 1992 to run for re-election as an independent.

Finally, it should be remembered that California has traditionally been an independent state, with a long history of weak parties, non-partisan elections, a knack for quirky and sometime fringe politics and a fondness for eccentric politicians. Where else but California could figures such as Ronald Reagan, Jerry Brown, S.I. Hayakawa, B.T. Collins, Tom Hayden and others garner such attention? The California electorate today is as volatile as ever, and far from moving in one direction or the other as some have argued, it is likely to go both ways, and may, in fact, continue to search for an alternative route. 🏛

**Graph 3**

## Mean Vote Share for Third Party Candidates in Legislative and Congressional Elections: 1966-92

source: Secretary of State, Statement of Vote, 1966-92

# Dollars from the right

## Conservative group is finding that even ideology has a bottom line

### By John Borland

Reprinted from California Journal, September 1995

The first time anyone picks up a musical instrument, the results are more than likely to be horrendous. Ask any parent with a child in the school band. But there's a learning curve involved, and the passage of a few years and a little bit of practice will eventually produce something like a recognizable melody.

There's a learning curve in politics too, and the California Independent Business PAC — until very recently known as the Allied Business PAC — has reached the song-making stage. Formed by now-state Senator Rob Hurtt (R-Garden Grove), wealthy Orange County financier Howard Ahmanson and several other conservative businessmen in late 1991, the group immediately became the state's biggest benefactor of GOP conservatives and a lightning rod for liberal criticism. Their early efforts were marked more by purchasing power than political sense, but the PAC is learning the art of picking their battles and targeting their abundant funds to races they have a good chance of winning. There may be no immediate profit in campaign politics, they say, but it still requires business sense to succeed.

The four young women who do the PAC's day-to-day political version of heavy lifting present something of a stark contrast to the group of older businessmen donors. Executive Director Danielle Madison has been on board since the group's inception, performing the jobs of district analysis and the unearthing of suitable candidates. Madison reports periodically to the PAC's board of contributing members, now reduced to Ahmanson; Roland Hinz, a publisher of dirt bike and motocross magazines; Edward Atsinger, the head of a nationwide string of Christian radio stations; and Richard Riddle, owner of a box-manufacturing company. The recent name change was a way of codifying the withdrawal of Hurtt from day-to-day activities and of distancing themselves from the Christian right connotations attached to the Allied name, but the PAC's goals remain unchanged.

**Rob Hurtt**

The group denies, vigorously and repeatedly, that they are the banking arm of a monolithic religious right. "Religion has never been a prerequisite of the group," Madison says, adding that there are significant differences of opinion even within PAC ranks. She points to Ahmanson, the member most often accused of being the state Christian right's banker for his affiliations with conservative Christian organizations, and notes that he opposed Proposition 187 and does not support mandated school prayer.

"They're obviously religious people with strong feelings," says Ron Unz, the conservative Silicon Valley businessman who challenged Governor Pete Wilson in last year's GOP primary, and a former contributor to Allied's coffers. Through much of last year, Unz travelled to Orange County every month to participate in the group's board meetings, at which they discussed races and candidates. Religion was no more than a very small part of these discussions if it came up at all, Unz remembers. "Really a lot of it was political strategy," he says. "Can we win this district? What are the polls saying? Should we put more money into the district? Things like that ... It was never a question of discussing people's religion."

But opponents are far from satisfied with the group's denials. "They were formed to elect Christians to office," says Jean Hessberg, California director of the People for the American Way. She points out that several of the PAC donors have long had strong connections to Focus on the Family or other conservative Christian organizations. "Our complaint is that they're not representing to the voters what their real agenda is." Aside from that, Hessberg adds, the PAC is supported by only the four wealthy members, rather than by the broad-based groups many PACs represent. "That's not really what the political action committee process is about."

With total 1993-1994 political contributions by the PAC and its individual members topping $5 million, Allied far outstripped any other ideologically grounded group. But it is the rise of a business-minded, professional husbanding of its resources, as much as the incredible size of its pocketbook, that is allowing the PAC to have an increasingly visible influence on the makeup of the state Legislature.

The 1992 slate of Allied candidates tilted to the right like an upended Titanic, conservative enough on both fiscal and social issues to raise loud cries of an invasion by the religious right. The strategy worked well enough in the primaries, where the well-funded conservatives edged out a competing list of Wilson-backed moderates across the state. But it backfired badly in the general election, and a number of Democrats won in marginal seats that would have been more friendly for moderate Republicans. Allied bettered this record considerably in 1994, spending close to $2.8 million on state legislative races alone and winning 24 of 29 general election races, mostly in the Assembly.

"We didn't do thorough district profiles in 1992," Madison says. She points to the example of Brad Parton, the Allied candidate defeated by now-Assemblywoman Debra Bowen (D-Marina del Rey). "That was a case of trying to fit a square peg into a round hole." A more reasonable look at the district, in which nearly-even party registration should benefit Republicans,

calls for an entirely different kind of candidate, she explains. She notes that the district has recently elected four women as legislators: U.S. Senators Barbara Boxer and Dianne Feinstein, Representative Jane Harman and Bowen. "It looks like this district leans toward moderate women," she says.

The group no longer moves reflexively towards any candidate that fits their list of conservative issues. Before going into a race, Madison and her staff will commission a poll, developing a detailed profile of the district and its high-propensity voters. "We'll find out what the district wants," she says. "We'll look at the vote histories going back 10 years or so, and get a good sense of the history of the district."

The histories are particularly useful in deconstructing areas like the Central Valley, which has tended towards the more conservative over time. "We won't go to a district just because it has Republican registration," she says. "We go to districts with a history of voting Republican." Madison points to the PAC's support of Assemblyman Brian Setencich (R-Fresno) last year. "That district has Democratic registration, but their vote history is Republican." In 1992, voters there supported conservative talk-show host Bruce Herschensohn by a wide margin over Boxer, and the district was one of the few in the state to give President George Bush its solid support. "Everyone wondered why I was so adamant about going into that district," she recalls. "They're Reagan Democrats. They're looking for that independent Republican type. Setencich fits."

None of this means the group has moderated its picture of an ideal candidate. The PAC maintains a list of its positions on a number of issues, ranging from low taxes and decreased government regulation to school choice to the statement that "government should do whatever it can to discourage and restrict abortion." But Madison and the four families of contributors have realized that an eight-out-of-eight-point candidate will not fit every district, that there are marginal districts that, if they are to be won by Republicans, must be won with five- or six-point candidates that reflect district voters more than the PAC's positions.

In most cases, the PAC conducts interviews of potential candidates, looking for someone who fits their district profile. "We'll talk to people, look at who we know, go through word of mouth,

sometimes even call them cold turkey," Madison says. But the latter is only a last resort, in important districts that need a strong candidate. "Usually there are too many [candidates]. We need to weed them out, and find the people that fit the district."

Assemblyman Bruce Thompson (R-Fallbrook) interviewed with Allied before his 1992 race. The group did not end up officially endorsing him, but did contribute to his campaign. "They asked me what my positions on business issues were," he remembers. "They asked if I had problems that would surface during the campaign." The conservative social issues, while addressed, he says, were not as prominent as economics, crime and the year's hot topics such as three strikes and Proposition 187.

But not every candidate will go through these interviews. Assemblyman Bruce McPherson (R-Santa Cruz), a moderate for whom Allied produced an independent mailer during his 1993 special-election campaign, says he did not solicit the PAC's aid in any way. "I didn't even know it was coming until it was done," he says. And in his case, the help was not altogether welcome, given Allied's reputation for supporting only the most conservative candidates. "I thought that effort actually hurt me in the campaign," he says. "I don't need their help." He asked them to refrain from supporting him in his re-election bid, and they stayed away in 1994.

Another tool in the PAC's political utility belt is a series of training programs for candidates and campaign staff. The group funds a joint effort in late August with the conservative Young Republican Federation, featuring most of the state's major GOP consultants and a number of national strategists. "We do this because it's hard to keep good trained people on site," Madison says. "There are a lot of candidate training schools, but this is for the campaign team, one of the most important parts of the campaign." The weekend session solicits sponsorships of up to $2000, and charges $75 per attendee. Any funds left over will go to the Young Republicans, rather than back to the PAC.

Allied is one of the few donor organizations that does not explicitly lobby its candidates after getting elected, according to its supporters. Candidates supported by the group agree, saying that they have not had PAC staff knocking on their doors to ask for votes. "I'm surprised that they're not up here asking people to vote against the budget because of the abortion issues," says Thompson. But he recognizes, as do other observers, that the group primarily backs candidates that support its conservative philosophies. "If you go through and get good candidates, then there's no need for [lobbying them]," Thompson says.

Nevertheless, some do report feeling pressure, largely through the actions of Hurtt, one of the leaders of Allied until his election to the Senate. "[Hurtt] goes beyond the bounds of propriety in the way he tries to lead people around," says one Republican legislator, who asked to remain anonymous. This influence was particularly felt during the recent speakership battle, he adds. But the same legislator notes that Hurtt's actions are not necessarily seen as identical to the PAC's wishes. "It's not a monolithic group."

The PAC's recent name change has another sidelight. Traditionally focused on legislative races, the group now intends to begin playing on the local level, aiming at developing a "farm team" of candidates for future elections. The move comes both as a response to the opportunities given by term limits and to frustration at past near-misses, according to Madison. "It's partly my frustration ... in finding people with local experience," she says. "It's vital in winning campaigns to have the pulse of the district. And no one does that better than elected officials."

A deep-pocketed group like Allied could be hugely influential in local elections, where candidates spend a fraction of the budget of a legislative campaigns. And the current volatility of local governments — fully half of state-wide county supervisory seats turned over last year — provides considerable opportunity for leverage. "It's a tactically wise thing to do," says Senate President pro Tempore Bill Lockyer (D-Hayward), who has kept a close watch on the group since its birth. "Anyone with mainstream or left-leaning candidates should be very concerned."

But local elections do have different rules. For one, the ballots are generally non-partisan. In addition, many municipalities have contribution caps limiting donors to $500 or less. And even if no limits exist, the usually tiny participating electorate in local elections may act as a brake on spending. "The awareness level of voters in municipal elections to outside influence is much higher than in the 60 percent that vote in generals," says Tom Shortridge, a Los Angeles-area Republican consultant. "It becomes politically a little embarrassing if you're a councilman and you get $10,000 of your total $20,000 from Allied."

Democrats note the PAC's increasing success rate and widening scope with a wary eye. Lockyer has made it a point to keep a microscope lens trained on campaign expenditures made by both the PAC and its individual members, and loses no opportunity to publicly underline the group's extremely conservative agenda. Assemblyman Antonio Villaraigosa (D-Los Angeles), a member of the Assembly Democrats' 1996 campaign committee, agrees that information is the best way to fight back. "What will be the key is to show who [the PAC] is and who they're giving to," he says. He acknowledges that fighting candidates tailored to their district will be difficult. But PAC support is ammunition to link even a moderate to a highly conservative agenda, he says. "We've got to tie them to each other."

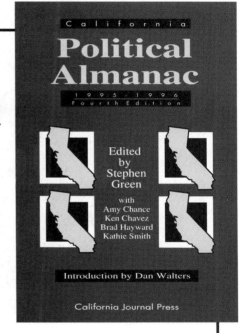

# The Virtual Primary

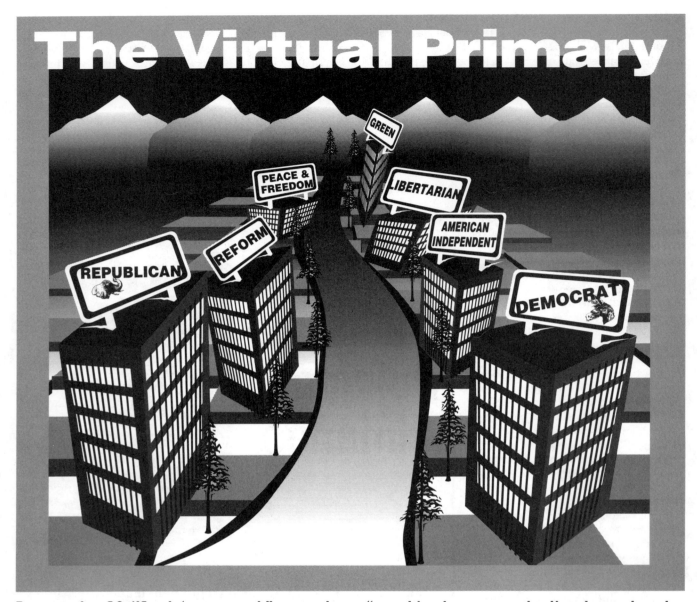

**Proponents of California's proposed "open primary" want to give every voter the chance to vote in primary elections. But opponents of the scheme say it will further weaken political parties and allow "enemies" to skew the results.**

## By Charles Price

Reprinted from *California Journal*, November 1995

"Too often, the choice in the general election boils down to a Leon Trotsky-type Democrat versus an Attila the Hun-type Republican," lamented Richard Ferrari, San Diego Republican activist and co-author of the so-called "open primary" initiative, which has qualified for the March 1996 primary.

Ferrari's lament bolsters the notion that California's current "closed" primary system often produces candidates who represent the extremes of both major political parties. That system requires that voters who want to participate in a party primary must register for that party.

But Ferrari and his allies want to change that system with an open primary that would allow participants to cross party lines to cast their ballots. Instead of Democratic voters restricted to voting only for Democratic candidates,

---

*Charles Price is a professor of political science at California State University, Chico, and a frequent contributor to California Journal.*

Republican voters for Republican candidates, and so on, voters would have the opportunity to vote for any candidate regardless of the office seeker's party affiliation. The party candidate receiving the most votes running for a particular office would be listed as that party's nominee on the general election ballot. Republican and Democratic county central committee members, however, would be elected on a separate party ballot available only to their respective party voters.

At present, 11 states operate under some form of open primary. In eight of those states, voters are allowed to choose which party primary to vote in on Election Day. Currently in California, if a registered Democrat decided he wanted to re-register as a Republican in order to vote in the 1996 GOP presidential primary, he or she would have to complete the paperwork with election officials at least 29 days before the primary. Three states — Washington, Alaska and Louisiana — have what is called a "blanket primary," where voters may vote for the candidate of their choice regardless of that candidate's party affiliation. California's open primary initiative is patterned after those states. Louisiana's blanket primary has a unique twist: if a candidate running in the primary gets 50 percent-plus-one of the total vote cast for that office, he or she is elected automatically in the primary.

The current primary system in California dates to the early 20th century, when Progressive reformers successfully promoted it to undercut domination of the nominating process by party leaders and activists, who created party slates at state conventions. While most states have followed California's lead, a few Eastern states still cling to the old convention system. Thus, Ollie North received the Republican nomination for U.S. Senate in 1994 at a Virginia convention rather than in a primary. North eventually lost to incumbent Democrat Chuck Robb. With Progressive prodding, California also became one of the first states in the nation to elect rather than appoint delegates to the national nominating conventions.

Originally, California's primary featured an embellishment known as "cross-filing," which allowed candidates to file for a particular office in their own party's primary, and also in the "other" party's primary as well. The notion was that people had the right to vote for the best person in a primary regardless of party. Since a cross filer's party affiliation was not listed on the ballot when they entered the "other" party's primary, voters often did not realize they were voting for a person of the "other" party. They simply voted for the familiar name; usually, the incumbent. Candidates winning both party's primaries — sometimes as high as 70 percent to 80 percent of legislative races — were listed on the general election ballot as hyphenated Republican-Democratic or Democratic-Republican (depending on the incumbent's party affiliation); they had no major party opponent. On rare occasions, cross filers won the other party's primary but lost their own.

Republicans, for the most part, were able to take better advantage of cross filing because they had more incumbents, superior campaign financing and greater newspaper support. Because of its disastrous impact on Democratic Party fortunes, cross filing was modified via a Democrat-sponsored initiative in 1954 and completely abolished in 1959. Occasionally, however, a candidate may receive two different party's nominations for an office. Senator Jack O'Connell (D-Carpenteria) accomplished that feat as an assemblyman in 1990 when he won his own primary, then won the candidate-less GOP primary as a write-in. Assemblywoman Jackie Speier (D-South San Francisco) did the same thing after no Republican opponent filed against her in 1994. Both Speier and O'Connell received a sufficient number of write-ins from Republicans (at least one percent of the previous general election total).

In terms of objectives, the open primary and cross filing are similar, but the way they work are quite different. Instead of having a single, hyphenated candidate on the general election ballot with no major party competitor, under the "open" primary, each party's top vote-getter for a particular office becomes its nominee. This ensures competition on the general election ballot.

The open-blanket primary idea has been proposed periodically over the years by various "good government" reformers. Until recently, however, the idea failed to develop sufficient momentum. Open-primary legislation has been introduced in the Legislature before, but it always died in committee. In 1984 an open-primary initiative was filed, but proponents failed to get the necessary signatures to qualify for the 1986 ballot. Many of the activists from that failed effort are involved in the new initiative.

For the most part, the key activists who organized to promote the open primary initiative are moderate Republicans, including Republicans For Choice and the California Republican League. They launched their drive because they have become increasingly disenchanted with right-wing nominees who frequently win Republican primaries. A smattering of Democrats and independents provide some bipartisan balance to the initiative effort. For example, Trish Hooper, a Democratic activist of San Mateo County whose daughter is married to former GOP Congressman Pete McCloskey, is co-author of the initiative. State Senators Steve Peace (D-El Cajon), Ruben Ayala (D-Chino) and Lucy Killea (I-San Diego) also are supportive. And, United We Stand volunteers have been involved in initiative planning.

Any effort to qualify an initiative requires money. To that end, one of the open primary's chief legislative proponents, Senator Tom Campbell (R-Stanford), said that he persuaded David Packard, co-founder of Hewlett-Packard and one of California's wealthiest citizens, to offer a matching grant of $200,000 to the cause. William Hewlett provided another $25,000, and the Hewlett-Packard Corporation contributed $10,000. The early seed money from Packard was invaluable. Open-primary proponents hired attorney Peter Bagetellos, a specialist in initiative law-making, to draft the initiative, and American Petition Consultants, a professional signature-gathering firm, to collect the required signatures. The effort to qualify began in February 1994.

"The [open] initiative was not the easiest to qualify," said Bill Arno of American Petition Consultants. "Our solicitors had to spend a little more time explaining the measure. It wasn't nearly as easy to qualify as [Propositions] 184 [three strikes] or 187 [illegal aliens]. We had to pay our solicitors a little more per signature in order to collect all of our signatures." Arno said about 75 percent of the signatures were gathered by paid solicitors, with the remaining 25 percent brought in by volunteers.

---

**Update**

The open primary initiative (Prop. 198), while being opposed by state Republican and Democratic leaders, was easily approved by voters in the March 1996 primary — 59% yes, 41% no. It will be in effect in 1998 when the next state primary is conducted.

---

Proponents of the initiative, such as Republican activist Susan Harding of San Diego, argue that their proposal provides three prime advantages. "First, it will increase participation in the California primary," said Harding, a Dean Witter executive and the measure's campaign coordinator. "Those registered as 'decline to state' will be able to vote ... in the primary, and this will increase their turnout. Second, it will reinvigorate the electorate by providing primary voters broader choices. Third, it will encourage parties to put forth stronger, more viable candidates."

Ferrari noted: "Those nominated in the Republican and Democratic primaries often have little in common with the great mass of voters. Our best officeholders tend to be mayors and supervisors — people who hold non-partisan office. Now, admittedly, many of these local officeholders are registered Republicans, but they're pragmatic Republicans like Mayor Richard Riordan of Los Angeles."

As moderate Republicans see it, conservative candidates tend to win GOP primaries because hard-core conservatives are more likely to vote in the primary. But these staunch conservative GOP candidates often lose to Democrats in the general. For example, moderate Tom Campbell lost to arch-conservative Bruce Herschensohn in the 1992 U.S. Senate Republican primary. Herschensohn subsequently lost to Democrat Barbara Boxer in the general. Cross-over Democrats voting in the primary for Campbell could conceivably have won him the nomination. And, it is possible that Campbell would have been a tougher opponent for Boxer in the general.

Open-primary advocates argue that most Californians live in legislative districts that are "safe" Republican or Democrat in registration. As a result, minority party registrants have no chance of influencing the legislative primary outcome and so often opt not to vote. Under the open format, their vote would have meaning.

Killea added that the open primary would "increase the opportunities for more moderate, less partisan candidates to get nominated. This isn't the complete solution to California's governmental problems, but it is one piece of it." Killea noted that moderate Republicans seem to be the prime instigators of the initiative because "they're suffering the most under the present system."

The prime opponents to the open primary are sure to be the Democratic and Republican parties and legislative party leaders. They argue that party registrants should determine party nominees, and the open primary will further weaken political parties in the state. "Our party hasn't taken an official position on the 'open' primary yet, but I suspect we will oppose it," said John Herrington, chairman of the state Republican Party. "Personally, I don't support it. It leaves room for a lot of mischief. The open primary would tend to blur the ideological lines between the two parties and more candidates would move to the center. That would be bad."

In a similar vein, Democratic consultant Bob Mulholland argued: "Would Lion's Club members invite Kiwanis members to vote in the election for the president of the Lion's Club? No way! I see the open-primary initiative mainly as a political agenda for David Packard to promote the candidacy of ... Tom Campbell."

Mulholland also argued that an open primary would encourage party raiding. "The open primary would work kind of like a special election, with all the candidates running on the same ballot. There would be all kinds of opportunities for Republican or Democratic party leaders to encourage their voters to switch and vote for the weakest candidate of the other party. We'll play under the rules that are adopted, but this would open the door to manipulation."

That fear has not materialized in other states, however. According to political scientist Hugh Bone of the University of Washington, the blanket primary in his state has not led to organized party raids by one party against the other. Bone said there is no evidence to suggest that Washington voters have been more energized to vote because of the state's blanket primary.

Assemblyman Phil Isenberg (D-Sacramento) was skeptical of the benefits of the open-primary initiative and felt there was an "Episcopalian" impulse to it. The backers of the initiative are "the white Protestant, well-to-do, highly educated pillars of the community who always want to dictate to the rest of society their values. I can't guess what the ultimate consequences of the open primary might be — it's a leap into the dark. It would further weaken parties and could conceivably bring a kind of recall fervor to primaries."

Sharing Isenberg's negative assessment, Assemblyman Bernie Richter (R-Chico) said that he opposed it because he felt "it would significantly reduce the effectiveness of political parties in California. I think a much better institutional reform that would accomplish the same objectives of the open primary would be to guarantee no more political gerrymanders. Having a large number of marginal seats [where both parties are competitive] would force Republican and Democratic candidates in these districts to look beyond their core party constituencies."

Senate Minority Leader Rob Hurtt (R-Garden Grove), on the other hand, said he had "no problem" with the open primary for statewide elections, "but I do foresee trouble in legislative races at the district level where a few thousand votes can determine the outcome." Hurtt was concerned that in a high-registration GOP district, featuring a crowded Republican primary, Democrats could play a spoiler role by voting for the weakest Republican. He pooh-poohed the notion that electing more moderates to the Legislature might defuse partisan conflict.

Republican campaign consultant Wayne Johnson admitted that he had mixed feelings. "I like clear contrasts between the Republican point of view and the Democratic — the spirit of debate and the give-and-take. The open primary would lead to less well-defined, rich man's candidates running for office."

Johnson also scoffed at the notion that electing more Republican and Democratic moderates would promote more legislative harmony and effectiveness. "Not at all," he said. "The pettiness in the Legislature is not ideological; it's personality-driven. Willie Brown had the power to keep bills locked in committee at the behest of special interests and their campaign contributions. He didn't want floor debate on these bills." While Johnson admitted that the open primary could stimulate more turnout in primaries, he contended this would not automatically make it better. "To register independent means you skip the primary. It's a self-absorbed act. The voter is saying, in effect, 'I choose to be irrelevant.'"

What are the prospects for victory for the open primary? At this point in time, chances of success for proponents seem reasonably good. A Charlton poll done recently and an older Mervin Field survey indicate that about two-thirds of Californians favor an open primary, once it's been explained to them. And that explaining may be the fly in the ointment. Open primary is not a hot-button, emotional issue, such as term limits, three-strikes, illegal aliens, or the pending Civil Rights initiative to eliminate affirmative action. Thus, winning public approval requires a substantial educational campaign by proponents. The question is: Will anyone listen? 🏛

# DIRECT DEMOCRACY

In California government the people have three tools that make them very powerful participants in the decision-making process. The initiative, referendum and recall were instituted by Governor Hiram Johnson and the progressives in part to break the hold of the railroad interests on state government in the early 1900's. With all three of the direct democracy devices, a simple majority of those voting determines whether the proposal passes.

• *Initiative*. The initiative gives the people the right to place local or state measures on the ballot if they obtain the required number of signatures. It has also been used by governors, legislators and special-interest groups to get what they want after the Legislature has rejected or been unable to meet their demands. To qualify for the ballot, a statewide constitutional initiative requires signatures equal to eight percent of the vote cast in the last gubernatorial election; initiative statutes require five percent.

After the 1994 gubernatorial election the number of signatures required is:

Constitutional initiative - 693,230
Statutory initiative - 433,269

Today, a powerful and sophisticated initiative industry has developed: signature-gathering firms, pollsters, political lawyers, and campaign management firms specializing in the qualifying and passing of ballot measures.

• *Referendum*. This is a procedure that can be used by the public, if they can gather sufficient signatures, to block a state statute or local ordinance pending a popular vote on the issue. It is not used often, but the threat of a referendum occasionally has the effect of blocking enactment of legislation. This procedure cannot be used to stop urgency bills, and for this reason emergency measures require a two-thirds vote rather than a simple majority in the Legislature. The referendum procedure was used successfully at the state-wide level to place four measures the Peripheral Canal and three reapportionment plans — on the ballot in June 1982.

The number of signatures required is the same as for a statutory initiative.

• *Recall*. The third of the Johnson direct-government reforms establishes a petition procedure for placing on the ballot the question of removing any elected official or officials from office. Recall elections are common in local government and have increasingly been used to target state legislators. Former President Pro Tem David Roberti in 1994 and Assembly member Paul Horcher in 1995 had to face voters in recall elections.

California's system of direct democracy does not stop here. The Constitution and local-government charters can be amended only by a vote of the electorate. Neither the state nor any local governmental agency may incur a general-obligation debt without prior approval of the electorate (although revenue bonds can be sold without such approval). At the state level, a simple majority vote is sufficient to approve bond measures for such purposes as higher-education construction, park acquisition and development, the Cal-Vet farm and home program, and water-pollution plants. But at the local level, all bond proposals — even school bonds — require a two-thirds majority.

In recent years, the potency of direct democracy in California has grown. This power was demonstrated by the far-reaching tax revolt, which started with Proposition 13, the Jarvis-Gann property-tax initiative in 1978. This was followed with the "Spirit of 13" spending-limitation measure enacted in 1979, a successful Jarvis-sponsored income-tax indexing proposal in June of 1982, the successful Gann Legislative Reform Initiative of June 1984 and a number of other Proposition 13 follow-up measures thereafter. Proposition 140 imposes term limits on California elected officials, plus it mandates a 38 percent cut in the legislature's budget. Proposition 164 imposes term limits on our U.S. Senators and Members of the House of Representatives. In 1994 two initiatives were at the center of state political debate: The "Three Strikes" (Prop. 184) and illegal aliens (Prop. 187) initiatives. In 1996 the much ballyhooed Civil Rights Initiative abolishing affirmative action programs is likely to be *the* issue of the year. The number of measures qualifying for the ballot shows no sign of abating in the near future.

With these tools, there is hardly any aspect of state government that cannot be controlled by the people. 🏛

# initiative reform
## Is it time to return to the "indirect" initiative?

*Illustration by Mike Tofanelli*

### By Charles M. Price

Reprinted from *California Journal*, April 1994

If public attitude toward state government was a radar screen, the little blip marked "confidence" probably has disappeared from view. And the reasons for it are myriad. Corruption unearthed in an FBI sting operation conducted inside the Capitol ensnared legislators, lobbyists and staffers. The economy has been blistered by defense cutbacks, an unemployment rate higher than the national average, a tidal wave of illegal aliens, a never-ending series of fires, floods, drought and earthquakes, and human maelstromes such as

*Charles Price is a professor of political science at California State University, Chico, and a frequent contributor to California Journal.*

the Los Angeles riots. When dealing with all of this, political institutions often seem mired in gridlock and unable to cope.

Thus, the public took matters into its own hands, using a process of "self-government" established more than 80 years ago — the initiative. Beginning with Proposition 13's overhaul of the property tax system in 1978, voters systematically restructured state political institutions and changed forever the way state and local governments funded themselves. They also put a cap on the amount of time state elected officials may serve in office.

But a growing number of critics feel that the initiative process, set up to curb the influence of special interests on government, has become instead a tool for those interests. Critics also feel that the laws that emerge from the initiative system are flawed. And they want the process overhauled.

The initiative — together with its cousins, the referendum and the recall — first saw the light of day in California back in 1911 when Progressive Governor Hiram Johnson led the charge to write them into the state Constitution. Initiatives allow voters the right, via the petition process, to propose and enact laws and constitutional amendments, and, by so doing, bypass the Legislature and/or governor.

Initiative critics, including elected officials and academicians, point to a number of problems with the current system.

• Initiatives are often authored by special interests or by ambitious politicians, not by average citizens, as Johnson intended.

• These measures are filed and approved for circulation without any in-depth analysis. Although the attorney general makes sure proposals don't violate the constitution, many slip into circulation with drafting errors or are flawed in other ways that must later be sorted out in court.

• Most initiatives qualify for the ballot through the work of professional petition firms rather than the efforts of volunteer citizens.

• Initiative propositions are laden with legalistic jargon, making them difficult to understand for the average voter.

• So-called "counter-initiatives" — two proposals on the same subject and the same ballot — often complicate the voter's ability to sort among conflicting measures.

• Initiatives add to the length of the ballot and number of decisions facing voters.

• Propositions are packaged into deceptive campaigns by slick professional campaign consultants.

• Finally, initiatives, once approved by voters, are amended with great difficulty.

Beyond these problems, a succession of fiscal initiatives have severely hampered the governor and Legislature's ability to provide fiscal leadership — or even craft a budget. Included in this group are Proposition 13's 1978 property tax relief; Proposition 4 of 1979, which imposed government spending limits; Proposition 6 of 1982, which abolished property and gift taxes; Proposition 62 of 1986, which required a two-thirds vote before cities may raise taxes; and Proposition 98 of 1988, which mandated a minimum funding level for K-14 public schools.

Finally, voter adoption of Proposition 140 in November 1990, the harsh term limits and legislative budget reduction initiative, was for many legislators, especially Democrats, the "last straw."

Thus, over the last several legislative sessions, various Democratic legislators have proposed "reforms" to stem the initiative tide: raise the filing fee from $200 to $1000, require that signatures be collected in a specific number of counties, increase the percent of signatures needed to qualify an initiative or require that the percent be geared to registered voters not to the total vote cast for governor at the last election, the current requirment. This proposal would double the number of required signatures (currently 615,958 for a constitutional amendment and 384,974 for a statute). Yet, none of these proposals passed even though Democrats had secure majorities in both houses.

Restrictions on the initiative process fail for a number of reasons. First, conservative Republicans are wary of undercutting a process they often have used with great success. Term limits, for instance, was proposed by former Assemblyman and former Los Angeles County Supervisor Pete Schabarum — a Republican conservative. Second, polls repeatedly show that the public supports the initiative process. And although that support has declined over the last several decades, it still is backed by more than 60 percent of the electorate, according to *The Field Poll*. Third, an alliance of interests united to help protect the initiative during the 1991-92 legislative session. This "Initiative Coalition" included political watchdogs such as Common Cause and the League of Women Voters, environmental groups such as the Planning and Conservation League and the Sierra Club, and conservative anti-tax groups such as the Howard Jarvis Taxpayers Association, People's Advocate (founded by the late Paul Gann), and Paul Gann's Citizen Organization. The coalition opposed restricting the initiative process because its members had successfully sponsored initiatives and were reluctant to see the process dismantled. Moreover, the Jarvis and Gann groups have used the initiative process as a money-making tool to help fund their activities.

One significant initiative reform emerged from the 1991-92 session, however — Democratic Assemblyman Jim Costa's ACR 13, which established a 15-member Citizen's Commission on Ballot Initiatives to study the process and propose possible remedies. Under ACR 13's provisions, the governor, Assembly speaker and Senate Rules Committee each selected four members, with appointees a reflection of the state's diverse population. The commission also included a designee of the secretary of state, attorney general and president of the County Clerk's Association. Retired Legislative Analyst A. Alan Post, one of the most respected former officials in the state, was selected to chair the commission.

The commission met periodically during spring 1993 to listen to various initiative experts recommend initiative reforms and to formulate a proposal. Two experts in particular played key roles in framing the commission's deliberations: attorney Robert Stern, former counsel to the Fair Political Practices Commission and author of "California's Fourth Branch of Government;" and Floyd Feeney, a University of California, Davis, law professor and co-author of "Improving the Initiative Process: Options for Change." The "Initiative Coalition" also provided input.

In the end, the initiative process gained a vote of confidence from the commission, although there was substantial consensus that it had some problems. As Post commented, "I don't think that commissioners felt the initiative process should be constrained nor that it was overused. The intent was to make it a better instrument." Post and his colleagues agreed a comprehensive package of initiative reforms was needed and, in January 1994, they presented their recommendations to the Legislature. Costa packaged these recommendations into an omnibus initiative reform bill introduced in February 1994.

The most dramatic change proposed by the commission involves reinstitution of a modified "indirect initiative." Currently, initiatives that qualify go "directly" to the next statewide ballot. The commission would detour those measures by requiring that qualified initiatives first go to the

Legislature for evaluation.

Under an "indirect" system, sponsors of an initiative would have 180 days (30 more than under the current system) to circulate petitions and gather enough signatures to place their proposal on the ballot. But instead of going before voters at the next state-wide election, the proposal instead would be sent to the Legislature, which would have 45 days to act on it. Lawmakers would hold hearings  where proponents and opponents could testify. Lawmakers also would negotiate with sponsors to iron out flaws or correct drafting errors. Sponsors then could amend the measure as long as the amendments were consistent with the "purposes and intent" of the original proposal. Each house would vote on the initiative and — if the Legislature passed and governor signed it — it would become law without going before voters. The governor and Legislature also could adopt their own law on the same subject, and proponents could choose to withdraw their proposition if satisfied with the effort. If, however, the governor and lawmakers reject a qualified initiative, it automatically would be placed on the next statewide ballot, where it would become law if approved by voters. If a statute, the Legislature subsequently could amend it after three years by a two-thirds vote of each house. Constitutional amendments could not be amended by the Legislature.

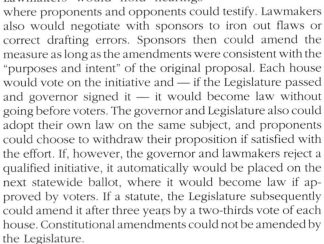

There are advantages to this approach, the commission argued. For one, proponents would have a little more time to qualify their petitions, and this might encourage more volunteer rather than paid signature collecting. More important, it would provide a mechanism for revising initiatives after they have been filed. Today, qualified measures go on the ballot, period. The commission's plan, however, would allow for hearings, complete with bill analyses, review and amendments. Oversights, ambiguities and gaffes in the initiative text could be corrected. For example, opponents of Proposition 165, sponsored in 1992 by Governor Pete Wilson to reform welfare and the budget process, focused on one significant drafting error: Although the proposal gave the governor emergency fiscal powers, the Legislature was not given the power to override his decisions. George Gorton, Governor Wilson's initiative campaign manager, admitted to the drafting flaw but contended the courts would take care of it. This could have been avoided had the commission's format been in force because Wilson would have had the opportunity to amend his proposal.

There are problems with the commission's recommendations, however. Hiram Johnson sought a procedure that would bypass a gridlocked or special interest-dominated Legislature. The proposal puts the Legislature back in the loop. Also, from 1911 to 1966, the California Constitution included both a direct and an indirect initiative, but the latter device was rarely used. Finally, *The Field Poll* reported in 1990 that 50 percent of Californians opposed the indirect initiative, while only 41 percent favored it. Also, if initiatives never reached the ballot, it would mean less money-making opportunities for campaign consultants.

In addition, opponents often want proposals killed, not amended, and see their best chance at the ballot. In this vein, they might not want to tip off proponents to drafting errors at a legislative hearing but would rather spring these shortcomings on proponents later in the campaign.

The Post Commission also included a smorgasbord of other fine-tuning reforms, including additional contribution disclosure statements, improved signature-verification procedures, better ballot design, and full disclosure of the top five contributors to the proposition.

The commission, however, did not deal with the role of money in the initiative process. Court rulings mostly have preempted the subject. Powerful groups like the California Teachers' Association or the tobacco industry are in a better position to qualify their proposals than is, say, an animal rights' group because wealthy organizations can spend a lot of money on professionals to collect the required number of signatures. The U.S. Supreme Court ruled in 1988 in *Meyers v. Grant* that states can not prohibit paid petitioning because the ban limits free speech.

Clearly, the side with the most campaign money, particularly if it's by more than a two-to-one or three-to-one margin, has a better chance of winning at the ballot box. This advantage is even more enhanced in the 1990s because the "fairness doctrine" — which once required radio and television stations to provide some free air time to proponents or opponents of propositions with modest financial resources — is, at present, dead. Yet courts also have ruled that attempts to set contribution or expenditure limits also violate free speech.

The contemporary initiative process seems to work. Since the 1970s, only about 20 percent of the filed initiatives actually qualified for the ballot. Of these, only about one-third were approved by voters. If "too many" initiatives get on the ballot, or if initiatives are too lengthy or complex, voters tend to play it safe and vote "no." Thus, in effect, the initiative process already has a self-correcting mechanism.

For his part, Costa has pushed ahead with plans to author legislation to implement some commission recommendations. At the end of February, the Fresno lawmaker introduced AB 3181, which incorporates those recommendations that received unanimous support from the commission. Among the bill's provisions are the requirement for legislative hearings on proposed initiatives, a procedure for proponents to amend their measures, an extension of the circulation period, an improved signature-verification system, and provisions for additional campaign statements.

Costa also introduced ACA 40, which puts provisions of AB 3181 before voters. Both bills are headed for their debut before the Assembly Elections and Reapportionment Committee. Randall Henry, a senior consultant to Costa, expressed guarded optimism about the fate of the two bills, saying that Costa packaged only those recommendations that had been given unanimous approval by the commission, with its varied representation.

Still, Costa's success could depend on how lawmakers perceive declining public support for the initiative, legislative anger over term limits and support from the Initiative Coalition.

Meanwhile, the public seems to be in for a breather — the June 1994 ballot contains only one initiative. 🏛

# In the shadow of Jarvis and Gann

# Citizen initiators tilt at the electoral windmill

## By Charles M. Price

Reprinted from *California Journal*, April 1995

**S**eventeen years ago, a singular success turned their names into household words, made them instant inductees into the grass-roots hall of fame, secured their places in California political history and launched a movement that even today has the power to turn normally forthright, sane and otherwise stalwart politicians into quivering mounds of Jell-O. One was a cantankerous Southern Californian, the other a gentlemanly Sacramentan, and prior to their success, they had a somewhat checkered history as authors and proponents of ballot initiatives. Both separately and together, they had logged a record of failure that might have caused ordinary mortals to develop a more rewarding hobby.

But these two had the kind of genius that comes from the dogged pursuit of a singular goal. Or, maybe they just had blind luck, for in 1978, Howard Jarvis and Paul Gann hit paydirt, nirvanah, the promised land. They offered up a property tax relief initiative that captured the imagination of beleaguered taxpayers, who endorsed their proposal — known then and forever as Proposition 13 — and made it the law of the land. From that day forward, Jarvis and Gann became mythical practitioners of initiative politics.

Jarvis and Gann scored a huge success, but many less-successful promoters push their ideas just as doggedly — often in the face of defeat after defeat.

Take, for instance, Robert W. Wilson, a Southern California artist and initiative proponent whose motto might well be, "If at first you don't succeed — try, try again." In 1964 Wilson qualified a ballot initiative that would have set up a statewide lottery — Proposition 16 that year. Voters, however, rejected it.

"I was 20 years too early," Wilson lamented, adding that Nevada gambling interests and California horsetracks poured millions of dollars into the effort to derail his initiative because they feared the competition for gambling dollars.

Embittered by his experience, Wilson in 1965 filed a new initiative that would have allowed casino-style gambling in Adelanto, a small San Bernardino County community in the Mojave Desert a few hours drive from Los Angeles. It also would have provided for extended pari mutuel wagering on horse racing. The initiative was a less-than-subtle swipe at the enemies of Proposition 16, but Wilson failed to gather enough signatures to qualify it for the ballot. Undaunted, Wilson has resubmitted his Adelanto gambling measure 25 times since 1965. It has yet to qualify.

Wilson and his band of allies remain undaunted. "Do you realize that Californians spend over $3.5 billion yearly gambling in Nevada?" asked John Brown, an Oxnard attorney who co-authored Wilson's 1994 gambling proposal. "That's why Nevada doesn't have to have a state income tax. Hang Nevada."

Brown may be correct, and a whole bunch of Californians may agree with him. But the act of qualifying

---

*Charles M. Price is a professor of political science at California State University, Chico, and a frequent contributor to* California Journal.

an initiative requires more than an idea whose time may have come. It requires big money. Thus far, Wilson and Brown have been unable to find the financial backing needed to hire professionals such as American Petition Consultants to secure the needed signatures. If they ever do find a bankroll, they might just qualify their idea. And given the mood of the electorate, it might pass. After all, that's precisely what happened to those old men of myth — Jarvis and Gann.

Meanwhile, Robert W. Wilson symbolizes the potentials and pitfalls of the initiative process. In a nutshell, the process that has so enmeshed Wilson goes like this:

A person or group drafts an initiative idea — whether a statute or constitutional amendment — into the proper legal form. Generally speaking, politically savvy proponents rely on experienced attorneys to put their proposals into proper legalese. Others may request drafting assistance from the legislative counsel if the request is accompanied by the signatures of 25 voters. The Legislative Counsel's Office lends this assistance as time permits. The proponent then submits the initiative proposal to the attorney general, along with a $200 deposit for processing costs that will be refunded if the measure qualifies. The Attorney General's Office gives the proposal a title and summary, after which it is sent to the Secretary of State's Office, which sets the deadline for turning in enough valid signatures to qualify for the ballot — currently, 432,945 for statutes and 692,711 for constitutional amendments. In addition, a fiscal analysis is prepared by the Department of Finance and Joint Legislative Budget Committee. Finally, if a sufficient number of valid signatures are collected by the deadline, the measure goes on the next statewide ballot where voters approve or reject it.

Over the last 30 years, initiatives have increasingly occupied center-stage in California politics. Among the most prominent were Proposition 4 — the Political Reform Act of November 1974; Jarvis-Gann's Proposition 13 of June 1978; Proposition 140 and its imposition of legislative term limits in November 1990; Proposition 174's school-voucher proposal of June 1993; and Propositions 184 and 187 of 1994, better known as the "three strikes" and "illegal immigration" initiatives. Already approved for the March 1996 primary election is an "open primary" initiative that would allow voters the right to vote for any primary candidate regardless of party label. In addition, another school-voucher bombshell is in the works, also aimed at March 1996, while a measure to abolish the state's affirmative-action laws could land on the November 1996 ballot. All three promise to have substantial impact on the elections of 1996. Overall, since 1964, nearly 650 initiatives have been filed in California, approximately 17 percent have qualified for the ballot and about 7 percent approved by voters.

Initiative qualifying may have crested in the 1987-90 period when some 36 made it to the ballot. Of these, 15 were approved. Since 1990, the number of proposals qualifying for the ballot seems to have slacked off despite a continued stream of petitions circulated for signatures.

What sort of people file initiatives? Essentially, there are three types: elected officials, executives of financially powerful interest groups and private citizens. Most initiatives that qualify for the ballot are authored by the first two groups. These proponents are politically astute and often have the financial wherewithall necessary to promote petition drives. They nearly always hire professional firms to guarantee their measures make the ballot.

Elected officials have introduced a fair share of initia-

tives over the past three decades as well. In particular, conservative Republican officeholders such as John Schmitz, John Briggs, Pete Schabarum, Floyd Wakefield, Don Rogers, Frank Hill, Bill Dannemeyer and Ross Johnson have put forward ideas and, by so doing, have sought to bypass the Legislature, which has been controlled for the most part by liberal Democrats.

**N**ot that Democrats, too, haven't felt compelled to use the ballot. The likes of former Assemblymen Lloyd Connelly and Dick Floyd and Senator Tom Hayden and former Senator Alan Robbins have filed initiatives. A more recent trend has been for major statewide officeholders or candidates to propose initiatives as adjuncts to their campaigns. John Van De Kamp, Leo McCarthy, George Deukmejian, Pete Wilson and March Fong Eu are examples. Interest-group leaders such as John Henning of the AFL-CIO, Kirk West of the Chamber of Commerce and Carol Lee of the California Medical Association have been active initiative proponents as well.

Even political insiders frequently fall short in their signature-qualifying efforts, however. For example, no one is more keenly aware of the problems in collecting sufficient valid signatures in the right amount of time than the secretary of state. Yet, former Secretary of State Eu failed to qualify her "Dimes Against Crimes" initiative in 1987.

It was average citizens like Robert Wilson, not political insiders, whom Progressives wanted to empower when they first placed the initiative procedure into the state Constitution not long after the turn of the century. After all, elected officials and lobbyists had access to the formal institutions of lawmaking — Legislature and governor. The initiative was designed for those outside the regular process.

Who are these average Joes and Janes? And why are they willing to plunk down $200 for their initiative idea? How do they hope to collect the hundreds of thousands of signatures needed to place their measure on the ballot?

Some private-citizen initiators believe strongly in their issue but have little appreciation or understanding of the costs of printing thousands of petitions and coordinating a massive signature drive. For example, builder Norman Bedford of Healdsburg was the subject of several expensive lawsuits. Bedford became angered by what he considered to be excessive costs for attorneys, and he filed an initiative to limit their fees.

"I thought I would receive financial support from the insurance industry with my proposal," Bedford admits. But, the money never appeared. He has filed seven initiative proposals over the years, but none has ever qualified.

In 1973, in a one-week period, Patrick O'Shaughnessy of San Francisco filed 20 separate initiatives on a wide variety of subjects. None qualified, and O'Shaughnessy was out $4000 for his trouble. And, in 1994 one proposed initiative on "Forfeiture of Office" listed an all-time high of 57 co-authors. It, too, failed to make the ballot.

**S**ome citizens launch initiatives aware that qualifying them will be difficult but do so to get media coverage for their measure, or to give their issue legitimacy. For example, Barton Gilbert, in the 1970s and '80s, and currently Jack Herer have promoted efforts to legalize marijuana under certain circumstances — an issue the Legislature has been reluctant to take on. None has ever made the ballot.

Said Robert Wilson, "I didn't even try to qualify many of my [gambling] initiatives. I kept reintroducing them because this was my idea — my way of maintaining a kind of patent on the idea."

A fair number of private-citizen initiatives are filed because particular interests such as doctors, lawyers, teachers or insurance companies have a virtual veto over hostile legislation. Thus, to circumvent the power these groups hold over the Legislature, proponents resort to initiatives such as single-payer state health system, school vouchers or "pay at the pump" no-fault auto insurance.

*Illustration by Mike Tofanelli*

Some citizen initiatives promote non-traditional approaches to government. Some of those filed over the last two years:

Matt Dillon proposes a 24-hour-a-day, 365-days-a-year telephone voting system on propositions submitted to voters.

Former Alaska Senator Mike Gravel would allow California citizens a chance to participate in a world constitutional convention to establish global governance. It appropriates 25 cents per California resident from the general fund to help finance the effort.

Cheryl Fort wants to amend the preamble to the state's Constitution.

Norman Bedford wants to implant facial identifying numbers subcutaneously on released violent felons.

Robert Bell proposes that California secede from the Union and become an independent nation.

Eurica Californiaa wants laws on nudity to apply to males and females equally, bare chests and all.

Occasionally, initiatives sponsored by private citizens have qualified. In the 1970s Ed and Joyce Koupal, after failing to qualify a recall of Governor Ronald Reagan, left Sacramento and moved to signature-rich Los Angeles. Activists — mainly students and housewives — were organized into the People's Lobby, a petition-sponsoring group that promoted

liberal causes. With minimal financial resources but dedicated volunteers and a no-nonsense approach to gathering signatures, they succeeded in qualifying several of their initiatives. Ironically, one novice who learned at their knee was Howard Jarvis, himself a right-wing ideologue.

And then there were Jarvis and Gann. Prior to Proposition 13, Jarvis and Gann had failed to qualify any of their six initiatives. After Proposition 13, they jointly or separately succeeded in qualifying a number of measures, with several winning voter approval. They also established two organizations that promote conservative causes via the ballot box.

The most-recent heir-apparent to the Jarvis-Gann legacy is Mike Reynolds, a Fresno native whose 18-year-old daughter was murdered by a paroled felon after she refused to give him her purse. Reynolds labored for years to pass stiffer penalties for violent felons, only to see his effort crushed in a Democrat-dominated Legislature. In 1993, Reynolds went the initiative route — his cause helped when Petaluma 12-year-old Polly Klaas was kidnapped and murdered by an ex-con with a history of violent crime. His proposal became the "three strikes and you're out" initiative of 1994 — Proposition 184.

In addition, public-interest lobby groups with modest financial resources — for example, Common Cause, the American Cancer Society, Campaign California and Californians Against Waste — using mostly dedicated volunteer signature collectors have sometimes been able to qualify petitions. Another, the California Planning and Conservation League, has enlisted high-powered and high-paying allies to fund its initiatives, mostly by writing shares of the spoils into the initiative on behalf of those it seeks as co-sponsors. This "Christmas tree" approach has succeeded in qualifying and passing ballot measures in the 1990s. In addition, the Ross Perot-inspired United We Stand, led by state chair Kirk McKenzie, attempted to qualify four separate initiative proposals in 1994 but failed.

Much of the criticism concerning ballot-box lawmaking — use of counter-initiatives; paid signature-gathering; partisan game-playing; and expensive, duplicitous campaigns — can be tied to elected officials and financially powerful interest groups who seem able to buy their way onto the ballot at a whim. But it is the Howard Jarvises, Paul Ganns and Robert Wilsons of the world — underfunded grass-roots citizens or groups with altruistic, irksome, wacky, innovative, naive or even unconstitutional proposals — that more closely reflect what Progressives had in mind when they advanced the initiative process nearly a century ago. 🏛

# Paying the tab for recall elections

Assemblyman Mike Machado was the target of a recall election in 1995. The attempt failed, but the Linden Democrat wants the state to pay the nearly $1 million it cost Machado to defend himself.

## By Charles M. Price

Reprinted from *California Journal*, June 1996

Mike Machado seems an unlikely target for Republicans. A conservative Democrat from the rural San Joaquin Valley, Machado now and then breaks with his Assembly Democratic colleagues to throw his lot in with the GOP on policy matters. Only this past April, for instance, Machado was the lone Democrat to vote in favor of Governor Pete Wilson's proposed 15 percent tax cut.

But a year ago, Machado was very much in the GOP's crosshairs because he was the wrong guy in the wrong place at the wrong time. The setting was the speakership wars which wracked the Assembly following the 1994 elections. Machado had voted for his own party's nominee as speaker — then-Assemblyman Willie Brown Jr. (D-San Francisco). And that vote gave Republicans the pretext to employ a little-used tactic to try to oust Machado from office — the recall election.

**Machado**

The recall effort against Machado ultimately failed. But the Linden lawmaker was not one to forgive and forget. If the recall itself was rare prior to 1995, Machado's subsequent action was even more extraordinary: He asked the state of California — through the Board of Control — to reimburse his campaign for the $889,000 cost of defending himself against the recall. Machado and his allies contend that the state constitution provides for the reimbursement, and that it is fair that he be made whole after voters turned back the recall effort. Critics of his action argue that the notion of reimbursement, if upheld, might deter recall efforts against other officials.

Machado found himself at the heart of this controversy because he was caught up in recall mania — the "string 'em up" attitude fostered by Assembly Republicans who sought revenge on two of their own members: Republican-turned-independent Paul Horcher of Diamond Bar and Doris Allen of Cypress. In separate incidents, the pair had deprived Republicans of the speakership after the GOP had gained a 41-vote majority in the lower house during the 1994 elections. First, Horcher voted for Democrat Willie Brown Jr. for speaker. Then, Allen took the speakership for herself with the help of Democratic votes, a maneuver also engineered by Brown.

To punish the dissidents and keep other potential malcontents in line, Assembly Republican leaders applied the seldom-used recall procedure. Under this process, recall activists collect sufficient signatures from registered voters in a member's district within a stipulated time period, and the member is forced to stand for election. If a majority of those voting in that election opt for recall, the member is removed from office immediately and is replaced by whichever candidate receives the most votes from a slate of hopefuls who run in the same election. Both Horcher and Allen met this fate and were replaced in the Legislature.

But Machado was targeted for a different reason. On the surface, Republicans said that Machado ought to be removed because he had promised during his 1994 election campaign to exercise independent judgment when voting for speaker. Then, these Republicans claimed, Machado had the audacity to vote for his *own* party's choice — Willie Brown Jr.

But the real reason that Republicans went after Machado is more simple and more crass: They thought he could be had, and his removal would provide personal gain for the recall leaders — Assemblyman Larry Bowler (R-Elk Grove); Dean Andal, a member of the Board of Equalization who formerly represented Machado's district in the Assembly; and Senate Minority Leader Rob Hurtt (R-Garden Grove), who provided seed money for the recall's signature drive.

Machado was viewed as vulnerable because his 1994 margin of victory was only a few hundred votes. In addition, had the recall succeeded, Bowler would have been well positioned to challenge Senator Pat Johnston (D-Stockton) in his 1996 re-election and thus provide Republicans — and Hurtt — with another vote in a closely divided Senate.

But the plan misfired. As Republican political consultant and recall expert Tony Quinn noted, "In Horcher's and Allen's Southern California, high Republican registration districts, there was intense opposition to Willie Brown and those Republicans who collaborated with him. In Machado's Stockton district, Democrats turned the tables on the Republicans. They argued that Southern California politicians were trying to tell them who their assemblymember should be. It was a very effective message."

Even some Republicans thought the Machado recall effort was unwise. For example, Assemblyman Bernie Richter (R-Chico) considered the Machado recall wrong. "It was an attack on the validity of the election results," he argued. "That's banana republic."

Using the recall to oust a state legislator still is a rare event, although less rare today. Prior to 1994, only three had had to fight off such a threat in the 83 years since the recall was first placed into the state constitution in 1911. Since 1994, however, four members have faced recalls — Horcher, Machado and Allen in 1995 and former Senate President pro Tempore David Roberti (D-Van Nuys) in 1994. Roberti successfully defeated an effort launched by gun enthusiasts angry over his sponsorship of a ban on assault weapons. Although the Allen recall last December was the last in the current spasm of recalls, the successes against recalcitrant colleagues suggest the procedure could be used again as a disciplinary tactic.

But the spate of recalls also has renewed a long-standing debate over their value. Critics contend that recalls are too easy to put on the ballot, are costly to local governments and taxpayers, foster "down and dirty" campaigns, poison the already bitter mood in the Legislature and should be used only as a last resort, not to discipline measures or to reverse the results of a close election. Proponents, on the other hand, say that the threat helps keep public officials attuned to their constituents. Citing the godfather of recalls, Progressive Hiram Johnson, they argue that the recall was never intended as a last resort but as a "precautionary measure to remove recalcitrant officials."

"The original idea for the recall was to reduce the power of the political boss and party machine," noted Quinn. "Progressives were angry with elected officials who did whatever their boss told them to do." According to Quinn, the recent GOP-inspired recalls were aimed at overthrowing the formerly, all-powerful speaker, Willie Brown, and very much in the Progressive tradition.

But one facet of the recall law has yet to play itself out. Article 2, Section 18, of the California Constitution reads, "A State officer who is not recalled shall be reimbursed by the State for the officer's recall election expenses legally and personally incurred." Evidently, it was placed in the constitution to discourage capricious use of the procedure. Incumbents who were vindicated in a recall would have their recall election expenses paid.

This reimbursement feature applies only to state recalls, not to local efforts. Nor is it a feature in any of the other 14 states that provide for recalls of state officials. To date, only three California legislators have beaten back recalls and thus were eligible for reimbursement: James C. Owens in 1914,

Roberti in 1994 and Machado. Neither Owens nor Roberti filed a claim. Roberti said that he considered requesting a reimbursement for recall expenses but decided against it.

"I didn't apply for reimbursement because this recall provision is very vague," Roberti explained. "The major problem is you'd have to establish the fact that the money you're requesting was your's personally and not the campaign's. Also, it's a very long process. The claim has to go to the Board of Control and, if they approve, to the Legislature and governor. There would have been a lot of public debate about whether I deserved the money." For Roberti, it wasn't worth it, and now his one year statute of limitations has run out.

Machado, on the other hand, is pushing forward. He thinks the amount he should receive "should be defined as the total amount of money I spent to defend myself, $889,000." Machado has promised that if his request is approved, he will give San Joaquin County $150,400 to pay for half of the cost accruing to the county to conduct the election.

"I think that Larry Bowler and Dean Andal ... should put their money where their mouth's are," Machado said. "They should offer to pay the other half of San Joaquin County's expenses for the recall." For his part, Bowler tried with House Resolution 18, designed to compensate San Joaquin County for conducting the recall election. The measure died in Rules Committee.

Machado's reimbursement claim has been submitted to the State Board of Control by his attorney, Joe Remcho. The board is responsible for governing claims against the state for money or damages. After input from its staff and Department of Finance consultants, and following a public hearing on the matter, the three-member board will make its decision. The board currently is made up of Democratic state Controller Kathleen Connell and two appointees of Governor Pete Wilson — Chairman and Director of General Services Peter G. Stamison and a public member Bennie O'Brien. If they recommend reimbursement, the Machado claim, along with other civil claims against the state and victims of crimes claims, will be incorporated into an omnibus bill introduced in the Legislature. If the board rules against Machado or recommends an amount of compensation less than what Machado believes is fair, he may take the matter to court. In the Legislature, the Board of Control's claims bill goes to the two houses' fiscal committees for approval, floor votes, and then submission to the governor for is signature or blue pencil.

Given the fact that Machado's request for reimburse-ment is unprecedented, and because the constitution is vague on this point — "expenses legally and personally incurred" — and due to the highly charged partisan nature of the three speakership-related recalls, how much money Machado will receive is very much in doubt.

Not surprisingly, some are contemptuous of Machado's request. "We view this as a publicity stunt," said Bowler Chief of Staff Don Ediger. "It's not a legitimate claim. He's trying to manipulate the media and portray himself as a victim. ...Why should state taxpayers have to fund Machado's recall expenses when he displayed zero restraint in spending on the race? Should we reward financial mismanagement?" Ediger argues that the reimbursement feature was designed when a recall campaign's total budget might be a few hundred dollars — most of it being the incumbent's own money. "But it was never intended to cover the [incumbent's] total expenses in a modern recall campaign." Echoing this senti-ment, Quinn said, "I think this reimbursement feature is a bad idea. Why don't we just reimburse everyone who wins an election for their expenses?"

Richter, on the other hand, thinks "[reimbursement] a good idea, although it should be made crystal clear in the constitution exactly what expenses should be reimbursed."

Besides being compensated for his recall expenses and providing San Joaquin County money for conducting the election, Machado has one further objective in pursuing this quest: to quell what he believes is abuse of the recall process for partisan advantage.

"Progressives put the reimbursement feature as a protec-tive mechanism," said Tim Riordan, Machado's chief of staff. "By providing a reimbursement, some people may think twice about pursuing a frivolous recall in the future."

But Assemblyman Phil Isenberg (D-Sacramento) doubts that reimbursement will deter future recall efforts. "Machado will be reimbursed by state taxpayer funds, not [by] the people leading the recall drive," he said. "The people you want to deter are those using the recall as an election technique or strategy."

Machado himself has introduced AB 2782, which would require the state — not local governments — to pay for the costs of recalls aimed at state officials.

Meanwhile, his unusual request for reimbursement adds yet another wrinkle to a recall saga that already has changed the face of the Legislature. 🏛

*Charles Price is a professor of political science at Califor-nia State University, Chico, and a frequent contributor to California Journal.*

# LOCAL GOVERNMENT

One reason why Californians have so many elections and frequently such long ballots is that the state has a complex system of local government. Every citizen in the state probably is a resident of a dozen or more units of local government, among them:

*Counties.* The state has 58 counties (counting San Francisco), some of which are governed by general state law and others by charters (similar to constitutions) voted by the people.

*Cities.* Most Californians live in one of the state's 470 cities, but some live in unincorporated areas in which municipal services are provided by the county and special districts. General law cities (384) operate through a structure established by state law. Charter cities have more flexibility in their structure and procedures.

*City-county.* San Francisco is a combined city and county operating under a charter.

*School districts.* Public schools from kindergarten through 12th grade are operated by independent districts with directly elected governing boards. There are about 1200 school districts in the state.

*Community college districts.* Directly elected trustees also run community colleges, which provide freshman and sophomore courses.

*Special districts.* These can vary from large regional districts such as the Metropolitan Water District in Los Angeles to a local mosquito-abatement district. There are more than 3400 special districts formed to provide specific services for a defined area. Most directors are elected by the public.

*Local Agency Formation Commissions.* Each county has a commission that serves as clearinghouse for annexation of territory by a local agency and for formation of new cities.

*Regional governments.* There are no all-powerful regional governments in California, but there are numerous limited-purpose regional agencies such as the Bay Area Air Pollution Control District, Rapid Transit District and Sewer Service Agency. Efforts have been underway for years to enact a powerful regional government for the San Francisco area. There are several voluntary associations of local governmental agencies designed to help resolve regional problems; these include the Association of Bay Area Governments and the Southern California Association of Governments.

## City and county government

Counties are run by boards of supervisors elected by the public, usually by district. In most counties, the board appoints an administrative officer to supervise the details of county government. Counties also have other directly elected officials, such as the district attorney, the sheriff and the assessor.

Cities are operated under a variety of systems. Under one basic arrangement not widely used, the strong-mayor system, the mayor is the chief-administrative officer of the city, and policy is set by the council. The more common system establishes the mayor, who may be elected either by the people or by the council, as the ceremonial chief of the city and puts the administration of municipal affairs under the control of a powerful city manager or administrator. The council has the power to appoint and remove the manager. Under this council-manager form of government, the council is supposed to be limited to the setting of policy, but there have been a few cases in which a mayor, by virtue of a strong personality, had been able to run the city government, relegating the manager to the role of errand boy.

More frequently, however, the manager, by virtue of the fact that he is a full-time employee with a large staff, plays a role as large as or even greater than the council in establishing policy.

Special districts are usually administered by a superintendent, general manager or other executive selected by the governing board. 🏛

# Hizzoner — the mayor of Los Angeles

## Richard Riordan has inserted a CEO's perspective into a sensitive political environment. Has it worked?

### By Sherry Bebitch Jeffe

Reprinted from *California Journal*, June 1995

April 11, 1995, was a good day for Los Angeles Mayor Richard Riordan. He was a big winner in the city elections, and he wasn't even on the ballot. Los Angeles voters approved eight City Charter amendments aimed at cutting government waste and red tape and making the bureaucracy more accountable to citizens and their elected leaders. That's what entrepreneur–and–neophyte pol Dick Riordan promised to do in the 1993 mayor's race.

But there followed some not–so–good days. When Riordan recently laid out a $3.89 billion budget, it called for the elimination of about 1200 city jobs and cut $8 million from the Fire Department. Already under attack for mismanagement and allegations of harassment and discrimination by his department, City Fire Chief Donald O. Manning abruptly resigned. In the midst of the maelstrom that followed, Riordan chose to demand the resignation of Fire Commissioner Leslie Song Winner, a Manning critic and the commission's most active supporter of affirmative action. That put the mayor at odds with public–employee unions, council members and almost every other major player in city politics.

That's the way governing had been going for Los Angeles's new mayor. Riordan will do many things incredibly right and then stumble over something astoundingly wrong. By and large, the "saves" have showcased his sure–footed, business skills. His fumbles highlight his impatience with and — some critics say — his insensitivity to the political environment of Los Angeles. These slips also have tended to occur on issues of particular concern to the city's poor and minority populations.

What does that say about Richard Riordan — the person and political leader? Riordan's view of the world has been shaped by his life, training and career before he entered electoral politics. And that world view has influenced his leadership style and philosophy of governance. Riordan is the product of privilege and preparation. A philosophy student–turned attorney, he moved to Los Angeles in 1956. He became an entrepreneur and venture capitalist, amassing a fortune estimated at more than $100 million. He has donated millions of that to charity, and as mayor accepts a salary of only $1 per year.

Venture capitalists make their mark in business by investing in fledgling companies in exchange for a big chunk of equity. But the way Riordan has operated Los Angeles government is more reminiscent, say some critics, of a take–over artist, who takes control over a corporation, pares it down, tightens its belt, and then takes

---

*Sherry Bebitch Jeffe is a senior associate at the Center for Politics and Economics at Claremont Graduate School. Her column on Southern California politics, "Southern Exposure," appears several times each year in California Journal.*

missions that oversee city departments cut across partisan and ethnic lines. But they rely heavily on the mayor's bases of support — middle and upper–class Angelenos, Republicans, like–minded business people, whites, Valley and Westside residents. Minorities and poorer residents of the city's urban core have lost some ground. A similar emphasis can be found in the mayor's budget — which continues Riordan's drive for more police, slashes business taxes, and proposes further cuts in the government payroll. As a result, critics charge that Riordan is the mayor of "the white and rich" Los Angeles. Groused political consultant Felicia Bragg, who has run inner–city election campaigns, "Somebody ought to tell him 'The Brady Bunch' was just a movie."

Riordan, the man, tends to view the world through the prism of class. And that impacts policy outcomes in a city increasingly defined in terms of conflicts between a politically active, influential group of primarily Anglo "haves" and a powerless aggregation of largely Black and Latino "have–nots." Riordan's tilt also reflects his grounding in both venture capitalism and politics. Simply put, to the victors belong the spoils.

Riordan, the politician, is an odd combination of Ronald Reagan and Bill Clinton. Like Reagan, Riordan gives off an aura of being "centered;" he is at ease with himself and his persona. Like Reagan, Riordan radiates a central core of values. His values are not framed by conservative ideology; they reflect his pragmatism. Also like Reagan, Riordan focuses on the "big picture," locking onto the broad policy goal he wants to accomplish and happily turning the challenges and problems of implementation over to an aggressive staff. The mayor also shares another quality with Reagan: Even his critics admit he's "so damn likable." Said Councilman Mike Hernandez, both a critic and supporter, "He means to be a good man." Riordan is a self–styled optimist who radiates a Reaganesque belief that it's morning in Los Angeles. Both men also came to elected office bent against bureaucracy and "Big Government;" both rode a wave of voter frustration with those institutions. And, Reagan biographer Lou Cannon observed, "Riordan [like Reagan] has a certain authority that comes from his being a citizen–politician." Finally, as with Reagan, Riordan found his lack of government experience an early disadvantage — and is working to overcome it.

Riordan says "the biggest mistake" of his early administration was "not learning how to effectively work with the City Council." Council President John Ferraro believes that Riordan came to office "not realizing [what it means] being mayor of the city when the governing body is the City Council."

Riordan has been moving to improve relations with the council and bureaucracy. Opinion among council members appears divided on his success. But Ferraro believes the mayor has "a greater grasp of government now."

The missteps, such as those surrounding the Fire Department, occur, and that's when Riordan begins to look like Clinton. Riordan, like Clinton, sometimes steps on his message or stumbles over strategy and finds himself sidetracked by damage control. Like Clinton, he's been criticized for his handling of personnel matters, while controversy and conflict–of–interest questions have dogged some Riordan appointees. Early in his administration, staff turnover was high. Clinton has come under fire from the left for abandoning Democratic core constituencies; Riordan has been attacked as an apostate by disgruntled conservatives. Last year, for instance, RINO

off for other pursuits. Critics say Riordan has brought "the art of the deal" to City Hall, with a style more suited to a corporate CEO than to the temporary head of an entrenched bureaucracy. But his activist philosophy is infused by his Catholicism and a culture of "noblesse oblige."

Riordan, the politician, came out of nowhere — if you consider years of quiet civic involvement and contributions to political and social causes "nowhere" — and spent over $8 million dollars ($6 million of it his own money) to position himself as a political "outsider" in the race for mayor against then–City Councilman Michael Woo. Riordan handily won election to Southern California's most visible political office.

Riordan's electoral coalition provides a map for his governing priorities. In Los Angeles, Anglos account for about 37 percent of the population. But in the June 1993 mayoralty election, they were 72 percent of the city electorate. Anglo voters sided with Riordan over Woo 67 percent to 33 percent. Riordan garnered a healthy (for a Republican) 43 percent of the Latino vote, and 31 percent of the Asian vote. But he got only 6 percent of the African–American vote. Riordan scored his most striking victory in the vote–rich, moderate–to–conservative San Fernando Valley — defeating Woo by a 71 percent–to–29 percent margin. Riordan took the more liberal Westside, too, with 55 percent of the vote. Riordan's vote reflected the appeal his campaign themes — jobs, safety and government reform — had with moderate and swing voters. And the mandate Riordan and his people read in those results has driven his policy agenda.

Riordan's appointments to the powerful citizens' com-

buttons appeared at GOP functions, blasting Riordan for being "Republican in Name Only." Bill Wardlaw, Riordan's close friend and key adviser, chaired Clinton's California campaign. And Riordan has supported Democratic candidates and hired staff across party lines.

Riordan's biggest success so far spotlights his leadership style. For many, including the mayor, last year's Northridge earthquake defines his image. It was, said Hernandez, "this mayor's baptism." "He was in charge," marveled another City Hall observer, "competent, calm, supportive. He was everywhere."

In terms of policy, the charter victories and the two budgets Riordan has submitted since taking office are generally viewed as stand-outs in an otherwise spotty record. The passage of Charter Amendment 2 was particular impressive. The reform, which gives the mayor and council more clout in hiring and firing city department heads by exempting them from civil service, represents a sea change in Los Angeles governance. Said one longtime City Hall watcher, "It was only Riordan's personal political popularity that got [it] through. People don't trust government, but they trust him."

**R**iordan has had his policy failures, however. "Privatization," for instance, is viewed by City Hall watchers as a significant failure. Riordan campaigned on — and has since backed away from — a plan to privatize Los Angeles International Airport (LAX) to pay for more police. And the City Council has rebuffed all his efforts to turn city services over to private contractors. The mayor found himself stymied by the political clout of the city's public employees unions — which supported Woo in the mayor's race. But Riordan insists, "I'm not an ideologue on privatization. I'm an ideologue on efficiency and the threat of privatization has helped us ... with the unions and management working with us to make the departments more efficient."

"Empowerment" is a word the mayor often uses; it is a concept central to his approach to both business and government. To Riordan, it means "giving [people] the power to make decisions, the power to make mistakes and the power to correct mistakes — all with confidence."

"Empowerment" became a linchpin of Riordan's plan to revitalize the local economy. It also made another Riordan setback particularly bitter. In December 1994 the Clinton administration decided *not* to award Los Angeles a federal empowerment zone. Ironically, the empowerment zone program was created largely in response to the 1992 Los Angeles riots. The designation would have meant $300 million to $600 million in social-service grants and tax breaks, which would have directly benefited poor communities in Pacoima and east, Central and South Los Angeles. But, the feds said the Los Angeles application was vague, lacking in focus and specificity. City leadership was criticized as disorganized and overconfident.

Los Angeles received a "consolation prize" of $250 million in federal funds — including $125 million that must be repaid with interest. But Riordan was so angry at the loss of the empowerment zone designation that he snubbed Clinton by refusing to participate in a press conference call arranged by the White House to announce the awards. That amount subsequently was increased to $400 million, and Vice President Al Gore came to Los Angeles himself to announce it.

A large percentage of Los Angeles' population is minority, but thus far, Riordan's relationship with the city's diverse ethnic communities has been shaky. His relationship with Police Chief Willie Williams, the city's highest-ranking African-American official, has long been characterized as "uneasy." Councilwoman Rita Walters, who represents a Black part of Los Angeles, argues that "from the time [Riordan] took office, he set up [his] relationship with the chief for failure."

Some African-Americans believe that the mayor's office has been encouraging criticism of both Williams and Metropolitan Transit Authority Chief Executive Officer Franklin E. White, who is Black. Riordan has been faulted for, as Walters put it, his "failure to communicate with all parts of the city and lay the groundwork for doing substantial outreach with all parts of the community."

And although he leads a city where Latinos make up nearly 40 percent of the population, Riordan was invisible on Proposition 187. In addition, the mayor's take on the hot-button issue of affirmative action satisfies few African-Americans. Riordan has ordered a review of city affirmative-action programs, with the idea of making them better on the issue of contracting out. "Too often," he says, "they help the usual, wealthy suspects and not really the people that they're designed to help ... the small, medium-sized businesses."

Will Riordan run again? Nearly everybody — including the mayor — says "Yes." "It's fun!" he says of his job. And City Hall watchers see no one on the horizon to run against him. With Riordan's popularity high, local politicians appear content to wait until the mayor's two-term limit — which he championed during the campaign — kicks in. A recent attempt by disaffected African-American leaders to plot strategy for the 1997 election — including the possibility of fielding their own candidate against Riordan — yielded little. And despite rampant speculation that Riordan has set his sights on the governorship — or higher — Riordan demurs. Vice president? No, he says. "I never want to be anonymous in life." Governor? "No. It doesn't appeal to me" because it's the mayor's office "where you can do things."

Riordan has a lot to do in the next two years to make good on his campaign promises. He pledged to deliver 3000 new police to the city or not run again. Ironically, the Republican mayor's progress toward his goal relies heavily on Clinton's federal crime bill. But the new GOP Congress could upset his plans, although such an upset probably is not fatal. As *Los Angeles Times* columnist Bill Boyarsky observed, "No one will care if he doesn't reach 3000 if he tries."

In the wake of the empowerment zone fiasco, Riordan launched, and the City Council has approved, a proposal for a "community development bank." The novel public/private initiative would use federal grants, loan guarantees and venture capital to stimulate business development in the city's poorest neighborhoods. His administration is looking at the Community Development Bank as the new linchpin of Riordan's job-creation strategy. "It does," says Deputy Mayor Robin Kramer, "exemplify the mayor's approach and an effort to leverage some lasting results here."

The Los Angeles economy is likely to help Riordan toward that goal. Hard-hit by disasters and recession, it is beginning to show signs of recovery. Politics is, after all, a matter of luck and timing. And City Hall players agree that Riordan has been blessed with an ample amount of both. Riordan, says Boyarsky, is "where people are politically. He came along at the right time." 🏛

# Counties in crisis

Problems assailing Los Angeles and Orange counties once again raise questions about the relationship between state and local governments, and the need to pay for increased services with diminished resources.

## By Laureen Lazarovici

Reprinted from *California Journal*, November 1995

Lassen County no longer has a department of animal control. If any critters get out of hand, residents have to call the cops. "In egregious cases, a deputy goes out," says county administrative officer William Bixby. In the Sacramento County suburb of Elk Grove, the special fire district is considering charging homeowners $500 dollars to put out a blaze. Los Angeles County came only days away from virtually shutting down its public health-care system, and Orange County has the dubious honor of being the largest municipal entity in the nation to declare bankruptcy.

Why are California counties in a seemingly continuous state of crisis — and what are leaders trying to do about it?

Observers agree that the 1978 passage of Proposition 13 and the property tax shifts in the early '90s from municipalities to the state are the root causes of the counties' woes. How to solve these problems yields less agreement, however. Liberals argue for more taxes, while conservatives focus on privatization of services. Transcending ideology is a larger debate over a total overhaul of the relationship between state and county government.

Southern California this year provided stark case studies of counties' dire straits. In Los Angeles, years of stop-gap measures to balance the budget and of increasing demands on services — one in five residents receives some sort of public assistance — resulted in a $1.2 billion deficit. County officials considered closing Los Angeles' largest public hospital, raising the specter of people literally dying in the streets. Plans for only slightly less drastic closures of other public-health facilities were drawn up as alternatives. Only after President Bill Clinton came up with $364 million in federal funds to rescue and restructure the ailing county health-care system was a complete meltdown avoided (see "Washington Perspective," page 40).

Neighboring Orange County, meanwhile, struggled to climb out of bankruptcy. During the 1980s, then-Treasurer Robert Citron leveraged the county's investment pool into risky and exotic investments. No one raised an eyebrow as long as the financial markets were going his way. At one point, up to one-third of the county's budget came from interest income, making up for losses from other sources. But then the market started going the opposite direction than the way Citron bet, resulting in $1.7 billion in losses. Creditors couldn't be paid, and the county sought protection from the bankruptcy court. Under pressure from an emergency chief administrative officer, county supervisors reluctantly placed a sales-tax measure on the ballot to pay for the shortfall. It failed miserably. But in the closing days of the legislative session, relief came in the form of funds shifted from transit, flood control, park and redevelopment agencies.

Both counties have solvency in sight — for now. But as California State Association of Counties deputy director Dan Wall points out, "What brought Orange County to the edge of the cliff were the same forces that brought L.A. — and other counties — to the edge. The underlying circumstances are identical." Moreover, he adds, "None of the fundamental relationships have changed with these patchwork solutions."

Those underlying circumstances and fundamental relationships can be traced back to Proposition 13. That taxpayer revolt initiative capped property taxes and shifted revenue-raising authority away from counties and to the state. But counties still retained the responsibility for providing services. Proposition 13, in effect, delinked raising revenues from providing services. In the post-13 environment, the state government cushioned the blow to counties by taking over some of their health and welfare programs and by returning some property tax money to them. That worked — as long as the state could afford it. When the recession hit statewide, Sacramento in effect told the counties, "We want our money back." In 1992 and 1993 the state budget shifted tax money away from the counties and into the schools. For a large county like Los Angeles, that meant a loss of $1 billion. The legislative analyst's office cites the shift as one of the primary reasons for Los Angeles' budget crisis.

Proposition 13 changed the relationship between the counties and the states. The property tax shifts merely papered over, but didn't change the structure of that relationship. "The root problem is county boards have control over neither revenue nor expenditures," says Wall. On the revenue side, counties can't raise property taxes at all. They are allowed to raise general taxes with a majority vote of the people and special taxes with a two-thirds vote — a requirement recently upheld by the State Supreme Court. On the expenditure side, counties are bound by state and federal mandates, and much of their spending is indexed to ever-growing caseloads. Ten years ago, 15 percent to 20 percent of a county budget was discretionary. Now, it's down to 5 percent to 7 percent.

Liberal critics look at the revenue side of the equation. "Ultimately we're going to have to reform Prop. 13," says Lenny Goldberg, executive director of the California Tax Reform Association. "One simple sentence would do it: 'Non-residential property shall be assessed at market value,'" he says. Simple, but politically explosive. Ending Proposition 13's protection of commercial property has been a non-starter for years. Other tax measures have passed — notably 1993's Proposition 172, which permanently extended a special half-cent sales tax for public safety — but most don't fare well. This year, Los Angeles County sought the authority to tax alcohol and tobacco, but bills allowing that authority didn't even come close to getting out of the Legislature, although some officials now talk about a statewide ballot measure next November to that effect. Orange County's bankruptcy relief tax flopped by a wide margin at the polls.

In contrast, conservative critics focus on the expenditure side of the ledger. Early in Orange County's bankruptcy crisis, for example, the all-Republican legislative delegation introduced a carload of measures to privatize county services and relax state mandates on services. The bills went nowhere, but they did dramatize the difference in approaches to fixing county financing.

Tinkering with taxes and mandate relief within the current structure is just a shell game, according to those trying to look at the big picture. The Constitutional Revision Commission, empaneled to examine a whole range of state dysfunctions, has drafted an ambitious plan to bring together local governments — county, cities, special districts — in community charters to consolidate local services. Both general and special local taxes would be subject to majority votes, and property taxes would be allowed to be raised with the consent of two thirds of the voters.

Other reformers are examining the relationship between counties and the electorate. "A board of supervisors is a 19th century institution," says Peter Detwiler, former consultant to the Senate Local Government Committee. "A board blends legislative and executive responsibilities, and it doesn't do either well. The California Constitution ought to separate these functions and reduce the size of districts, increasing the number of supervisors. There should be a directly elected county mayor and reduce the number of directly elected department heads." The fact that some counties can't solve crises within their own governmental structures is proof of the need for reform, says Detwiler. "Why did L.A. appoint a health czar?" he wonders, referring to former Assemblyman Burt Margolin (D-Los Angeles). "We have to do extraordinary things when ordinary things don't work."

Many political pitfalls stand in the way of reform. Not the least of them is a large gulf of distrust and rivalry between state and local elected officials. Orange County Supervisor Marian Bergeson has a unique perspective on that issue, given that she was a Republican state senator for 16 years before taking her current post. "Until I actually served as a supervisor, I hadn't realized the damage Sacramento had done, especially in terms of mandates," she says. Lawmakers trying to solve the Los Angeles and Orange county problems were constantly laying blame on one another. Orange County legislators chastised the board of supervisors for dragging its feet on coming up with a recovery plan. Los Angeles legislators said supervisors got themselves in the mess, while supervisors shot back that it was their own delegation that went along with the devastating property tax shifts. When Los Angeles state officials finally put together a plan authorizing a loan from the local transit agency to the county, supervisors snubbed them by turning it down.

Any type of reform would necessarily trample on turf and gore some sacred cows, including police agencies. "No one is talking about the inefficiencies in law enforcement," says CSAC's Wall. "Why do we need city and county departments? Why not consolidate? It's politically taboo. It's about turf."

Perhaps the starkest political reality is that counties serve politically powerless constituencies: those on welfare, those who use public hospitals, those going through the court system. They are not the ones going to the polls every time a special tax is on the ballot. "Our clients are not the ones who show up for fund raisers," observes Bergeson ruefully.

Increasingly, voters are asking themselves not which governmental entity ought to be providing these services but whether government should be providing them at all. This larger question haunts the debate over reforming counties or even doing away with them altogether. "What kind of Hobbesian choices are we going to have to make?" asks Dave Oppenheim, senior legislative analyst for CSAC. "The safety net that everyone depends on — the courts as well as health and welfare — is in jeopardy. The service responsibilities don't go away. Doing away with counties doesn't get to the real problem." 🏛

# The California dream of higher education

## Throughout the years, Californians have enjoyed unparalleled access to colleges and universities, but it will take a renewed commitment to maintain the dream.

## By J.W. Peltason

Reprinted from *California Journal*, September 1995

The California dream has proved remarkably durable. It has survived wars, depressions, migrations, natural cataclysms, social and politi-cal unrest. That is because the California dream, like the American dream, rests on the availability of high-quality education to all who want and are prepared for it. For over 200 years, we have built a higher-education system premised on a few simple but powerful ideas: that education would serve as a path to social and economic mobility for those who lack inherited wealth; and that higher-educational opportunity thrives best in a system with a diversity of institutions — from small liberal arts colleges to large research universities — so that students have the widest possible range of educational options from which to choose. Somewhere within our system there is a college or university education suited to the talents, aspirations, income and academic preparation of just about everyone who has the motivation to seek it out.

It is still easier to get an excellent college education if you are affluent, of course. Expanding access to higher education has meant, however, that a college degree is increasingly within the aspirations of the poor, as it has long been for the rich. There's nothing surprising about the fact that it is possible to go to Harvard or Yale and end up as president of the United States. What is surprising, and what sets this country apart, is that it also is possible to go to Whittier or Elmira or Southwest Texas State College and be elected president. The American system of higher education would not score high on orderliness or organization, but it has succeeded beyond the imagination where it counts — in providing social and economic mobility, not to mention such intangibles as productive and rewarding lives for more and more people.

No state has demonstrated a clearer understanding of these realities than California. We have consistently encouraged our public universities to be as excellent as our private institutions. The celebrated

---

*J.W. Peltason is president of the University of California. He is scheduled to retire in October 1995. Patricia A. Pelfrey assisted in the preparation of this essay.*

1960 Master Plan for Higher Education made that aspiration possible by reorganizing California's public colleges and universities into a coherent system that emphasized quality and discouraged unproductive competition, while promising a place to any California student with the talent and motivation to benefit from higher education. The Master Plan has been, by just about any measure, an outstanding success. The University of California can carry out its special missions of providing instruction at the doctoral level and of producing the knowledge upon which our economic future depends because the California State University and the community colleges do such a splendid job of fulfilling their special roles. Our strong system of independent colleges and universities offers its own array of excellent educational options. As a result, more than any other society in the world, California has made good on the promise of educational opportunity for all of its citizens.

The system is still working, but today the doors of opportunity are beginning to close. They are closing with little public debate and less public understanding of the drastic consequences for California. Several trends threaten our system of higher education and although they are national in scope, as in so many other ways, change comes first to California.

First is the chronic underfunding of higher education. The fiscal problems facing California higher education today are more serious than those we faced during the Great Depression. Steep declines in support have occurred not because our leaders will it but because of a combination of constitutional requirements, federal mandates and expenditures for public safety that drain resources away from higher education. More than 85 percent of the state budget is protected by constitutional or statutory provisions that may only be altered by changing the law. UC, along with CSU, has the unfortunate distinction of being part of the unprotected 15 percent of the budget.

As a consequence, the share of the budget devoted to UC and CSU has declined from 13 percent in the late 1960s to 8 percent today. Unless something is done to reverse the trend, that figure will continue to decline as each year the percentage of the budget available to support higher education becomes smaller and smaller. And this is happening at a time when we are on the cusp of a reduction in federal funding for research and student aid that is so massive that it could dwarf even the radical cuts in state support we have faced over the past five years.

Solutions to the state's severe budgetary and structural dilemma have been proposed but as yet none has been adopted. The California Constitutional Revision Commission, appointed jointly by the governor and Legislature in 1993, has the formidable challenge of proposing answers to California's budgetary gridlock. The commission has released its preliminary report, and its recommendations deserve close attention by the people. The stakes are high.

Unless decisive action is taken, the long-term consequences for higher education are clear. As the California Postsecondary Education Commission put it in its report, "Challenge of the Century," public insistence that priority be given to corrections and other state activities at the expense of education means that "more criminals will be in prison, and more students will be denied college." The irony is that it is much cheaper to send someone to college than to prison; it costs over $20,000 a year to keep someone in a California state prison, while it costs little more than $12,000 annually to pay for the housing and education of a UC student.

The second trend is related to the first. A tidal wave of criticism is engulfing higher education. Even foundation heads, traditional boosters of higher education, are joining the chorus. The list of complaints is long and, if you are a college or university president, painfully familiar. There is no vision in higher education, critics say, no long-term planning, no coming to terms with the changed fiscal environment facing higher education. In particular, there are no proposals for fundamental change in the state's public universities. If professors would do less research and teach more, if fewer administrators would accomplish more, if unnecessary schools and departments and specialties were eliminated, if the various higher-education segments would cooperate more, if thousands of students were taught via distance technology and persuaded to graduate in three years rather than four, if enrollment projections were better and more consistent, then higher education's problems would be solved.

There is much to be said for a number of these proposals. Most of them already are being examined and many of them are being implemented. Some seem to miss the point, such as the assumption that research and teaching occur only at the expense of each other when every survey at UC shows that more than 70 percent of our students believe they have received a good to great education in our research-oriented environment — a record unrivaled by most human institutions, including marriage.

It should also be noted that in the contest for media attention, what we do systematically and well oftens loses out to the colorful anecdote. On an average day at UC, 160,000 students attend class unreported. One takes off his clothes, and the next day it is the "naked guy" we read about.

We will never purge our institutions of all their human and organizational imperfections, and it is not clear that it would be a good idea if we could. The worry is not the existence of criticism — which no public institution can or would expect to be exempt from — or individual criticisms themselves, some of which are true. The worry is that critics of higher education seem to have captured public attention and the public imagination. Much of their criticism is dramatically overstated and venomous in tone. But it is coming from people with tremendous influence on public perception and policy.

This criticism has not yet undermined public confidence in higher education, which still is highly sought after by parents for their children. But it has clouded and sometimes confused the public dialogue on higher education's future. That dialogue has yet to reach the level of accuracy, thoughtfulness and respect for opposing views that the subject itself deserves.

The third potentially damaging trend for higher education is what might be called the "illusion of the quick fix." There is growing support, among critics and the public, for the idea that planning will bridge the gap between what we give our colleges and universities and what it costs them to educate the young and discover new knowledge. It is a matter of vision and will, it is said, and the determination to make fundamental changes in the American university.

Universities are complex institutions that are built for the centuries. Major change tends to be incremental, not revolutionary; universities have survived as well as they have because they have not transformed themselves with every passing trend. But they must — and do — respond to the society that supports them. The very nature of what they do requires them to assess regularly changing demographic, economic, educational, public policy, and a host of other trends. This includes, of course, the likelihood of long-term resource constraints. Obviously, the transition to this new and difficult environment won't happen without will and vision and much more, but it also won't happen without minimal resources to pay the costs of educating the next generation, in addition to the other things that higher education does for California. The postsecondary education commission estimates that over the next 10 years, some 455,000 additional students will knock at higher education's doors, including an increase of 32,000 students for UC. Although UC's estimates are lower, they still are significant. The commission also anticipates that California's public institutions will need $1 billion more per year over the next 10 years to pay for new construction, repair and maintenance of existing buildings, and equipment.

Clearly, higher education in the next century will not have the resources per student that it has had in this one and will have to learn how to be more efficient and effective. But there is no way higher education can plan itself out of this budgetary straitjacket. California's public colleges and universities have made enormous efforts, in some cases with remarkable success, to increase support from private and other alternative sources. They have reluctantly raised student fees. They also have made draconian cuts in libraries, laboratories, maintenance of campus grounds and buildings and, most of all, in their people. There is no more fat to cut.

And although there is increasing discussion of privatization of professional schools within public universities or even the universities themselves, there are definite limits to that option. Increases in private gifts and research funding are helpful, but they will never bridge the funding gap. The state's share of UC's total budget, for example, has dropped in recent years until today it constitutes on 24 percent. But to say that state funding constitutes only 24 percent of our budget is like saying that your heart constitutes only 24 percent of your body. State dollars pay for the core educational activities that are at the heart of everything we do and that make every other activity possible. And no matter how small a proportion of our budget state dollars becomes, we will remain accountable to the people of California and to their elected representatives.

I also am skeptical of what may be called the "technology fix." Perhaps the most popular form of this idea is the virtual university — shorthand for the use of informational and other technologies to substitute for the traditional labor-intensive process of teaching and learning. The more enthusiastic among us even believe that the university as a physical place will wither away as information and instruction speed along the Internet to anyone who wants to take advantage of them.

Informational and similar technologies offer wonderful possibilities for expanding the scope and efficiency of teaching and research. Just as the invention of the book had a revolutionary impact on the teaching and learning process, so will the computer. We are experimenting with some of those possibilities within UC, and in cooperation with other educational institutions.

But as Stanford President Gerhard Casper has argued, in weighing the advantages of the virtual university, we also must consider "what learning and which skills can *not* be taught at a distance." Students and teachers will continue to need to get together. Despite the fact that, in the future, knowledge will be dispersed and readily available on CD-ROMs, there still will be the human and social need to meet for face-to-face confrontations, intellectual stimulation and social intercourse. Knowledge can be transmitted by a cable, but wisdom is acquired in social contexts.

Informational technologies and distance learning are not inexpensive, moreover, and the initial investment is the least expensive part of it. Nor will technology make the traditional classroom obsolete. The invention of the book and the creation of the library didn't make professors obsolete or education less expensive; they merely gave professors and students new tools for learning. The essential functions universities perform have remained intact over the centuries and will remain so into the future.

It also is worth noting that when some people talk about delivering education inexpensively through distance learning, they generally have in mind the education of other people's children; for their own, they seem to prefer traditional, residential face-to-face experience. It always is tempting to look for money saving ways for everyone else's kids to go to college. But the reality calls for something more from all of us.

The trends described here are exerting increasing pressure on our colleges and universities. Even more serious is the tremendous strain they impose on California's longstanding social consensus that public universities should be as good as private ones. The danger is that public higher education will gradually evolve into a two-track system, as has happened in many places with respect to K-12 education. If public education is allowed to drift into mediocrity, those with resources will send their children to private colleges and universities, just as they have moved their children at the lower grades into either suburban or private schools.

It must be emphasized that the governor and Legislature, despite recessions and a declining share of the state's general fund available for higher education, have buffered us from the worst consequences of California's fiscal crisis. And for the moment, at least, there are some hopeful signs. I am very much encouraged by the four-year compact Governor Pete Wilson announced in January. Through a combination of a modest increase in tax dollars and reasonable fee increases, coupled with additional aid to needy students, the compact will stabilize higher education during the next four years and give us the chance to make the changes we will need to move into the next century.

Important as it is, however, stability isn't enough. As earlier generations of Californians have done, we must invest in our future. And for the first time in a long while, California is not getting ready for the next generation.

The Master Plan hasn't failed. Our colleges and universities, despite their imperfections, haven't failed either. What has failed is public understanding of the unyielding fact that we can't go on simultaneously insisting on more prisons and refusing to pay for them through increased taxes. As a result, we are depriving ourselves of the chance to build California's infrastructure, including the educational infrastructure that has helped make this state into the sixth-largest economy in the world. We are asking our colleges and universities to run on empty. If we don't begin questioning our willingness to live with this situation, it will not be long before California and the California dream both will be going nowhere. 🏛

# Affirmative action and the UC vote

## Presidential politics put regents in the national spotlight and on the spot for a vote to end racial preferences.

### By Kirsten Mangold

Reprinted from *California Journal*, September 1995

t's rare that those who take opposite sides of a disagreement claim the same battle cry, but that's what seems to have happened in the politically charged debate over affirmative action — particularly in the case of the recent University of California Regents' decision to abolish affirmative-action policies within the university system. Both supporters and opponents said they were rallying for "fairness" — in other words, a system that does not discriminate based on the color of one's skin. For many who attended and many more who observed last month's bitter 12-hour debate on the issue before the UC Board of Regents, the issue wasn't one of race, ethnicity or economic background. In their minds, to re-work a Mae West aphorism, "Fairness had nothing to do with it."

Politics did.

According to many observers, and some regents, the political circus surrounding the meeting itself was unfair — to the board. There was anger at how a customarily apolitical board had been hijacked to become a forum for a major national identity crisis. There was anger at the way supporters and opponents of affirmative action tried to browbeat them with warnings, protests and even bomb threats. And there was more than a little anger at the man whose ambitions had thrust them into this acrid political miasma: Governor Pete Wilson.

As the state's chief executive, Wilson is automatically a member of the Board of Regents — indeed, he has the right to preside over any meeting he attends. For the last three years, however, Wilson has eschewed that right. What drew him to last month's meeting were two resolutions, sponsored by his longtime friend and financial supporter Ward Connerly, a Sacramento consultant who is African-American. The first sought to end affirmative action in university admissions; the second in its hiring policies. Although Connerly began his crusade to end affirmative action long before Wilson announced for president, the governor has gained much mileage from the issue, and the meeting was held only one day after President Bill Clinton delivered a major national address in which he defended affirmative action.

It was clear from the get-go that Wilson intended to gain even more mileage from the regents' meeting. There were only slightly fewer television cameras than cover a Simpson trial press conference, and reporters had come from as far away as Great Britain. The atmosphere was made even more

politically charged by the presence of a former Democratic presidential candidate who is himself eyeing another run — the Reverend Jesse Jackson. Jackson, in what one observer described as his "getting arrested clothes," energized public opposition to the affirmative-action proposals and pleaded with regents to reject them.

The deck seemed stacked against opponents from the start. Nineteen of the regents are appointed by the governor (the remaining six serve because they hold some other elective office), and 17 of the 19 appointed regents currently owe their regency to Republican governors. Most have been reappointed by Wilson after their first terms expired. Although the position is unpaid, it bestows a great honor on those who sit on the board.

The meeting opened with a host of legislators reminding the regents of the event's importance. Former Assembly Speaker Willie Brown Jr. (D-San Francisco) asked them to "be responsive to the people of the state of California." Senator Bill Leonard (R-San Bernardino) spoke in favor of the proposal, then noted that he would "oppose any legislative attempts to punish the UC system or its students" — regardless of the regents' final decision. Assemblyman John Vasconcellos (D-Santa Clara) implored the panel to "please, take your time," echoing the sentiments of others who argued that there was no real reason to rush a decision. Assemblyman Phil Isenberg (D-Sacramento) said that regents did not have enough information at their disposal. And then there was the entire university hierarchy, from UC President Jack Peltason down through the nine campus chancellors to the Academic Senate and to a host of individual professors and student leaders — all of whom opposed the proposals.

For his part, Wilson dismissed notions that his efforts to abolish affirmative-action programs were motivated by anything but the best interests of the university. Yet the governor seemed less than interested in how the final decision might affect another critical issue facing regents — the selection of a new president to succeed Peltason, who is retiring in October. Critics, including Peltason and Regent Roy Brophy, head of the presidential search committee, have speculated that approval of the resolutions will make it harder to recruit a university chief. When pressed to respond to rumors that some candidates already have said they would pull out of the nominating process should the proposals pass, Wilson appeared indifferent. "I don't think that's true, because nobody is in a position to [say] that," Wilson told the *Journal*. "If it *is* true, then [candidates] *should* pull out."

The political nature of the debate, and the ramifications inherent in the growing perception that regents had bowed to political pressure, split even those appointed to the board by Wilson. Dean Watkins, a wealthy Southern California businessman, fell in behind the governor, saying at one point

that "I follow my leader." On the other hand, Brophy — described by friends as a stalwart Republican — voted against both proposals and took the unusual step of addressing regents as a private citizen. Brophy, who has felt personally responsible for recruiting a new president, expressed his deep disappointment that the university was being dragged through a political swamp.

"Years ago, I would have assumed that [Brophy] would side with the governor, but ... he stood up as a citizen and said he was ashamed of the regents," said fellow Regent William Bagley, who abstained from the admissions resolution. "That was a very forthright statement, and in my mind, he's my hero."

While Bagley denies he was personally lobbied for his vote, it seemed clear that political pressure was brought to bear on other participants. Brophy publicly decried lobbying and several others suggested privately they'd been contacted about the vote. Regent Meredith Khachigian, wife of longtime Wilson supporter Ken Khachigian, was one of those who seemed uncomfortable being forced to make a choice. "It's not a clear-cut issue; some have clearly made their decision, but all the rest of us are fighting with it," she noted before the vote was taken. "There is no doubt [our decision] will have a tremendous impact." At the time, Khachigian wouldn't say which side she had chosen, but three hours later, she delivered a speech in favor of the proposal and cast an "aye" vote. When it was finally over, she left the room in tears.

"I didn't make phone calls or ask people [how they would vote] before the meeting, but it was pretty evident by putting a sensitive finger to the political wind ... there were several regents who were worried about the politicization of the process," said Bagley. "I was disappointed in them, disappointed that those people helped pass the resolution. They are the ones who should have stood up for the university."

If, as seems clear, regents were lobbied on the issue, the lobbying paid off. The board voted 14-10 to end affirmative action for admissions (with one abstention), and 15-10 to end it for hiring and contracting. Assembly Speaker Doris Allen (R-Cypress), who also sits on the board, was absent.

The vote was a badly needed attention getter for Wilson's presidential campaign. Coming one day after his nationally televised response to Clinton's speech, Wilson's blunt-but-effective presentation cemented his place as the national respondent to Clinton on the issue of race- and gender-based preferences. "It is a two-person debate on this issue," said political analyst Sherry Bebitch Jeffe. The Washington-based pundit corps, keepers of the conventional wisdom, viewed Wilson's performance as his ticket to the coveted "first tier" of presidential candidates. In the aftermath of the regents' vote, Wilson made the talk-show rounds, getting into the kind of heated on-camera exchanges with Jackson that make GOP political pros salivate.

"Taking Jesse Jackson and Bill Clinton on at the same time elevated his stature considerably," said GOP political consultant Sal Russo.

In the days and weeks following the affirmative action vote, however, Wilson had reason to withhold a declaration of total victory. Public opinion surveys conducted at the height of the controversy showed an overall majority of people more inclined to support Clinton's "mend it, don't end it" approach. Two prominent Republican conservatives — former HUD

Secretary Jack Kemp and former Education Secretary William Bennett — accused Wilson of fanning racial fears in his tirades against "reverse discrimination." Bennett publicly detailed Wilson's recent conversion on the issue, using ammunition thoughtfully provided by the Clinton White House.

Perhaps most embarrassing for Wilson was the pronouncement from Richard G. Butler, a leader in the neo-Nazi White Aryan movement. Speaking from a hate-fest in Idaho, Butler said Wilson is "beginning to wake

Bagley

Brophy

Peltason

Connerly

up." Wilson's spokes-people quickly distanced themselves from the comments, emphasizing Wilson's continued insistence on tough enforcement of anti-discrimination laws. Still, a *New York Times* photo of the Nazi gathering with the quote praising Wilson took a little of the joy out of the victory.

"It is in our long-term interests as a party to address some of these issues in a way that makes people feel a part of us," concedes Russo, a Wilson supporter. "The tone of the affirmative action discussion can get us off in the wrong direction."

In addition to affecting the long-term interests of the GOP, the vote last month also raises questions for the Board of Regents. Was it pushed into the political arena against its will over the issue of affirmative action? And is Wilson responsible?

The man at the center of it all — Ward Connerly — says no, insisting Wilson has been on board with his crusade since last August. "I raised this whole question back in August of last year; our first hearing was back in November," Connerly said, noting that Wilson was involved from the get-go. "In August of 1994, with Pete Wilson just beginning to catch up with Kathleen Brown [in governor's race], people would have laughed at the idea of him running for president."

While he concedes politics did enter the affirmative action debate, he insists the issue does not portend a more overtly political Board of Regents. He also takes care to point out that in this case, the governor was not the only one to use political clout to elbow the regents. "I'm told by one regent that he got a call from [Lieutenant Governor] Gray Davis," Connerly said, launching into a long list of opponents with possible political motives. "Certainly Willie Brown has a political interest; this will play very well in San Francisco. Barbara Lee is running for the Senate. All of those members of the Black caucus and the Legislature have something to gain. So while this did become political, Wilson wasn't the only one with a personal interest, and he wasn't the only one who lobbied."

Connerly also insists the regents' decisions were based on personal beliefs and nothing else. It is true, he said, that most of the regents are strong allies of the governor, yet he doesn't understand how it might be thought that "yes" votes were tantamount to paying back the favor of appointment.

He dismisses the notion that the regents are greatly concerned with furthering Wilson's career, and uses himself as a potential case in point: "Everyone knows that I'm a heavy donor to Wilson's [presidential] campaign. How am I repaying the governor by voting the way he wants? If I've given that much to his campaign, haven't I already paid my dues? That argument just doesn't stand up."

Conservative think tanks such as the Pacific Research Institute join Connerly's assessment. "It is true that Pete Wilson is the president of the board, but he's still only one vote," said senior fellow Lance Izumi. "If the regents really felt that what Wilson and Connerly were doing was wrong or purely politically motivated, they didn't have to adopt the resolution. I can't say whether the governor was calling in favors or not, but the fact that he appointed them doesn't mean that they had to vote with him."

While Wilson's defenders maintain he has not corrupted the regents process, others aren't so sure. Tim Hodson, executive director of the Center for California Studies at CSU-Sacramento, was hesitant to speculate on the regent's motivations or future, but he noted that there might be a correlation between the kinds of people a governor appoints as judges and those he appoints as regents. Former Gov. Pat Brown, Hodson says, appointed roughly the same number of Republicans and Democrats to the bench, but all subsequent governors — Ronald Reagan, Jerry Brown, George Deukmejian and Pete Wilson — have chosen the majority of their appointees along party lines.

"Observers have said that once upon a time, it was your standing, your reputation among your peers that got you an appointment," said Hodson. "Now it's more about your political affiliation."

Dave Merkowitz of the American Council on Education in Washington, D.C., said that his organization is concerned about the entry of partisanship and presidential politics into university governance.

"This sort of thing has happened on public boards before, and it does set a dangerous precedent, and it's quite an intrusion," he says, adding that UC is unusual because it is the only university system nationwide in which the state's governor also is a regent. "California has its own traditions, and generally those traditions have worked well, as evidenced by the reputation that the university enjoys. But i'ts dangerous to have this kind of political interference ... [it can] cause its own kind of political reaction."

Wilson, of course, is hoping that reaction is the sort that will transform his presidential campaign, and if it continues, Wilson's stand could make the difference next November. If, on the other hand, Wilson is viewed as having overplayed the race card, the governor could find his success with the regents to be a Pyrrhic victory.

"The governor had a clear political interest in getting the reaction that he did," said Merkowitz. "I don't know if there will be public tolerance for that kind of thing happening very often." 🏛

# Managed care struggles to come of age

## After more than a decade of explosive growth, HMOs find themselves at the core of a controversy over their priorities. Are they driven by the corporate urge to make money, or by the societal ethos to provide quality health care? And are the two compatible?

### By Mary Beth Barber

Reprinted from *California Journal*, April 1996

anaged care as a concept has been around since World War II, when a multi-faceted steel and ship-building conglomerate run by the late Henry Kaiser provided its own doctors to workers and their families. But the benchmark year for managed care is 1982, for that is the year that the Legislature pushed the concept for those who depended on government for health care — thrusting the world of medicine firmly into the competitive marketplace.

"Managed care" actually is an umbrella term for a number of health plans that try to control costs through preventive care and "capitation" of costs — establishing a set annual fee per enrollee, regardless of the level of health care that ultimately is provided. Its most common manifestation, the health-maintenance organization (HMO) also is varied, although most consumers think of the giant Kaiser Permanente — the current incarnation of Henry Kaiser's program — where doctors are employed by the organization.

But Kaiser actually is the exception. The more common forms are:
- contract HMOs, that deal with one medical group;
- network HMOs, that work with a handful of providers; and,
- independent practice association HMOs (IPAs), that contract with doctors who also serve non-HMO patients.

Managed-care programs didn't begin to spread, however, until after California started to feel fiscal pressure in the wake of Proposition 13 — the 1978 property tax-slashing initiative. Faced with shrinking government revenues, especially at the county level, the Legislature in 1981 found itself in

---

*Mary Beth Barber, a former assistant editor of* California Journal*, is a freelance writer in San Francisco.*

Steve Thompson

Quite simply, profits accrue and premiums are reduced if less care is rendered. The for-profit HMOs are in the business of making money.

— Thompson

a difficult position when it came to that part of the population that depended on government for health care — basically, those who were too poor to afford their own medical services and who were served through the state's MediCal program, which draws funding from federal, state and county sources. The state could either serve fewer MediCal patients or spend less money on each. The state chose to control costs.

Historically, most insurance companies and federal programs have reimbursed doctors and facilities on a "fee-for-service" basis. Patients could see the qualified doctor of their

choice, or go to the most convenient hospital or clinic, and those doctors, hospitals and clinics — known as "providers" — charged a wide range of fees for each service rendered to a patient. Insurance companies, or the government, then paid the fee. For a variety of reasons, including the increased costs of more sophisticated technology and the influx of additional money through federal programs such as Medicare and Medicaid, inflation hit the health-care field, increasing costs at nearly three times the national rate of inflation by the early 1980s. The cost of health insurance skyrocketed as insurance companies passed on their increased costs to the folks who paid for that insurance — namely, individual consumers and employers. Employers, in particular, complained to the Legislature.

But it took a MediCal budget near $5 billion to spur lawmakers to action in 1982. The state's solution, as health-care expert Soap Dowell points out, was to inject marketplace competition into health care by contracting with doctors who offered favorable rates — rather than by turning the MediCal population loose to see any doctor or hospital. The rates themselves were negotiated and bids were competitive. According to Dowell, the Legislature then was persuaded to give private insurers the same authority that had been given to MediCal, extending marketplace competition to the private sector as well. It also helped insurers compete more adequately with the few HMOs because it freed them from the requirement that their clientele be able to choose any physician or hospital and allowed them to contract with an entity known as a Preferred Provider Organization, or PPO. Rather than charge a capitated fee like an HMO, PPOs negotiate fee-for-service rates that are fixed for a given period of time.

If 1982 marks the birth of managed care, then the system now is entering its teen-age years. Like all teen-agers, it occasionally requires a stern guiding hand. Sometimes, the system behaves responsibly toward its enrollees; at other times, it displays a contemptuous side that often is highlighted by the media. Although it still is growing, managed care is trying to decide what it's going to be when it matures — with doctors, executives and government as mentors tugging it in different directions.

"Managed care is causing a revolution in the way medical care is provided in this country," said Dr. Arnold S. Relman, editor-in-chief emeritus of the *New England Journal of Medicine*. Because the traditional one-on-one doctor-patient relationship has been replaced by medical networks of physicians and other providers, "it erodes the bond between the individual and doctor," said Relman. "The doctor has two masters now: the patient and the company."

Reminding the medical establishment that someone has to foot the bill is not necessarily a bad thing, said Byron Chell, executive director of the California Medical Assistance Commission, the state agency that oversees MediCal hospital contracts, who adds that preventive medicine is the best way to reduce the cost of providing medical care. "I like the idea of a group of doctors working as a team for my health."

Most HMOs created in the early '80s were simply health-insurance companies that converted to a "capitated model,"

one that limited physicians and encouraged primary, preventive care. Kaiser, the only major HMO to survive the '70s, was thriving and growing, and nearly all HMOs at that time were non-profit — a situation changed by a proliferation of HMO conversions from non-profit to for-profit over the past 10 years. Currently 13 non-profits exist, including Kaiser. There are 23 for-profit plans available, eight of which once were non-profit.

Exactly how the for-profit factor affects health care is at the core of the current debate over managed care. Profit motive is nothing new in health care. "Since the days of Florence Nightingale, there has always been a for-profit motive in health care," said Kurt Davis, a spokesman for Foundation Health, a for-profit organization.

Yet consumer studies have shown that patients really don't like the notion of a company making money off their health. Myra Snyder, executive director of the California Association of HMOs, pointed out that health care was initially supplied by missionaries as charity. "I don't think we can ever in the United States have ever shed that belief," she said. But whether a company is for-profit or non-profit has little to do with the health care they provide, she contends. "These are not monetary titles, but rather how they are structured. Some non-profits make money, and some for-profits go bankrupt."

The California Medical Association, however, doesn't see the differences as structural. "Quite simply, profits accrue and premiums are reduced if less care is rendered," said Steve Thompson, CMA vice-president for legislative affairs. "The for-profit HMOs are in the business of making money."

Relman is especially critical of the percentage of profits that go for administration and into stockholders' pockets. Non-profits typically dedicate around 10 percent for non-medical costs; similar costs for for-profits can vary anywhere between 15 to 30 percent.

CMA has been pushing legislation to discourage non-profits from converting to for-profit. Doctors feel their judgment and control over patient care is jeopardized by the profit motive; HMOs charge that doctors bear a grudge because their incomes are dwindling and because many medical specialists are finding themselves squeezed out by organizations that rely more and more on general practitioners.

Government officials like Chell disagree that for-profits can't provide good medical care at low costs. "If they provide the service, who cares?" he said. "You don't have to be dishonest or unethical to make money in health care."

Consumer groups tend to disagree. "The concentration on the bottom line is not what health care needs," said Harry Snyder of the Consumers' Union. He and others cite numerous horror stories to show that HMOs are concerned primarily with the bottom line, at the expense of sound patient care and treatment.

The place where these disagreements are sorted out tends to be government, where managed-care organizations are regulated. But even here, the trail of regulation can be confusing. The law most directly affecting HMOs is the Knox-Keene Act, passed in 1975 and designed to set regulations for all HMOs in California. But from the outset, Knox-Keene regards HMOs as businesses because they are under the purview of the Department of Corporations, not the Department of Health Services or the Department of Insurance.

"I am a long-time HMO enrollee," said Senator Herschel Rosenthal (D-Van Nuys). "Yet it wasn't until I became chairman of the Senate Insurance Committee that I realized that the DOC was responsible for regulating HMOs."

Lately, HMO regulation has been shadowed by a bigger question: What does the government do when a non-profit wants to convert to for-profit? The companies enjoyed tax benefits as non-profits, and executives in those companies stand to make a lot of money from conversion.

"I am disappointed in the non-profits," said Assemblyman Phil Isenberg (D-Sacramento) a few weeks after listening to a pre-conversion process. "The board members emphasized the lack of charity cases they took as a non-profit. Traditionally, non-profits wouldn't ever say that they didn't do charity cases. They all want to convert, so they say they didn't do much."

Many HMOs contend they have had to convert. Making ends meet without the benefit of having access to large amounts of capital — as for-profits do by selling stock — is almost impossible, they say. Competition has made health care a vicious world, and staying afloat is not easy.

"We found ourselves in the worst possible situation," said Leonard Schaeffer, CEO of the recently converted Blue Cross. Established in 1937 as non-profit insurance coverage, Blue Cross wanted to continue providing health care but was in grave danger of going bankrupt. The initial solution, said Schaeffer, was to create a for-profit subsidiary, called WellPoint Health Networks, that would be controlled by the non-profit company board.

In the past, non-profits heading down the for-profit road were required to compensate in some way for the years of tax breaks accorded to them as non-profits. In the case of Blue

Cross, all of its assets — valued at $3 billion — will be contributed to a pair of new charitable foundations. WellPoint will raise additional cash via the sale of stock. Approval of the conversion was announced in mid March.

The creation of WellPoint was well underway and almost approved in the fall of 1994 by the Department of Corporations when then-DOC Director Tom Sayles left and was replaced by Gary Mendoza, who had a different take on the conversion. Blue Cross had assumed that the money it would be required to donate to charity would be low because the conversion to for-profit was only partial, in accordance with the deal Blue Cross had struck with Sayles. But Mendoza required a much larger set-aside — a move that Blue Cross representatives say forced them to completely convert to for-profit status. "It's ironic," said Blue Cross lobbyist Bob Scarlett. "Their actions basically forced us to convert."

Blue Cross agreed to $3 billion, and the company is further required to set aside 5 percent of its assets to the foundations every year as long as Blue Cross exists. The requirement was a move away from the DOC's "hands-off" attitude. But Mendoza thinks that the foundations set up by converted HMOs can solve some of the concerns the public has with for-profit companies. "For the not-for-profits, daily operations are their societal contribution," he said. For-profits have something separate, Mendoza adds. "If the foundations are led in a meaningful way, they can make a significant contribution." Mendoza says he's gotten phone calls from insurance commissioners in other states where Blue Cross plans also are considering converting.

Hospital conversions are the next area that lawmakers such as Isenberg are watching. HMO conversion legislation that mirrors some of Mendoza's requirements for Blue Cross was passed last year. But Isenberg notes a large number of non-profit hospitals are being bought by large for-profit chains. He's working with the Department of Health and the attorney general for future regulation.

The explosion in managed care, and the concern about its growth, isn't confined to the private sector. Both MediCal and the university teaching hospitals have been affected — MediCal for the better and university hospitals for the worse. MediCal is a huge potential market for managed-care companies. "The state is somewhat belatedly recognizing the benefits of managed care," said Department of Health Services Director Kim Belshe.

California has two different HMO models for MediCal. The 12 counties with the highest number of MediCal enrollees are implementing what's called the "two-plan" model. Patients will have a choice of a county-run HMO or a private plan that has contracted with the state. The second model, a pilot project in Sacramento County called geographic managed care (GMC), allows any HMO that meets state requirements to participate. Sacramento MediCal patients now choose from seven different plans. While there have been some implementation problems with the program, such as confusion from school officials

> I am a long-time HMO enrollee. Yet it wasn't until I became chairman of the Senate Insurance Committee that I realized that the DOC was responsible for regulating HMOs.
>
> — Herschel Rosenthal

about students' health coverage, "geographic managed care is a very positive story," said Belshe.

The biggest advantage for patients is access, continued Belshe. Finding primary-care doctors who would see MediCal patients has never been easy. "They'd end up in the emergency room for something like a child's ear-ache," she said. Now, MediCal patients are on an equal footing with people covered by private insurance.

Opening up MediCal to managed care is also slowly changing managed care, said Belshe. The plans approved for the two-plan models and for the GMC had to adjust for the MediCal population, especially expanding their language capabilities for the culturally diverse MediCal population. "The plans balked at first, but they're coming around," said Belshe. The more culturally diverse a plan is, the more patients it can attract. "Ultimately the plans will conclude that these type of standards make sense in a business way."

Educational institutions, on the other hand, have been hit hard by the managed-care explosion. "For-profit HMOs are not doing their part in education and research," said Dr. Gerald Lazrus, dean of the University of California, Davis, School of Medicine. Only 15 percent of the school's budget comes from the University of California. The other 85 percent is from research grants and clinical reimbursement. "We had previously been able to cross-subsidize from the money that comes from patient care."

If UC-Davis is not able to continue seeing patients in a normal setting — especially primary-care patients — "the opportunity to teach while seeing patients is really compromised," said Lazrus. Before, when teaching hospitals received the majority of MediCal patients, the federal government's medical dollars supported education. "Now the educational dollars are going into those for-profit HMOs," said Lazrus.

The universities aren't the only ones feeling out of control in this brave new health-care world. Rosenthal contends that consumers feel at a loss when it comes to evaluating their insurance. "Who protects their interest in getting reliable information to help them secure quality HMO services?" he said. HMO-initiated studies and polls lack credibility, he contends. The one national organization that monitors and accredits plans, the National Committee on Quality Assurance, has a reputation for independence. But the NCQA was recently sued by an HMO that received an unfavorable report, and Rosenthal thinks the case may taint future analyses.

Proposals for report cards and analyses are floating around the Legislature to encourage HMOs to base their companies on care not costs. But Californians are unique in their acceptance of medicine as a business, said Relman — a concept that has not caught on in the east. Part of the HMO-for-profit trend could be linked to California doctors' attitudes towards medicine. "I think California will be one of the last states to realize that a profession is not a business," said Relman. 🏛

# The role of government in health care

## By Lynelle Jolley

Reprinted from *California Journal*, April 1996

Thirty years ago, with a stroke of President Lyndon Johnson's pen on the Medicare and Medicaid legislation, a new era in health-care policy began. From that day forward, the government made a commitment to bring the nation's elderly and its poorest citizens into the mainstream of American medicine. Hospitals and doctors started getting paid for what they'd been giving away. And with the establishment of this "mainstream" principle in our social conscience, it has become clear there is no going back.

Now Medicare is the proverbial "third rail" of politics: Touch it and die. For the nation's growing number of senior citizens, universal coverage has been achieved, and its beneficiaries guard it as carefully as life itself. As for Medicaid, while there is a national debate over moving it down the government food chain in the form of block grants to states, few seriously propose a return to reliance on charity to serve the poor. But the huge bill that government, at all levels, now pays for these two programs — estimated to be $328 billion in 1995 — combined with the fact that 40 million people nationwide still are uninsured either publicly or privately, raise fundamental questions about what the government's role should be in health care.

"While many argue that the marketplace can drive health-care reform without the hand of government, experience has shown us that in fact government has an important role to play," says Burt Margolin, former Democratic assemblyman who chaired the Assembly Insurance Committee and now is a private consultant.

The shift from a system where a third party paid for each service with a fee — fee-for-service — to a system of managed care appears to solve the inflation problem in medical care, at least temporarily. In California, with its highly competitive managed-care marketplace, the growth in health expenditures is far below the national rate. According to a study by the RAND Corporation, California's pro-competitive approach to controlling costs resulted in significantly lower growth rates from 1980 to 1991 than in states with well-established government rate regulation. Does this mean we should leave it to the private sector to control costs? The authors of the RAND study say that there needs to be research on the question of how managed-care plans achieve savings — increased efficiency or reduced access and/or quality. They cite evidence, for instance, that in California, such competition has contributed to a reduction in access for the uninsured population as hospitals find it increasingly difficult to absorb the costs of uncompensated care.

Harold Luft, a health-care economist at the University of California, San Francisco, says that the marketplace is indeed downsizing the system, a trend he feels eventually will allow everyone to be covered, but he cites pitfalls along the way. "Unfortunately, some people are losing coverage and some institutions are being forced out of business, but not necessarily the low-quality ones which should be forced out," said Luft. "In the long run, the profits will be driven down and expenditures that aren't directly helpful to good health will be eliminated, so that eventually the government will be able to step up and provide coverage for the uninsured."

Government's role goes beyond that of financier, however. Traditionally government has been the regulator of quality, whether it's the licensing of physicians or other providers, the licensing of hospitals, or the licensing of insurance plans and health-maintenance organizations. "The marketplace can be pretty unforgiving to people who think they are getting a good health plan that turns out to be a lemon," says E. Richard Brown, director of UCLA's Center for Health Policy Research. "Government needs to assure that plans meet basic standards for financial stability, [cover] a comprehensive range of benefits that includes preventive care and appropriate access to specialty care, and actually deliver on what [they] promise people who join the plan."

Physicians have long resisted governmental interference with the practice of medicine, but many are frustrated with today's carrier-dominated system. Recently reports have surfaced of disgruntled physicians who feel that financial considerations are taken more seriously than their professional opinions. "In our zeal to control costs, we have allowed corporate concern over profit to compromise medical decisions," says Steve Thompson, vice president of the California Medical Association and its chief lobbyist. "Most physicians don't believe that medical decisions should be legislated. But to the extent those decisions are being made in corporate boardrooms, without any physician involvement, legislation — where physicians at least have a chance to have input — is preferable to a corporate mode of decision making."

To illustrate his point, Thompson cites the example of insurers who require mothers and newborns to be released from the hospital within 24 hours, putting doctors in the position of having to argue why mothers should be allowed to stay longer in some cases. Legislation has been introduced in several states, including California, to return that decision to the doctor. When New Jersey passed such a law last year, economist Uwe E. Reinhardt at Princeton University wrote in a *New York Times* op-ed piece that it symbolized "a pervasive distrust of the private health-care market. For years voters have clamored for government to get off their backs. Yet now, at the first sign of discomfort with the private market, they have clamored for government to climb right back on."

Is the current regulatory model the only way govern-ment can protect the public interest and influence the health-care marketplace? Not according to former Assemblyman Bruce Bronzan, now associate dean at UCSF's Fresno Medical Education Program. "Government needs to think of itself as a purchaser, not a regulator, and use its purchasing leverage to get the best possible health outcomes for the price," Bronzan says. He notes that many county governments in California, responsible for providing medical services to the state's 6.5 million uninsured persons, are finding they cannot afford to care for medically indigent patients and compete with private hospitals for patients under capitated health plans — those that pay a fixed fee for each patient. Bronzan says this is leading more and more local governments to consider purchasing indigent care from the private sector rather than provide it themselves. The state also is moving to a purchasing role by negotiating with public and private managed-care plans to serve Medicaid beneficiaries. Bronzan sees governmental entities holding great untapped bargaining strength in their collective Medicaid, indigent and public-employee populations. With so many people to purchase health services for, he feels government can negotiate concessions in the marketplace, including the release of data that can be used to measure quality, more effectively than by using direct intervention.

Nothing the government has done so far has been focused directly on making health care available to everyone. Instead, its role has been shaped by the public's demand for quality, affordability and other issues of concern to the population that already has access. Attempts to achieve universal coverage by requiring employers to provide health benefits have been largely unsuccessful. The 1993 reform plan put forward by the Clinton administration mandated that employers foot the bill, as did Proposition 166, defeated by California voters in November 1992. Meanwhile, a growing number of employers are opting not to provide health benefits, swelling the ranks of the uninsured. What's a government to do? "Either we will have to require all employers to help pay for coverage for all their employees, or we have to turn to government to do it. A single-payer system is the most efficient and effective way to cover the entire population," E. Richard Brown says.

Arguably an expanded version of Medicare, a single-payer system would leave the actual delivery of services in the hands of the private sector, with the government financing a comprehensive set of benefits for all citizens. Proponents say it is more equitable and would be less expensive than what the private and public sector already pay for health care — $938 billion nationally in 1994, or 14 percent of the gross domestic product.

So, why hasn't a single-payer plan been adopted? "We have this belief in this country that government can't do anything right," says Congressman Jim McDermott (D-Washington), sponsor of a single-payer bill in Congress.

In California, voters rejected Proposition 186, a single-payer initiative on the November 1994 ballot. One of its authors, Dr. Vishu Lingappa, a professor of medicine at UCSF, says that long-term care, which would be covered under single-payer, is a more serious problem than most people realize. To receive assistance under the current system — unless one has private long-term care insurance, which most people don't — a person has to spend down to the Medicaid eligibility level. Unless we adopt a single-payer system, Lingappa is concerned that most individuals won't be able to afford this care, and the need for it will go up as baby-boomers reach old age. Medicare's long-term care benefits are restricted and capped; California's cost to provide long-term care under Medicaid is expected to double or triple through 2020.

One of the arguments used against single-payer is that it would lead to rationing, a sticky subject that society generally avoids. For example, should the government spend as much of our health care budget on extending the life of a 90-something adult as a 10-year-old kid? Richard Lamm, former governor of Colorado and now director of the Center for Public Policy and Contemporary Issues at the University of Denver, is one of those who says we have a bigger duty to the 10-year-old. "The genius of American health care has led us to develop more medicine than we can afford. We have to set limits," he says. Lamm urges Americans to engage in a "community dialogue about how we put our health dollars to the highest and best use."

UCLA's Brown cautions us not to pit elders against children, but acknowledges that the rationing in our current system — by price for those who are uninsured and by utilization controls imposed by health plans for those who are insured — needs to be done in a more thoughtful and deliberate way. "We should remove financial incentives that enable doctors, hospitals, and health plans to make more money either by giving more care than is necessary or even desired by patients or by withholding care that would be beneficial," says Brown. "We also need to involve patients and their families in these decisions, rather than allowing them to be made arbitrarily by government or health care providers."

Where does this leave us? Is there consensus emerging on the government's role here, or do the life-and-death issues involved in health care not lend themselves to easy casting? The comments of Soap Dowell, longtime veteran of the health-care wars as a former lobbyist for Blue Cross of California, reflect the conundrum: "The bottom line is that I do not know what government should or could do because the only things that might help are politically impossible. I have worked at it as long as anyone, and I am stumped."